Erkki Lehtiranta

UNIVERSAL LAWS

AND SPIRITUAL PROGRESS

A Manual for a Meaningful Life

WISDOM OF MASTER HILARION

Erkki Lehtiranta:
Universal Laws and Spiritual Progress - A Manual for a Meaningful Life
Wisdom of Master Hilarion

Published by Smiling Stars, Helsinki 2019
www.smilingstars.fi

Printed by Books on Demand, Norderstedt, Germany
ISBN 978-952-99832-8-5 (paperback)
ISBN 978-952-99832-9-2 (EPUB)

Original name (in Finnish):
Universaalit lainalaisuudet ja henkinen kehitys – hyvän elämän käyttöohjeet.
Mestari Hilarionin viisautta.
Smiling Stars 2012, Helsinki.

Translation: Meri Lehtinen
Layout and cover: Tomi Leporinne, Avendis

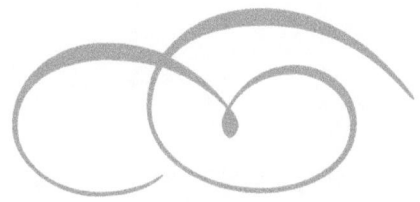

I DEDICATE this book with love
and gratitude to my dear friend
and incomparable Hilarion-
interpreter Jon C. Fox.

Acknowledgements

MY THANKS go to the innumerable people, known and unknown to me, who have influenced this book. Their presence at my lectures, courses, consultations, and other events has given me sparks of inspiration and brought enthusiasm and joy into my life. This book could hardly have been possible without the reciprocal energy of these contacts.

For the central message of the book's content, the universal laws and their application, I thank my great teacher and friend, Master Hilarion, for his infinite love, gentleness and patience with a hard-headed student. It is my humble hope that the book gives sufficient honor to his cosmic wisdom. I give warm thanks and love to my own guides and helpers, who have in many ways furthered this book project from other levels.

From my heart I thank the God of Love, who is finally the subject of this book. The excellent Hilarion-channel Jon C. Fox has contributed greatly to the book and supported its publication in many ways. Jon, who lives in California, has allowed me to use a series of recordings of 12 long Hilarion-sessions, which he channeled in the late 80's and early 90's. Their content is still most relevant. My warmest thanks also to John Keebaugh, who has edited and organized this profound material, and Jill Fox, who has conducted so many remarkable Hilarion sessions throughout the decades.

My translator and friend, Ms. Meri Lehtinen, has done excellent work all the way. Thanks, Meri! I also appreciate the suggestions very much and help from my spiritual friends, Ms. Seija Aalto and Mr. Seppo Ilkka, who have read the manuscript with the eyes of an eagle and the gentle heart of an angel. I thank my dear friends Vesa and Hannele Koponen and David Ward for their profound support to this book project.

Last but not the least, special thanks to my partner Leena Niemelä who's love, support, patience and understanding knows no boundaries. Leena has been my best mundane teacher of these Universal Laws.

Erkki Lehtiranta

1.

2.

3.

4.

5.

6.

7.

8.

9.

10.

11.

12.

Universal Laws and Spiritual Progress

Preface (Hilarion)

THE PRINCIPLES OF UNIVERSAL LAWS presented in this book can give a great many insights and aha-experiences about many kinds of questions, for example about life situations, or about one's personality or one's life. It is through this that most people are attracted to the immediate possibilities of practical application of the laws. If you have some particular problem or matter in mind as you read this, these practical applications are of great usefulness in this respect.

However, the most important application is the anticipatory use of these laws. When you attempt to be conscious of the principles of these laws **before** you begin some project, **before** you enter into some human relationship or **before** you have a child, you can best utilize them in your various life situations.

This is usually difficult for people who have not previously worked with these principles, but as the idea of them is transferred to the next generations, it is more likely that these will gradually begin to accept their existence and will transfer knowledge of them to future generations. Transferring this knowledge is important because it concerns principles that guide everything that exists, that extend into every aspect of life. Society, civilization, technology, and so many other things in the world flow, function and create continually in accordance with these principles.

These principles extend even beyond the three-dimensional world that you know into multidimensional realities, into what you were before you were born and who and what you will be after you die. But the Universal Laws have many practical applications in numerous areas of daily life. At the point where you notice that they are in fact the root point of everything, the creative principle and force through which matter, spirit, the earth itself and indeed humanity and all of its daily life function, you will see your own role in all this.

Many individuals have behind them lives where the struggle with one or more of the Universal Laws has become a kind of theme, an aspect of life that they have worked with and from which they have increased their understanding **on the soul level** for the improvement, development, extension and deepening of their consciousness. However, **these principles have not been explained to them in their physical life.**

On the non-physical level just before birth there have been many opportunities to gain understanding about these matters. But if a sufficiently strong pattern of thought that resists these principles or understandings has been formed already during physical life, it is often continued into the non-physical levels, and therefore the individual has great difficulties in accepting and working with these kinds of principles.

Therefore, in addition to bringing the information now within people's reach, there is another kind of need for this kind of introduction to the Universal Laws. The purpose is to bring these principles forth as an idea, as an existing principle or a simple announcement of the fact that there **is** a kind of **Handbook for humanity**, an operator's guidebook for your own life and for everyone else's life. It exists for the sake of formulating questions. It exists in your consciousness on many levels, and it is an idea that you can concentrate on more deeply if you so wish.

Concentrating on these ideas develops extremely necessary solutions to many of humanity's most pressing problems. This is difficult to present because it sounds like a magical cure, like something beyond the capacity of human understanding. But this is precisely the great gift of the Universal Laws. When the principles have been understood and applied in practice, even the most vexing problems may be solved. This is because matters originally **changed** into problems precisely because of the misunderstanding of some universal law, through ignorance, resistance or some such. People did not concentrate on the solutions to the problems, but they rather concentrated on resisting the universal law itself, either because of ignorance, or by misunderstanding it or misusing it.

Because of this life often becomes messy and difficult. People feel hurt and resentful or they struggle with things that somehow seem very familiar to them, but which nevertheless are troublesome or difficult. Thus, after struggling with an aspect of some law or with several laws from one life to the next, the individual has decided to come to just this life in order to work with them again. This time the difference is that people now have the opportunity to read this Operator's Guidebook and to notice what it means for them personally, and to recognize the sides of themselves that are able to accept these principles.

For this reason, we suggest that you see the laws as something else besides just neutral information that is now being presented to you and which allows you to take it or leave it. Attempt rather to observe how one or perhaps two or even three of these laws arouse significant resistance, emotional energy or other reactions in most people. And how, where every one of these laws is concerned, you can in a sense give birth to it again in your own heart and life.

You can for example think about: "If this information is really true, what would I myself do differently in my life? Or what would I say in a different way? Or how would I feel differently?" Or from a more intellectual point of view: "How would I myself apply this information in my own life?" Or how could you use the Law of Reflection – which is the most significant law in humanity's present situation – for teaching humanity and at the same time apply it to others?

Do you know someone who is struggling with a certain law? Should that person who is struggling with the problems know something that you could tell him, and which of the Universal Laws might apply to his situation? Then, by using the Law of Reflection, **turn the entire thought around.** In what way can you apply that conclusion to yourself?

Could that person tell you where he would apply that insight to yourself? As you play with these ideas in all possible ways, they will remind you of how all those things apply to yourself as well. They apply to different sides of your personality, to the way that you have related to other people, to what is important in life and to what things you have struggled with – but also to things that you have enjoyed, such as to your gifts, to mercies, to fun and to pleasure in life. All things in your life are greatly affected by your willingness to work with these laws.

In the end the most important thing is how you apply these laws **mainly to yourself, not to others**. The Universal Laws could be introduced in any part of the world for humanity's higher life path or for a deeper level of understanding. But our hope has been that when these laws were first presented to people with a Scandinavian view of the world, a European philosophical outlook and a consciousness of the application of these principles, in this way they could be embraced in their entire core. Thus, each individual could first apply them to himself and to understanding his own life, and they could then be adopted also in the fields of jurisprudence and economics, and they could be applied to economic enlargement, to the expansion of consciousness, to cooperation with other people and to many other matters where Europeans are generally skillful. Finns have repeatedly demonstrated how skillfully people can teach things to others with their own example, by showing how things have worked for them and how they could be universally applied in every country. In this way we have been able to expand global consciousness.

It is not however a question of expanding consciousness in the Eastern mystical sense, but rather of practical communication and of a strong understanding of unifying the heart and mind of all people, and of a deep respect for life. The Scandinavian base has felt fruitful for the broader acceptance of the Universal Laws, and for sharing them worldwide. Even more important is for them to be shared in a way that makes it possible **for the collective human consciousness to be willing and able to accept them as universal principles and to awaken them to life in their own lives** in all spheres of life, in all cultures and in all nationalities.

- Hilarion

Universal Laws and Spiritual Progress

Introduction

Heaven and earth so close to each other
- Within ourselves they come together.

DISCOVERING A THEORY to cover and explain everything has been one of the central scientific efforts and challenges of our time, and many kinds of answers have been attempted. Finding such a theory has proved to be difficult and challenging. On the other hand, it has served as a spur and an inspiration, especially in the field of physics. The great questions, such as the meeting of matter and spirit and their mutual influence, the existence and operation of a universal intelligence, the nature of life itself and the place of humankind in the cosmos – all these still await their final answers. While we wait life goes on and offers ever new sides of itself. Our book, The Universal Laws and Spiritual Progress, attempts for its part to answer these questions and to provide explanations of the principles which underlie all phenomena.

Over the years we have dealt with these questions in hundreds of our lectures and workshops, and now the time has finally come to collect these teachings of Master Hilarion under one cover. The starting point of our research has been the booklet Vision, published in the beginning of the 80's, which was given by Hilarion to his Canadian student and channel, Maurice B. Cooke (d. 2012). This work, small in number of pages, but colossal in content, contains these 12 Cosmic Laws in very condensed form, but their flood of information was already immense. Many matters that I had pondered over for years received masterful illumination from this teaching, which is one of the treasures of my library.[1]

---

1   Hilarion, *Vision Beyond the Apocalypse: A New Age Model*, pp. 13-30.

As for myself, I started to explore these principles in the mid-nineties and wrote about them at that time in a Finnish magazine, among other places. Still, every year of life has brought with it new understanding of the deeper meaning of these principles and especially of their application in practice.

As Karl Marx so aptly put it, practical applicability is the highest proof of a theory. In my opinion nowhere is this as true as in the matter of spirituality, since these days, along with true and authentic teachings, we are offered false spirituality, fast food that simulates authentic spirituality. In it magnificent-sounding words have behind them only the hollow rumble of empty barrels. There is no by-pass to the higher dimensions without confronting, practicing and learning these cosmic laws.

In this book I have sought to bring these matters to a practical level. Without practical application even the best spiritual teachings remain only unused possibilities. My principle has been that things can be simple without being naïve. The message of the book is meant not only for the head but for the heart as well. It is meant to inspire the intuitive capacities, which exist outside of logic, and to bring new insights through these capacities.

In this book I have tried to fill the barrels of knowledge with Hilarian wisdom and with the insights that come with experience. It is again a question of the mutual influence and cooperation of master and student. The masters do not want their students to be incapable of discernment, people who merely repeat mechanically the teachings they have received, but they should rather be active participants who think with their own brains, whose hearts beat in the rhythm of helping humankind, and who want to bring their own contribution to the spiritual progress of humanity.

These pages were born through experience and as the result of almost 20 years of endeavor. Hopefully they will offer you, my dear reader, new ideas and also new techniques that will support and further your own spiritual progress. The book is in fact designed for all those who want to clarify the markers of their own spiritual life with the help of the eternal principles coded into the structures of the universe.

So, test these laws, make them a part of your own world of experience. Otherwise they will remain only a dead letter and an intellectual factor, which give neither warmth nor light. This is not what they are in reality. It could be said that in these laws there is the presence of divine warmth and light.

Knowing the spiritual laws of the universe is not only desirable, it is essential on the path of spiritual growth. These 12 principles could well be called a practical guide to a good, meaningful life. A life of enduring happiness and wisdom depends on understanding and practicing them. We can in fact say that the path from knowledge to wisdom leads through the understanding and practical application of these principles. These laws give direction and meaning to life.

In addition, it is good to understand that the Universal Laws receive different emphases at different stages of evolution, both where individuals and where nations are concerned[2]. For example, we Finns are working in particular with the Law of Thought, while for our dear Swedish neighbors the most important cosmic law is currently the Law of Love. For the people living in the States the fundamental law is the Law of Reflection, while the Canadians study the Law of Thought, the French people the Law of Speech and the British people concentrate on the Law of Symbols etc. But of course, an understanding of all the 12 laws is present in the evolutionary goals of each nation.

It is interesting that these laws function at all times and in all places in this world of resistant matter; otherwise they would not be Universal Laws. Nevertheless, we often act as if they did not exist at all! Breaking the basic principles of the cosmos brings with it many troubles, difficulties, delays, and often health problems as well. For these we then blame circumstances, mere happenstance, or other factors outside of ourselves. But we cannot afford such self-deception in this era of rapid change, which presents the possibility of rapid spiritual progress.

The origin of the immense upheavals and conflicts that confront our planet is in many ways connected with a lack of understanding or the

---

2   See Appendix B.

abuse of these laws. Humankind has not yet thoroughly understood that beside and behind the physical laws of nature there exist these spiritual laws as a kind of umbrella or mother science, which you can act against, but only with your own responsibility. Perhaps you, as the reader, can see the same thing I see as the writer, namely that these laws are built into the nature of reality, into the deep structure of being itself. Besides, these laws have no loopholes, as man-made laws often do!

The abuse of the universal principles, for example in the sphere of technology, is visible to everyone currently in various areas of life. In medicine this can for example be seen in the sphere of vaccination, in physics in matters concerning radiation and environmental problems, in biology in the rapid increase of diseases, in chemistry for example in problems with pollution. The list could be extended almost without limit. Our mutual dependence, which brings us into connection with each other more powerfully every day, makes this particularly important and critical.

Social, economic and technological systems unite our world. In the economic turbulence of our world it is easy to see that we are all in the same boat, no-one is outside it. The total oneness of things is what is essential in this. Therefore, breaking these laws and various abuses of them are reflected throughout the planet, in time leading to problems that we must face and solve collectively.

For example, denying, rejecting, or blindly following one of the laws without understanding it deeply, can lead to serious consequences, great destruction and a variety of difficulties, all of which have manifested or are about to manifest. A misunderstanding of the Law of Love, and replacing it with money or other material things, is currently perhaps the most flagrant example of this. These problems can be and must be solved, but the solutions must contain a growing understanding of the laws behind everything, otherwise the number of problems can only multiply. Modifying Einstein's statement, we can say that problems cannot be solved on the level of consciousness on which they were formed. We need a new kind of consciousness, where an understanding of cosmic principles is present.

According to Einstein's theory of relativity nothing can move faster than the speed of light. New results of scientific research concerning neutrons tell us something else, however. In this way ideas and theories that we have held dear turn out to be untenable. In other words, the truths of today are the half-truths of tomorrow. The Universal Laws, on the contrary, are eternal truths in the changing stream of time. As you practice them you are at the same time connecting with the eternal in yourself. The byproducts of a good life, such as enduring inner peace and harmony and unconditional love, result from following the cosmic principles in your own life.

The Universal Laws are the oxygen tank of our spiritual growth. The further someone travels on the path of spiritual progress, on the higher path of the pilgrim, the better he understands these laws and knows how to apply them in practice. The laws are our guide book on the path of return to union with God, to light and to love. These laws transcend all cultural, religious and racial boundaries. They cannot be patented, they are not anyone's property – they belong to all humankind, and to greater entities as well.

In this context it is important to note that during the known history of humankind no major religion has been able to correctly interpret and explain the Universal Laws so that they became a harmonious understanding that could be integrated into daily life. This task has been left to the secretly functioning mystery schools, which throughout history have carried the thread of truth, out of range of spying eyes.[3] However, now the time has come to bring these principles out to wider extent, so that we can survive the great problems of our times and grow to full human adulthood.

Our planet is, from the point of view of humanity, a kind of research laboratory where the resistance of matter, inertia, contends with the flight of the spirit and the progress of consciousness. The light within us brightens as our spiritual muscles strengthen when we wrestle with these difficulties and resistances, which we ourselves

---

3   Hilarion, *The Letters of Paul*, p. 1.

have created for ourselves. In this work we increase our muscular strength by studying the cosmic principles and testing them in the stress and pressures of life. Our spiritual progress can be compared with the journey of coal from a fragile element to a diamond, which finally shines bright and perfect, and reflects the pure light of spirit flawlessly. Every universal law that has been correctly understood and practiced is like a single pure bevel in this diamond of the spirit.

Why Study the Laws of Spirit?

We are immortal divine beings, citizens of the galaxy, time travelers and adventurers in the interaction of spirit and matter. The time has come to fulfill the promises that we have taken on over the eons as the guardians of this beautiful planet. In my opinion we can best succeed in this precisely through understanding the cosmic laws and applying them wisely. There are certainly many good reasons to study these principles and to test them with the acid test of life.

12 such reasons:

First of all, the universal principles **analyze reality** better than any other factor. In other words, these laws organize life itself and form a rich and, at its core, a just cosmos out of seeming chaos. The universe is a benevolent place and attempts in many ways to help us on our path toward light and greater self-knowledge. From this point of view the laws are the navigation rules of the cosmos. By following them we sail wisely on the sometimes stormy seas of life.

An unanalyzed life remains a vague idea, a kind of draft or sketch, which has never served as the basis for beginning to build a house. Just as an architect needs a great deal of knowledge about structures, materials and measures, so do we need knowledge about the principles that underlie the phenomena of life. Through these laws life unfolds as a perfect, ever inspiring fresco.

In this, the laws shed light on the universal order that underlies everything. The classical Greek word *cosmos* means, among other things, an ordered, harmonious, systematic universe. Such a universe must be lawful, not coincidental. A person believes in coincidences when he has not understood the lawfulness behind the matter. The belief in coincidences is in fact another name for mental laziness.

The Universal Laws are in some sense the ultimate conditions of our reality. How could it be otherwise? Without these laws total chaos would prevail in the world.

The Universal Laws have a tremendous power of **explanation.** In the philosophy of science, a theory is often termed a good theory when it explains the maximum possible number of things. The Universal Laws are behind all phenomena, therefore they have the maximum explanatory power when properly understood. They form the integrative principles of the modern sciences, and they are more fundamental and more important than for example the basic laws of physics.

The cosmic principles **work**. I will give many examples of this in the following pages. I have tested these laws in my own life for almost 20 years, and have found them to hold true, sometimes even in very miraculous ways. Small miracles, and even large ones, start to flow into a life when a person learns about these laws and integrates them into his daily life. Very interesting, nearly magical, things start to happen, as difficulties dissolve, health problems disappear, and a new kind of knowing and understanding flows into the person's life.

That something works in practice is in fact one of the criteria of the truth. If something works time after time, we have reason to suspect that there is something real in it – even if for example materialistic science is not able, or perhaps not willing, to explain it. If on the other hand something does not work at all, no matter how fancy the terms that it is polished with, in my opinion it might as well go in the trash basket as fast as possible.

The Universal Laws are **comprehensive** – as even their name tells you – and they do not apply only to humanity or to this small planet, this small cosmic particle of dust. Therefore we dare to say that both the laws created by humans and the physical laws that the natural sciences study strive toward the universal principles. In some cases we can say that the laws decreed by humans are still only distant reflections of the creative principles of the cosmos. Nevertheless, we can observe in this process of laws and in this research project, that the striving of mankind to clarify the laws of the material world will inevitably lead to the discovery of and an understanding of the Universal Laws behind the phenomena of matter.

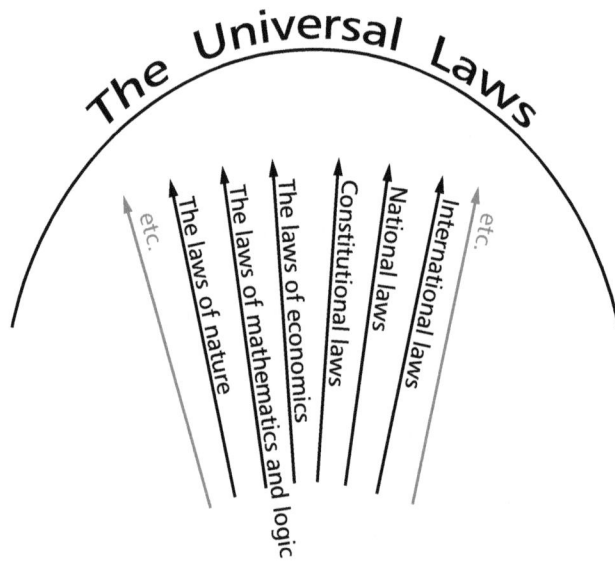

The universal principles are something like an "umbrella", a cosmic mother law under which the other laws fit and toward which they also strive.

The Universal Laws are an **economical** way of understanding the supporting pillars and the basic principles of the entire cosmos. They contain the maximum amount of information recorded in the smallest possible space. In the broadest sense of the proverb, they do see the forest for the trees.

The presence of any difficulty in a person's life is almost always the result of denying some fact or law, which causes disharmony between the individual and the universal law. The difficulty also leads to a narrowing of consciousness in relation to the person's true nature. All the same, you can rapidly get to the root of the problem when you learn to look honestly to see which Universal Laws demand your attention in the situation in question. In that case you do not allow the details to blind you or to cause tunnel vision.

Following the basic principles of the cosmos also brings with it an **ethical** way of life, so that we can respect and appreciate our fellow human beings, other realms of nature, our own environment, and this beautiful planet. These principles in themselves respect, to the maximum extent, the sacredness of life from the point of view of sustainable progress. These laws also contain in their essence full respect for the freedom of will, which lies at the core of all genuinely ethical action and choice.

The Universal Laws are **the basic principles of creation**. They are not separate principles, disconnected from each other. Rather, they form an undivided whole, which if seen from a higher plane unites into the basic laws of creation and the roots of creativity. By applying these laws a human being can learn to create, again in the higher meaning of the word. He then becomes a Co-Creator.

The laws connect seamlessly with each other. One of the goals of the book is in fact to bring out the interconnectedness of the laws. As we learn to understand and follow one of them, we at the same time acquire a better possibility of practicing the other universal principles as well. This is usually reflected in an increase in creativity. Combining the laws and understanding their interaction can help in creating your own daily life as well as in artistic endeavors. In fact, each of us is asked to bring our own contribution to the Universal Laws and their expression, for we ourselves are creative principles, whether we know it or not.

Understanding and following the Universal Laws can be seen as **a factor of spiritual success**, which guarantees optimal progress and expansion of consciousness. Why then would we choose to go forward or backward an inch or two during one incarnation when we could make a leap of miles and miles, an actual quantum leap upward in our spiritual progress?

The Universal Laws are loaded with **integrating energy**. With this energy they can integrate people, among other things. They are the energizing and expanding principles that govern the way that matter and energy interact. In other words, the laws are the cosmic integrating and energizing principles of everything that exists or can exist.

The Universal Laws increase our **self-knowledge** in an incomparable way. We are children of the universe, at our core we are immortal divine beings who on their path of pilgrimage learn to know themselves and their true measure through their understanding of these laws. As we study each of these laws, our individual consciousness increases and our interactions in human relationships and in society evolve. In concert with the cosmic Law of Reflection, increased self-knowledge is then reflected in the surrounding society, and for its part contributes to the progress of the whole.

Working with the universal principles **increases our health** and **our well-being**. Understanding and following these great principles in our daily life creates success and harmony and supports our spiritual progress, as I already noted above. In contrast, breaking or denying them results in difficulties and often in health problems as well, problems in the use and focus of energy, in nutrition, and in the various bodily systems and symbols, as we will see in the chapter concerned with the cosmic Law of Symbols.

These laws **are understood in the realms of higher vibration** – in fact the laws open the connection with, and provide the ticket to, those realms, and are the guidance used in those realms. The universal spiritual laws are the central principles of the three-dimensional slice of reality and are at the same time something like fractals in a much larger cosmic geometry. These laws show the direction of progress toward the fourth dimension, which opens itself to us only after we have thoroughly clarified the central doctrines and principles of the three-dimensional world. We must begin at the base, not at the top.

Some philosophies and doctrines speak very self-confidently about the higher dimensions and about working consciously in them. But the question is: are the issues of the three-dimensional world already mastered? If not, it is quite possible that in these doctrines the cart is placed before the horse and there is an illusion that the journey might progress forward in this way.

The Laws and Folk Wisdom

This book is not so much about diving into abstractions and into the world of mere intellectual perspectives, but rather about bringing up many practical and experiential aspects which will help the reader to apply these laws in daily life and at the same time to reach a higher level of evolution with their help.

We can gain useful knowledge about the more mundane level of these cosmic laws from for example the wisdom of proverbs and from the wisdom literature of different cultures, which contain many golden nuggets. Here are some examples:

What goes around comes around///As you sow so shall you reap/// As you make your bed so you lie in it/// - **The Law of Karma**

Speech is silver, silence is golden///My word is my bond/// - **The Law of Speech**

Don't count your chickens before they hatch///The mills of the gods grind slowly///To everything there is a season, and a time for everything under the sun///Time will tell///History repeats itself – **The Law of Cycles**

God created man in his own image///The eyes are the mirror of the soul///As above, so below, as in the macrocosm, so in the microcosm///A people has the leaders it deserves///When in Rome do as the Romans do///No smoke without fire///A tree is known by its fruits///A sound mind in a sound body – **The Law of Reflection**

Don't let the sun set over your anger///Love conquers all///It endures all things, suffers all things – **The Law of Love**

Ask and you shall receive, knock and it shall be opened///A friend in need is a friend indeed – **The Law of Help**

God sleeps in stone, dreams in plants, awakes and moves in animals, and finally becomes conscious of Himself in man///You cannot

step into the same stream twice///A rolling stone gathers no moss///
Practice makes perfect – **The Law of Progress**

These sayings and many other apt sayings shed light on the spiritual laws in folk speech and in religious texts. The laws are present in our daily life, in our ordinary world. They are not merely theory, but rather something like the air we breathe, like an inexhaustible cosmic oxygen tank. You just have to comply with the laws if you wish to rise to the level of human possibilities in this miraculous phenomenon called life.

The Universal Laws are presented in this book in the order in which they appear in Hilarion's book *Vision* except for the Law of Love. There are certain reasons for this, which should become clear as you read on. Each law has its own chapter in the book, and each chapter has a meditation connected with the law in question. If you want to get even more out of the meditation you can read it onto a tape, or have a friend read it. In this way you can concentrate better on the meditations themselves. They are very healing and empowering. In addition, at the end of the presentation of each law there is a summary of the essential points of the law, and hints about books which can help you to gain more understanding of it.

Come along on the path of discovery of your own life – with the guidance of the Universal Laws!

Literature:
Hilarion 1982: *Vision*. Marcus Books, Queensville, Ontario.
Hilarion 1989: *The Letters of Paul. A New Spiritual World View*. Triad Publishers, Ashland, Oregon.
Laszlo, Ervin & Currivan, Jude 2008: *CosMos. A Co-creator's Guide to the Whole-World*. Hay House, Inc., Carlsbad, California, New York City, London, Sydney, Johannesburg, Vancouver, Hong Kong, New Delhi.
Templeton, John Marks 1998: *Worldwide Laws of Life: 200 Eternal Spiritual Principles*. Templeton Foundation Press, Philadelphia, London.
Ward, Mark 2001: *Universality. The Underlying Theory behind Life, the Universe and Everything*. Macmillan, London.

1.

Manifestation

"Many different universes were created precisely
and solely so that the beings behind the form
could know themselves."

- Hilarion

ACCORDING TO HILARION, this is the most important of all the Universal Laws. At the same time it may be one of the most difficult laws to understand. It does not open itself completely through the intellect alone, but rather through experience, through personal inner work and perhaps through powerful experiences. Therefore it is important to understand this central universal principle not only mentally and with the intellect, but also with the emotions, with love, and with personal experience.

Understanding the principle of manifestation requires distinguishing spirit from physical matter. The spiritual core of some being or thing should never be confused with its form on the physical plane, or with the vehicle that this spiritual being is animating. The being or thing in question is only using its material garb for a time for its own purposes.[4]

This law holds true for a flower, an animal, the mineral kingdom, human beings, as well as for the whole planet and even for the galaxy.

---

4   Hilarion, *Vision*, p. 13

Many different universes were created precisely and solely so that the spiritual beings behind the forms, the entities, could know themselves.

Why then does a spiritual entity need to take on some form? Could it not simply observe itself and find its inner truth in this way? Of course you can learn a great deal by inner reflection, but through numerous experiences the being usually becomes too complex for complete self-knowledge to be possible with the help of inner reflection alone. Besides, the entity in question has probably in the course of its evolution gotten used to experiencing itself in the garb of some outer form or vehicle, so that it may be very difficult for it to analyze itself in the form of a purely spiritual essence.[5]

The above explanation may not help very much in understanding the question, for we are so deeply rooted in the world of matter that we do not always recognize our spiritual core and base. Even our language is anchored in understanding and describing the three-dimensional slice of reality. In the higher realms a different language of light is used. Nevertheless the sky above us with its dizzying heights, and the familiar and safe, solid and stable Mother Earth under us, tell us exactly this in their own way. They tell us of unlimited spirit and limited matter, whose resistant world we can nevertheless transcend into spiritual heights, enriched and ennobled by the experiences gained on the physical plane. If we understand the importance of the Law of Manifestation, we receive simultaneously an understanding of the timelessness of all things.

Hilarion tells us that in order to completely understand the Law of Manifestation we have to be enlightened, to be a conscious part of divinity, of All That Is, of the essence of things. That is what we are at bottom. It is good to ask yourself, "What is essential being? Does it have place and form, and if not, what is it formed out of? Can some being expand into space and time?" Yes, of course. "Does such a being have a form?" Yes. Patterns define form, but patterns are also defined with the help of form, which is created of something, whether of energy waves, of matter, or of the way in which things are put together.

---

5   Hilarion, *Vision*, p. 13

Essential being cannot be any of these things. In some fundamental way it must precede the things that have some form. This leads us into some of the great dilemmas of existential philosophy, for example: does essence precede existence or does existence precede essence?

The Law of Manifestation includes the proposition that the spiritual entity attempts to understand itself by taking on form. This proposition answers the question whether we can understand ourselves: the essential being and form are one, and in this union there is something greater than in either. This discovered greatness and specialness is a beautiful reflection of God, because God, in creating all this, allowing it and welcoming it, allows you to do the same. In every way each one of us is a reflection of God, and there is nothing without God. The Bible tells us that man was created in the image of God. But we are more than images: we are Co-Creators, and we have the capacity to attain everything, to be everything. There is God in us on every level, or otherwise what is involved is not a true essential being.

We are generally unwilling to accept this in ourselves. As a wise person has once said, we are not so much frightened of our smallness and darkness as of our greatness and glory! This unwillingness to accept our own divinity is the fundamental reason why the Law of Manifestation has been so poorly received, and that it has in fact met with much resistance. What if we stopped diminishing ourselves? (A habit which, by the way, suits the agenda of certain groups that like to enslave mankind.) What if we at the same time stopped resisting the God-part in ourselves? It is illusion, *maya*, that we are not this divine being, and that creation is something separate from us. We have to be reminded again and again to accept this law as the channel for every kind of complex creativity, as the route to individual expression, and one route among many to finding the truth.

It is a universal experience that most people – whether on a spiritual Path or not – begin, at some point in their lives, to ask important questions about consciousness and the possibility of its continuation after death, about survival, and, as the most important question, about themselves. The question of existence itself arises inevitably. We exist in order to understand ourselves, our universe and God. In this sense the Law of Manifestation is also the fundamental law of self-knowledge in the universe.

At the same time we see the first philosophical corollary of the Law of Manifestation present itself easily and beautifully. A corollary is a proposition, which in a simple way follows from a previously proved proposition or theory. **The existence and operation of free will** is sacred and unassailable; it has to be, it has to be preserved and allowed.

This means that when we begin to study and search for answers to the ultimate questions, we note the same impulse in other people, and begin to respect their seeking. Along the way there may of course be many kinds of difficulties, resistance, mistakes, struggles, and everything that could be called the negative aspects of free will. But these are also important. Without them, no free will would genuinely exist.

The next corollary of the Law of Manifestation is **desire**. It may be an important tool where it presents itself. When you concentrate totally on what you desire, more of you comes forth on the inner planes and what you desire may manifest. At the same time your desire also changes. The desire to know yourself causes you to know yourself in some new way. When you are in harmony with the fact that you want to know yourself, the thing you desire – whether something material, some relationship, or something else – manifests, because it is in many ways in line with your essential being.

The Permanent Atom

Esoterically, in addition to the God-spark or divine spark, sometimes a permanent atom is mentioned. This is often physically located in the chest area and resembles a jasmine flower. In each incarnation, our physical body is built around this original point or atom, which continues on from life to life. The soul builds a physical body for the personality, its "satellite" in each earthly life. The physical body corresponds to various developmental needs, reflections from previous lives, karmic conditions etc. There are other atoms on other planes, but we do not need to consider them here.

This essential being must exist beyond the limits of the three-dimensional world, of time and space, in the higher dimensions. The essential being is of God, the source of existence, time, space, dimensionality, and ultimately of the beings that carry within themselves the God-spark.

Our Own Uniqueness

Our seeking to know ourselves is a reflection of God's acting to know Himself. But we do not all reflect God's activity in the same way. If we did, there would be nothing to know. We must find our own path, our own uniqueness, our own individual way of expressing divinity.

What follows from this, what does this knowledge create? It creates differences: differences in the reality of God's existence, differences on many dimensional planes. This difference is qualitative. In our own frame of reference that difference is in most cases positive and useful.

It is very important for the individual to accept his own personal path, which has to do with love and an understanding of love in his own personal way. In it there is also a wonderful connection both to the universal Law of Love and to the idea about knowing oneself. Self-knowledge gained through one's own uniqueness and humanity, and working with love in a personal way contributes something to God. When I change, grow, evolve and progress, God changes, evolves and progresses in an analogous way. The cosmic lawfulness of progress is expressed in this way.

It has been noted time and again on the highest level of vibration that attachment to matter, and lowering the rate of vibration, bring very few results. It is a bit like a pile of trash or crushed stone, which does not particularly interest anyone, neither us nor God, nor any other beings. Over the centuries it has been observed that a positive direction of progress offers something more interesting, exciting and attractive, in its own nature.

If you ask why you seek to know yourself, why God seeks through you to know His own divine being, why this greater existence seeks manifestation in order to understand, play, create and in this way to know Itself, the answer is: because it feels good. Each of us has this same feeling when we see ourselves in a new, more positive way.

Manifestation and the Other Cosmic Laws

Everything we create includes the cosmic Law of Reflection, the Law of Karma i.e. the law of cause and effect, and the Law of Love, which has to do with the connection between all things. All of this is an expression of some part of yourself, a consequence of some part of yourself, and therefore your environment must naturally reflect this. We have here the third corollary of the Law of Manifestation: the lawfulness of the environment tells you that **your circumstances tell you something about yourself.**

This of course also has to do with the Law of Reflection: as above, so below, as in the microcosm, so in the macrocosm. But deeper in the environment, which is a reflection of yourself, there must also be keys to who you are. Do not just look at your body (your physical environment), your friends (the environment of your human relationships), your planet (the environment of our collective consciousness which we create and share together), also look at your work environment, the way you structure your life, and other similar things: **what surrounds you tells you about who you are.**

If you remember this, you will have a beautiful insight into the fact that your environment is a reflection of something very profound that is connected with the ultimate questions: who you are, what you are attempting to do here, how you exist and what you have found. You will then be able to accept your insight. This is difficult in the sense that not everyone accepts the environment of his life or understands that that environment is a reflection of himself.

You must take care here, for if a person limits his understanding of the fact that other people also have a need to come to know their essential being, he limits his understanding of this in himself at the same time. This is how it works because of the laws of corollaries, the Law of Reflection and the Law of Permanence. Outer harmony appears as inner harmony and outer disharmony similarly as inner disharmony, according to the universal Law of Reflection. In observing any living things it is important to remember that manifestation of a high order is taking place all the time. Accepting exactly this is very difficult for many people: that we ourselves create our own reality.

Even if a person accepts this, he does not necessarily take responsibility for his immediate or more distant environment. But it is worth taking a closer look, for the reality you create exists in order for your essential being to learn to know itself. Therefore every part that you see – whether you create it consciously or unconsciously – is a symbol, a reflection or an aspect of other laws, an aspect of some part of your own being, with which you can play. And even more: each one of them attempts to know itself, quite independently from you. The idea of creating your own reality feels difficult because of this, because the reality you create has its own reason for being.

Manifesting the things we want seldom succeeds completely in spite of the assertions of some doctrines. Why is this? Usually this involves some part of your own being that does not wish for the desired thing to manifest. You must develop and observe this part of yourself more closely. Accepting it, observing it, liberating it, changing it and bringing it into balance will help you to know yourself better. This is how the matter can be viewed through the Law of Manifestation.

It can be said through the Law of Karma that you have to balance your karma before you can, for example, have a certain car. Karma sets its own demands on what we can have. This is often forgotten in various "get-rich-quick" doctrines that abound. And through the Law of Symbols you must be able to understand what your environment and your life express. You must be able to read symbols and work with them before you can manifest things on the physical plane.

Before any attempts to manifest things on the outer level, you should respect a higher principle, the divine nature of the thing you are attempting to manifest. This results in a change in your own being, as well as in a new way of answering the burning question: "Who am I?" See if you are ready for this, or if you will have to struggle with this fundamental matter. You really should answer this question before you start to manifest anything.

In relation to manifestation the healthy attitude is represented by the idea that **freedom and process are more important than result**. The process can be very useful and valuable. It may be a questioning process, where we ask: "Who or what is experiencing this right now? How is it seeking its essence? How will it know itself?"

According to Hilarion we are wasting our time if a product or result is all we want. If we understand how important the Law of Manifestation is in its essence and dimensions, we gain an insight into the timelessness of all things. Even before anything exists that could be reflected in something else, even before anyone exists who could create karma, there exists a desire to feel, to know, to create, to become conscious and to discover. It is at the core of existence and creation.

To a certain extent all people resist the Law of Manifestation. Nevertheless, we exist and appear in this world of resistant matter, so why should we resist it? This is a good question, for if a person does not accept the full effect of the cause of manifestation – a powerful human nature, the need for spirituality and self-knowledge – or does not recognize it at least on some level, the result is usually confusion. Confusion attempts to balance itself through the help of the Law of Karma and the other laws. This results in a lot of work for people: a lot of busyness and many experiences are needed in their lives.

He Who Knows Himself Knows Everything

Working with the Law of Manifestation leads almost inevitably to the core question: Who **am I?** This may feel like quite an uncomfortable question that resonates deep in the core of our being. In some ancient cultures it was known as the door, or the gate.[6]

---

6   "Gnothi seauton, know yourself", were the words written in the temple of Apollo in Delphi, Greece. Another wise saying written in the temple was, according to Pausanias, "moderation in all things", i.e. nothing in excess. A significant part of the entire culture and thought of Greek antiquity was coded into these two aphorisms.

Asking this question in different languages is a very powerful tool. If you ask in all the languages you know, "Who am I? Who are you?" over and over again, it becomes a profound expression of your self, which brings up something different and new about yourself. Every person uses his free will on this journey of discovery in a different way from everyone else. Astonishing aspects arise – multifariousness, a desire to be different – and new routes to self-knowledge, which is what the Law of Manifestation is ultimately about.

On this journey you cannot finally differentiate your feelings clearly from your experience, for the language you use already makes this nearly impossible.[7] Therefore it is better to accept that there is something deeply satisfying in examining and knowing yourself. So then, if it feels good and you also accept the need for it in others, perhaps you can more easily respect the Law of Manifestation in yourself and in others. You do not just respect it mentally or on the verbal level; rather, it feels good deep in your heart.

A wonderful corollary of the Law of Manifestation is the Law of Signatures, or the **Doctrine of Signatures,** as it has been known since the times of Paracelsus (1493-1541).[8] This Swiss physician, herbalist and occultist, who is known as the father of Western medicine, wrote that the handwriting of the Creator is seen everywhere in nature, if only people have eyes to see. The God of Love has equipped nature's medicines with visible signs of the best ways to use them.

This interesting thought has survived, and in fact it was one of the points of departure for studying the symbolic language coded into nature. Plants, as well as stones, among other things, communicate by their colors, their forms, their general structure and other characteristics, knowledge about their being, and also about their gift to humanity. It has been said that every plant has at least one clear use or gift for humanity. With the Law of Signatures, we can learn to discover these gifts.

---

7   We can in general note that a new energetic/spiritual grammar partly also requires new concepts, and a deeper understanding of energies, vibrations and cosmic lawfulnesses as basic background for our reality. The clumsiness of the extant concepts often makes a description of the universal energy reality challenging.

8   Lehtiranta & Niemelä, *Suomen luonnon valkoista magiaa*, pp. 19-26.

Here there is also a connection to the Law of Reflection. As you examine the signatures and various hints about resemblances in your life, it is as if the environment you have created – your physical body, its substance and quality – is somehow related to your essential being, its basic quality and what it is trying to achieve.

The symbolism of signatures is powerful, and it is well understood in alternative medicine: in energy healing, homeopathy, flower essences, gemstone elixirs, and so on. But what about daily life? There it relates to the Law of Symbols. But fundamentally you can gain an understanding of and feel the quality of the essential being, become conscious of its indescribable beginning, the pure light which will know itself, in the manner typical of its signature and message.

What is your signature? I do not mean your handwriting, though that also offers wonderful support for the idea that you reflect your inner being in your outer expression. But at a deeper level your own essential experience differs from that of anyone else. Still, everyone has had, during his lifetimes, an experience of someone else's essential being. The eyes, as mirrors of the soul, will sometimes show this, when you look deeply into the eyes of another human being. You can call it love or infatuation. Sometimes it can be called sudden enlightenment or understanding yourself in another person. These experiences have many names.

Why not examine your own signature a bit. To begin with, think about some plant, look at its signature and see how its inner being is reflected in its outer form. As you look more carefully at the essential being of the plant, you can begin to understand the things that it can be used for, as a flower essence or as an herb in fytotherapy, or understand its effects when you grow it in your garden.

And what about your own signature, your way of being? What quality stands out, and is notable in your own being? That is exactly the quality with which you affect your environment, the people around you, and many other things. If you have not thought about this recently, here is an excellent way to answer, at least partly, the essential question: who are you? If someone shook you in a bottle and made an extract of you, what would be its basic qualities?

Universal Laws and Spiritual Progress

All the other cosmic laws are specifically connected to the Law of Manifestation. For example, an idea will manifest in an individual life if it is repeated often enough. Repetition makes the created thought compilations condense on the etheric level. As an effect of the thought, the condensing has to happen in the framework of the Law of Reflection, which offers a kind of mirror and creates a cause-and-effect relationship, or causality, while through the Law of Karma a cause-and-effect relationship brings out the result. The outer environment also has some effect on this, but mostly the effect depends on the original thought.

Trust is an important and challenging thing in relation to the Law of Manifestation, as well as in relation to the Universal Laws in general. How can you trust them when you cannot see them? They can always be questioned, you can always talk about coincidence and give thousands of other explanations. The universal quality of all these laws is precisely the fact that they cannot be seen. A deeper understanding of any of the universal principles involves trusting something that is not tangible, but which your own uniqueness can experience in some way. Such a cosmic principle cannot be proved from the point of view of rigid materialism, but it can be empirically tested, or it is something that can be **experienced** as true.

When you make space for trust, you at the same time awaken manifestation and welcome it in. This does not happen by pretending, but through your own experience and uniqueness. At the same time you increase considerably your possibility of manifesting on the physical level, satisfying your emotional needs, improving your human relationships, and so on.

Meditation: Who Are You?

Find a quiet, peaceful place, and relax. With your eyes closed, place your consciousness in some part of your body, perhaps near your navel, or at your root chakra near your tail bone, or perhaps in the region of your heart, or even in the middle of your head. Observe and focus on this place, breathe light into it and through it. Take your time, there is no hurry.

Then have a great cylinder of light stream into the place where you are focused and make it glow. With the help of your outbreath allow all unnecessary residues to flow out of your body into the Earth. Then, in this state of consciousness, say to yourself: "Who am I? **Who** am I? Who **am** I? Who am **I?**"

Let yourself feel safe, energizing and beautiful in this state. Let go of any sense of discomfort that may have arisen with the question but allow its power to remain with you. Allow the light that you have imagined in your center to glow and to pulsate. Who are you? Who are you? Who are you? Allow the question to resonate in you as if you were asking the light in your center, asking your very breath: Who are you?

Allow the answers to arise as they will: as colors, as forms, as feeling, as past or future feeling, as love, as consolation, as comfort or discomfort, as something concrete or perhaps as a symbol. It does not matter. The answer is yours, it is real, and it is loving.

Then focus your attention again on the state you are in. Let go of the answer and see whether it has changed you a little. You may want to share this experience with someone at some later time. Smile.

Summary:

★ God observes and learns to know Himself through us, Divinity looks through our eyes. We and the other manifestations exist in order to understand ourselves, our universe and our God, and to discover all this in each other.

★ God has detached a piece of his Divine Being, a piece which is a being with free will and which has been sent to find its own path.

★ The reality you have created exists in order for your essential being to learn to know itself.

✳ Essential being and existence itself are one, and this oneness contains something that is greater than both, and that is a beautiful reflection of God.

✳ Everyone must find his own path, his own uniqueness. The only means to this is a maximum use of energy and the expression of free will.

✳ In manifestation freedom is always more important than outcome, and the process more important than the product.

✳ Physical manifestation requires complete liberation from the connection of the manifested object with anything else. It also presumes consciousness of the inner ability of the manifested object to change you spiritually, and to help you to know yourself, as well as the object, in this process.

✳ Physical manifestation usually fails because some part of your being does not want it to be realized.

✳ A majority of humankind resists the Law of Manifestation because people do not want to accept that we are all a part of God and that God is within us. There is an attempt to balance the confusion.

✳ The Law of Signatures is a general observation about the way in which a human being or some other being creates a message about himself in his environment.

Literature:
Filosofian sanakirja (Ilari Hetemäki) 1999. WSOY, Porvoo – Helsinki – Juva.
Hilarion 1982: *Vision*. Marcus Books, Queensville, Ontario.
Lehtiranta, Erkki & Niemelä, Leena 2007. *Suomen luonnon valkoista magiaa*. Smiling Stars, Helsinki.

2.

Reflection

"The reality that surrounds any being on any plane of existence – no matter how high or how low its level – must ultimately correspond exactly with the true inner essence of that being."

- Hilarion

IN TERMS OF LEARNING, the Law of Reflection has great significance for humanity in its present stage of progress. In fact, according to Master Hilarion, it is the currently most important of these laws in the reality matrix of humanity. This principle is present in our daily lives in more ways than we notice, and we can learn a great deal about ourselves and our world through this law. The law is powerfully present in world events, and with its help we are best able to understand the possibilities that are connected with the survival of our species.

The Law of Reflection has been known since ancient times, and echoes of it can be found in the basic axioms of Hermetic philosophy: As above, so below; as in the microcosm, so in the macrocosm. We could add to this with, for example: as in the inner, so in the outer.

This third formulation of the law of course does not mean, for example, a correspondence between the inner and outer temperature or other such measurable conditions of the phenomenal world, but rather a correspondence between, say, the inner states of an individual and his outer appearance. The body is a wise display terminal of our inner states. Quite often the connection of inner and outer also points to the Law of Symbols, which we will take up a bit later, in chapter 10. These two laws have a strong connection. You can make use of the principle of reflection for example in examining and understanding your own state of health. There are some examples of this at the end of the chapter.

The principle of reflecting and being reflected penetrates the entire universe. According to Hilarion it is valid up to the 11th dimension. It is a question of the meeting of the macrocosm and the microcosm, which gives the student of reality a magnificent tool for understanding the great through the small, and the inner through the outer. A wonderful modern example of this is the world of fractals, where you can see the structure of the whole in the parts of a figure. Such a model of symmetry occurs for example in the hexagonal geometry of a snowflake.

In summary the law tells us that the surrounding reality corresponds to the real inner being of each being – whether great or small. In other words, the outer reality and the inner being are correlated. For example, the outer circumstances of an individual's life relate to the learning processes that are taking place in the soul, that is, at the level of the higher side of the being.[9]

The World Looks like Us

A fish in the water, a cactus in the desert, a person in daily life, a nation in a crisis of change, a planet in a galaxy, each has its story in which the great Law of Reflection is visible. While some of the other cosmic laws may be difficult to see on the level of ordinary life (I am thinking in particular of the Laws of Manifestation and Permanence), the Law of Reflection is present in our daily life.

Reality looks like us and places a kind of mirror in front of us. Whether we want to look into that mirror is another matter. As a rule

---

9   Hilarion, *Vision*, p. 14

of thumb, **never try to fix the mirror, fix the person who is looking at you out of the mirror. We ourselves create the reality reflected in the mirror.** In addition, the clarity or fogginess of the eyeglasses of our consciousness tells us how well we can comprehend this principle. The matter in question here may be difficult to digest all at once; after all, materialistic science has never told us about this kind of correspondence. Outside of us there is an absolute reality completely independent of us, or is there?

What then should we think of the experiences that we all know so well, where the outside world seems to echo our call? "You asked for it, you got it." Have you noticed how anger arouses anger in our environment as well? We project our inner states, our emotions and thoughts, into outer reality, and they in turn magnetize corresponding things to us from outer reality. In theory this may be a difficult equation, but in our experience it usually isn't, if we have the capacity to consider reality and know how to stay awake and be honest with ourselves in various situations.

Father Anthony de Mello has an amusing story that illustrates this point. I will borrow it here from memory. Once upon a time there was a wise rabbi who was often asked for advice in various difficult situations. Once there came to him a man who was about to move to a different area. He asked the rabbi what kinds of people he was going to meet there. The rabbi answered by asking the man, "What kinds of people have you met in this city?" The man said he had met greedy, selfish, sarcastic, dishonest people. The rabbi answered that he was going to meet exactly those kinds of people in the new place as well.

A little later there came another man, who also told the rabbi that he intended to move to another area. He too asked the rabbi the same thing, and received the same question in return, "What kinds of people have you met in this city?" The man answered that the people he had met had been friendly and helpful, with a good sense of humor, and who were in every way the best kinds of people. The rabbi said again that there would be exactly those kinds of people in the city where the man was planning to move.

Two Poles, Two Paths

This story, too, tells us how the world looks like us. Our emotional, psychological and mental equipment has something like a magnet with two poles.[10] One of the poles is a kind of "revulsion pole", which activates and attracts to us exactly the things, situations, circumstances and people that we loathe, despise and hate. This always involves a clear allusion to our own unfinished homework and inner lessons, which proclaim themselves in our own outer reality – more often than we would like. And these things happen over and over until we notice that we must become proactive about our homework.

The worst problem is usually the fact that we continue to project our problems onto the outer world and on top of it all, we are amazed that we bump into such and such a person or situation again. We have not learned an important lesson. On a deeper level, these situations and confrontations are the ringing of a kind of spiritual alarm clock, and we should draw the correct conclusions from them. For we have, on the level of the unconscious mind, a completely clear and transparent vision of the true nature of things, but our conscious mind often fights back, since it is so much easier to just continue to accuse the outer world: "It's not me but them."

Fortunately our spiritual equipment also contains that other, "positive" pole, which attracts to us the things, situations, and types of people that we love, respect and admire. It is wise to find, in the world and in people, the truly admirable, positive things, which you surely can find if you look for them, since the inner magnet activates, within ourselves, the things we admire. When a person lives in love, he reflects this high emotional state outside of himself – and the outer world of course answers his call and reflects love back to him. The same is true with all our other emotions.

In general, then, we meet in our outer reality the things that correspond precisely to our own inner states or the developmental is-

---

10   Lehtiranta, *Tien päällä ja taivaan alla*, pp. 450-451.

sues relevant to us at the time. It should be obvious which pole of the magnet I would urge you to strengthen and activate in every way possible.

The Law of Reflection tells you how you see and know yourself. It is a great point of departure for self-knowledge, and it can teach you much about your own nature and the nature of reality. In this it lines up very well with the Law of Manifestation, which was considered in the previous chapter, where I wrote as follows: Many different universes were created precisely and only in order for the spiritual beings, the entities behind forms, to be able to know themselves. If you are not a complete hermit – and who could be one, these days – you are working with the Law of Reflection constantly every day. In the outer world, you meet the energy that you reflect into it.

However, it is another universal law that most closely correlates with the Law of Reflection in human activity and interrelationships, namely the Law of Opposites, which we will return to more thoroughly in chapter 5.

Simplicity vs. Complexity

You can study the Law of Reflection along two routes. In the first, life is **very complicated**, but you can genuinely learn to understand many things through it. You can gain some understanding of the Law of Reflection symbolically or logically, or you can work with it experientially in your own life. You can proceed by using emotions to accuse yourself or others. You can criticize others and the circumstances of your life, and work on many things that become more and more complicated as time goes by.

Another route also exists, and it could perhaps be called **the path of simplicity.** As you journey on it, you come upon and observe things without understanding them completely, but there is something special and important about simplicity, and through it you can learn to understand the Law of Reflection. Thus, the possibility of choosing arises again.

The Law of Reflection is one of the areas of life where the choice of route is usually not compulsory, even though some karmic, or other patterns from the past, may have an influence on it.

Studying the Law of Reflection is usually difficult, because guilt, misunderstandings, perhaps the need to control, or resistance and denial often arise in situations of reflection. The idea here is that if you reject or deny something on any level, the rejected and denied exists all the same, and is nevertheless reflected back on to you. Remember that there are no innocent bystanders or accidents, nor unprovoked hostility. The things that exist in your being are reflected back on to you.

It is good to study these denied, forbidden, misunderstood, and guilt-inducing themes, but the solution to all of them is always the same. You must go back to the fork in the road and clarify why you chose that particular route where you needed resistance in order to recognize your own potential, where you needed guilt or struggle in order to know who you are. Or you chose the route out of experience, because it was safer, or you chose the route as an emotional reaction, or because you didn't know any better. This list could be expanded.

When you return to the fork in the road, where you made the choice, and recreate the event, change your energy at the same time in such a way that the energy reflected back on to you is something that individualizes, magnifies, or creates something beautiful in yourself. It could be called love, an aspect of love in your being.

It is also possible that you will receive the message of reflection immediately and realize its importance without complexity. You can choose surrender rather than control. Because, through control, you bring in conscious power and energy, which you then must endure with their consequences. Usually this involves greater denial at the same time, which makes everything more difficult. You can even choose the most difficult aspect of denial, i.e. addiction.

Does this sound too simple? It is because of this that Hilarion so often speaks about the heart and its wisdom. The Law of Love tells us much about the matter. There is a direct message in everyone's heart:

the eyes of your heart open to understanding and see better and with more love the things you manifest every time that you do not choose the path of difficulties and struggle.

If there is enough understanding and acceptance within you, and you are able to express maximum forgiveness, then bring love into a situation, because with it you can change things and understand immediately what is reflected in them. Much can be understood even in this simple way. The heart gives the best answer to the question of how to understand the meaning behind the symbols, the cycles, the ways in which things manifest, the energies that you receive etc. You can use this idea and this method in your meditation and see an image of yourself reflecting forgiveness in the situation in question.

When you ask for example: "Where is there a lack of love, how could love be used in this situation, in what respect have I denied some aspect of love in this?", you are already on the right course, and the ways this law functions start to become clear. The right questions are extremely important, as we will see in connection with the Law of Thought in chapter 7.

This is how you can work with any of the laws. For example the Law of Opposite Expression brings to you with precision the opposite of a matter: what is revealed in yourself is what you would often like to deny in yourself. Sometimes this is the most difficult thing to work with. Nevertheless through the Law of Opposite Expression you can bring to consciousness the emotion that is behind the denial.

Spiritual maturity is one of the finest fruits of understanding the Law of Reflection. Taking responsibility is in fact a part of the Law of Reflection, where you take full responsibility for yourself and your actions, without a stressed feeling or a heavy burden on your shoulders.

We can proceed further in our investigation by considering some other laws. The Law of Cycles is a very important law because it helps you to develop your understanding of the Law of Reflection: what goes around comes around. Here there is of course a connection with the Law of Karma. The connection with the Law of Karma is also important, because it shows you the mechanism by which you see the

Law of Reflection: cause and effect. What you create has the effect on the environment that corresponds to its nature.

This manifestation of energy is expressed as waves, which is true of most phenomena of the physical plane. You may think that this has more to do with particles and things like that, which you might call material. We may get stuck on the particulate nature of existence because we do not see or recognize ourselves as waves, which we largely are. It is precisely the waves of love in your heart, which bring to you directly the answers that have a new energy and a new resonance.

This is exactly what happens when you return to that fork in the road and decide that you will no longer take the route that tells you that you are separate from what you reflect. You are one with it. The Law of Love then shows you how you are united with all things, with all beings. By using the principle of love you gain knowledge on the heart level, which you may eventually be able to transform into energy that you can know and feel in your mind.

In many cases the Law of Reflection works immediately as a kind of echo effect. Nevertheless, the energies that are released often do not express themselves in a way that you can understand right away and be able to work with. They come at a time and in a form that you understand little by little. Perhaps they come into form, with other energies, in cycles which are connected with the symbolic movements of the planets and stars, with the cycles of the Earth, with other lives, with economic and political cycles, in which the Law of Reflection is also expressed.

Larger Reflections

It should be understood that these are not just laws that relate to planetary influences, but rather reflections from your world. For example, they are reflections where political unease, economic difficulties, and other similar things can be manifested in the stock market. Sounds familiar? For example the planetary cycles of astrology are more important for their symbolic value than for their direct influence and their predictability.

In other words, the Law of Reflection is valid in much larger spheres than just in our personal lives, even though recognizing and acknowledging this law in our daily lives is of great importance. Groups live in the sphere of influence of this law, as well, and can examine themselves and the current challenges to their progress through it, by observing for example their outer circumstances and troubles. In groups, problems connected with money usually indicate difficulties in sharing, in serving a larger whole – for example the society around them –, and in general, in practicing another great cosmic law, the Law of Love. Here it is possible to gain profound insights with the help of spiritual group dynamics and laws.

This is true of even larger contexts, for example large communities, nations, international organizations like the EU and the UN, for humanity as a whole, for the planet, for our life stream, for our soul stream, for civilizations, for the galaxy and the universe. To maintain full respect for each universal law and to work with it, we need to apply these principles in a greater context as well. Ultimately, since this reflection is the reflection of humankind's uniqueness back to God, God is able to understand and work with humankind on a new level: a level that humankind has created. Thus the Law of Reflection expands all the way to the largest imaginable source, and also recognizes the very smallest – there is no difference between them in relation to God.

The expression of the Law of Reflection on the level of communities, for example, is not very hard to understand, if you focus on the matter a little. For example, the collective consciousness of the population of larger communities is reflected in many things in those communities. The state of the zoo tells you about the collective relationship to animals, the botanical garden about the relationship with plants, the condition and safety of the subway about the relationship of the community to the unconscious, the weapons and aggressiveness (or the lack of these) of the police force about the relationship of the community to aggression.

The metro in Helsinki is relatively tidy and safe, the Paris metro on the other hand is very imaginative, complex and artistic: after all, that French metropolis has always attracted artists and creative people. The New York subway used to be very messy and even unsafe. Now it has become safer and cleaner. It should be remembered here that we are referring to collective consciousness, its general nature, not to individuals. [11]

Water as a Reflector

Let us take water as another, more active example. Water is an ancient symbol of the emotions, and one of the classical four elements (the others are earth, air and fire). I will write more about the symbolism of water in chapter 10, but the tales told by water extend further than the cosmic Law of Symbols, and they also involve the principle of reflection profoundly.

You may have noticed that water has been constantly present in all the communications media. Either there is way too much water somewhere, as in, say, the flood plains of Thailand, or else there has been way too little of it, as in the areas suffering from drought. Or else the water is polluted, poisoned, or otherwise threatened.

What does all this tell us, is it about coincidental events, or about something quite different? Coincidence, that lazy person's mental crutch, has nothing to do with this. Water is a reflector of the collective emotional life of mankind, and its symbolic value is immense. For example, in large communities, (which are almost without exception built next to water), the condition of the shores is a direct reflection of the conscious contact of the human collective with its emotional field, and of its values in relation to that field. Where the shores are attractively clean, well kept, beautiful, safe, and in the service of people's needs, there the emotional life of the collective is in good contact with the emotions and is notably progressive. In this case it is easier for the positive emotions to find their expression and to unite with the other important aspects of life.[12]

---

11   Hilarion, *Nations*, pp. 27-28.
12   Hilarion, *Nations*, pp. 28-29.

In the contrary case filthy, smelly, untended, and perhaps even unsafe shores, tell us that the majority of the people in the community have emotional problems. Contact with the emotions, and in particular with the cleansing streams of love, is in need of development.

As long as people wallow in negative emotions, in hatred, resentment, envy, lack of forgiveness, etc., so long water will also be out of balance on a planetary level. Many people have in fact already realized that the great natural disasters involving water, such as the tsunamis and the annual hurricanes, are Mother Earth's way of lightening her burden, which mankind in its heedlessness and immaturity has brought about.

When the emotions of mankind become calmer and cleaner on the collective level, and the positive emotions, unconditional love as the highest of them, become active and in control, the water system of the planet will also begin to come into balance. Hilarion has mentioned that this will be visible in, for example, the calming of storms in the oceans.[13] Calm water reflects the pure light of spirit, which is symbolized by the Sun, for its part. The Moon in turn is often astrologically linked with the water element and with the emotions, and this companion of the Earth can be seen as an important reflection in nature. It is, after all, a reflector surface of sunlight.[14]

Reflector Surfaces of Countries

In general it can be said that people have some kind of common sense understanding of the Law of Reflection, as when it is said that a people has the leader it deserves. "You asked for it, you got it" is an everyday expression, repeated with enthusiasm at coffee breaks and at work. But only a few understand the real reach and depth of this sentence.

---

13   Hilarion, *Symbols*, pp. 9-19.
14   Of the elements for example chromium is an excellent symbol of the Law of Reflection. For example as an energy elixir it can give a deeper understanding of this universal law. Chromium elixir has many powerful capacities to raise the level of consciousness of an individual as he accepts this universal principle. At the same time he is more able to understand the energies of other people and to reflect the best and highest of himself into his own environment.

Several Universal Laws meet in this sentence, for example the Laws of Reflection, of Karma, and of Thought. Among other things countries, peoples, cities, and families are a kind of spiritual magnets, which attract certain kinds of people who offer certain kinds of lessons.

We can give many examples that relate to, for example, countries and people. We Finns study and examine reality under the blue ray. This ray has served as the carrier wave for Finnish understanding and expertise, which connects with teaching, the sharing of energies, communication, and increased self-knowledge, among other things. I have written about this most interesting subject in my book *Tien päällä ja taivaan alla – kirjoituksia etsijän polulta* (On the Road and under the Sky – Writings from a Seeker's Path).[15]

A special characteristic of Finnishness is the study of the cosmic Law of Thought and its application in practice. Finland therefore attracts souls that want to learn especially about these things. The color blue is, interestingly, an essential part of being Finnish, after all, it shows up in our flag, in the multitude of our lakes, our longing for blue moments, and the amount of blue thoughts. The abundance of water in our country brings its own nuance to this symbolism and reflection: how do we become comfortable with our own emotional life? This is not altogether easy for a people whose special developmental needs are strongly anchored in the mental, in developing thought.

One of the central collective desires for us Finns is to be able to live by water for at least a part of the year. We feel that we are purified there, and just generally that we *feel* there. Now this is easy to understand as the unconscious (or partly already conscious) desire of the Finnish collective to gain a closer contact with our emotional life.

The spiritual magnet of the French also suggests the development of the mental faculty and a strong connection to the Law of Speech, in the light of Mercury. Spain, on the other hand, attracts individuals who express themselves powerfully through religious needs, or who want to study profound religious faith. Many who have incarnated in

---

15   Lehtiranta, *Tien päällä ja taivaan alla*, pp. 385-399.

Germany have a military past. Swedes, for their part, are particularly studying the expression of the Law of Love, the Estonians – who are strongly activated by the red ray at this time – the Law of Manifestation, and the Russians the Law of Opposite Expression. The USA is the prime example of a nation that is focused on the Law of Reflection at the current time.

All these examples illustrate the deep inner need to gain union and connection with the kind of universal law whose examination and application is perceived to be important from the point of view of the individual's own soul plan, and which possibly also indicates some neglect or denial involving that law. The denial of something in oneself always activates some important lessons, which relate to the Laws of Reflection, Opposite Expression, and Karma as well. We can again echo the view that what we deny and reject in ourselves, we attract to ourselves like a magnet. I will return to this very timely theme again in chapter 5, when writing about the Law of Opposite Expression.

As you can see, this opens a very expansive and many-layered view of the expressions of the Law of Reflection on the collective level. In addition to the Universal Laws, there are many different factors, such as the rays and the astrological energies, which come into the picture. These factors are very skillfully handled by for example Master Hilarion's co-worker, Master Djwhal Khul, a.k.a the Tibetan, in his books, which he has given to mankind through Alice A. Bailey.[16]

The Wisdom of the Human Body

It is time to return from these collective expressions of the Law of Reflection to the more personal level, where we can better understand our own life and our developmental needs. As I already noted in the beginning of the chapter, the Law of Reflection functions wisely in the human body, in which the inner appears in many ways in the outer. Almost every notable part or area of the body functions as a micro-

---

16   Among these are for example *"The Destiny of Nations"*, and *"Initiations"*.

cosm of the whole body – and if not as a reflection of the whole body, then of some other whole, complete level of the individual.

Reflexology is a wonderful example of this. The different areas of the foot are a direct reflection of the different parts of the body. Reflexology maps show this connection, especially in the sole and on the edges of the foot. Since the matter has been well coded and mapped, we will not go deeper into it here.

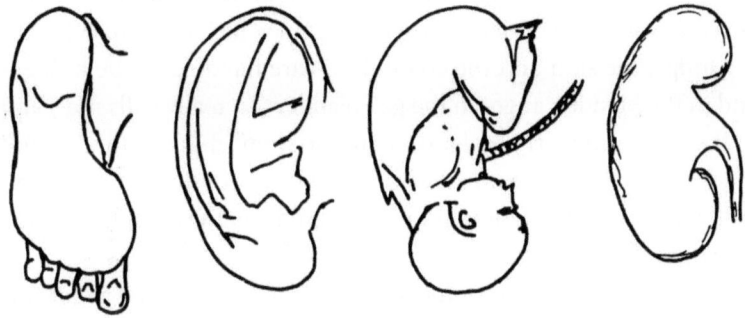

The similarity of form of the sole of the foot, the ear, and the kidney. Paul, Le Chant Sacré des Energies, p. 392.

On a more general level there are communication links between the different parts of a human being, both in the physical and the spiritual structure. Particularly in the etheric body there are innumerable channels of information and energy, which connect the interior organs and systems with some of the outer structures of the body: the palms, the feet (especially the soles of the feet), the ears, and the eyes. The energies that the reflexology therapist either awakens in the etheric body of his client, or that he adds to it, travel through these communication channels from the foot or the hand to the corresponding body part. According to iris diagnostics or iridology, you can see almost the entire state of health of a person from the eyes. But you can see even more from the eyes. The eyes cannot lie, even if the mouth does. An ancient wisdom tells us that the eyes are the mirror of the soul. This is a profound truth, which we will return to in connection with the Law of Symbols.

Esoterically the iris of the eye refers to the physical body, while the white symbolizes the etheric body, from which the physical body gets all its energy. The pupil in the middle of the iris symbolizes the higher essence, or soul, of the person.[17] Again, the large is visible in the small. In the gospel of Luke it is said, "If your eye is whole, your whole body is full of light." (Luke 11:34)

In Oriental body diagnostics the heart and the circulatory system are connected with hysteria and a lack of joy, while grief connects with the lungs, the skin and the colon. Fears are handled in the kidneys and in the bladder, anger in the gall bladder ("it really galls me") and in the liver, and worry and anxiety in the stomach, the pancreas and the spleen. The grammar of the human body opens through these and many similar understandings into a magnificent thesis on the cosmic Law of Reflection.

This law, more than any other of the cosmic principles, is a redeeming factor, which brings deep understanding and knowledge on many levels that are extremely comprehensive. Those who know and understand this lawfulness will in the future be the great guides of civilization, who will bring about the greatest transformation. They could be compared with the great leaders of the past, who brought blessings to their country because they had profound vision about these matters. In other words: use the Law of Reflection, get to know it, but also apply it to broader contexts as you listen to the news. Then you will understand how to relate to what happens in the world, how to relate to your neighbor, and of course also how to relate to your own personal life.

---

17   Hilarion, *Seasons of The Spirit*, p. 10.

Universal Laws and Spiritual Progress

A Meditation for Letting Go

If you are doing this meditation in a group, look around you in the place where you are meditating and notice all the beautiful soul sparks that are present. Notice these magnificent rays of light that struggle to recognize themselves in the world and to bring out the highest and the best of themselves in their own unique way and in harmony with their own God-nature. Trust your observations and now breathe into yourself the feeling that in this space there exists a strong love energy between people, all of whom are striving to know themselves.

Then let go of everything that you have to do or to be: make a living, take responsibility, feel guilty about not understanding others, accomplish things, be accepted or loved, look a certain way or act or make a living in a certain way, be healthy, survive, or exist. That you *have to* exist.

If you could leave all these things behind for a moment and just breathe – most likely you would confront the risk that you would no longer exist. But still, if you hear our voices and can read these lines, some part of you still exists, even if you let go of all these things.

Now when you close your eyes and sink into this state of letting go, you may notice that there is something joyous in you, something outside of the thought that you exist, or that you have to do anything or to make choices. In question here is precisely that place in you that continues to exist, to breathe and to live, and that is in fact the same place that understood the importance of light and life in order to grow and to understand itself. It is precisely this place that recognizes and respects love in the other people in the room and in yourself.

In this place it is easy to begin things and to reflect them, without compulsion, without having to do or to be this or that. This part of yourself accepts things and welcomes them because it feels good. If you have ever been through a significant health challenge, you may notice that you have now found a place where you can simply let go and be free. And at some time this place may give you strength, life force and energy, which will help you to heal or to have greater understanding, love, and many other things.

Now, slowly, let go of this. In other words focus your attention again on the space where you are, and on your own body, and notice at the same time how much humor is involved in your having to do all those things in the world. Give yourself a smile.

Summary

✳ The Hermetic axiom: as above, so below - as in the micro-cosm, so in the macrocosm - as in the inner, so in the outer.

✳ The Law of Reflection brings you everything you experience on the physical, the emotional, the mental and the spiritual level.

✳ The world around you shows you what you are and what you can become.

✳ In your life you are often at a fork in the road where you can choose the path of difficulties, denial and avoidance, or the route where surrender, love and forgiveness reign.

✳ The difficult things will not leave your life before you have met them with love.

✳ There are no innocent bystanders, accidents or coincidences.

✳ The Law of Reflection extends into the 11th dimension.

Literature:
Hilarion 1980: *Symbols*. Marcus Books, Agincourt, Ontario.
Hilarion 1984: *Nations*. Marcus Books, Toronto.
Lehtiranta, Erkki 2011: *Tien päällä ja taivaan alla*. Smiling Stars, Helsinki.
Paul, Maela & Patrick 1983: *Le Chant Sacré des Énergies*. Editions Présence, Sisterion.

3.

Karma

Every thought, emotion and action leaves a karmic residue, which 'clings' to the entity, whose thoughts, emotions and actions are in question.

- Hilarion

THE WEST AND THE EAST have traditionally had two different views of the Law of Karma, or the law of cause and effect. In our own times the west has taken a questioning, even a skeptical, stance toward it, and this attitude has been typical of both science and traditional Christianity. Science does consider causality to operate on the material level (perhaps apart from some phenomena on the quantum level), while for the traditional Christian believer there is no place for karmic thinking.

The usual western way of thinking emphasizes the significance of free will and does not believe in determinism except perhaps in the case of genetics and some environmental factors. In the east, especially in the cultural sphere of India, the most dominant view has been that a human being must surrender to his fate. " It's my karma, and I can do nothing about it" is a fairly typical comment in that culture. In the east the doctrine of reincarnation is closely connected to karma, since without that principle no-one could confront his karma completely within the space of one lifetime. Serial killers serve as a gruesome example of this.

In this book we try to build a bridge between the understanding of the west and the east. The east is correct in that much of what we confront in life is predetermined. The west is correct in that there is also a lot of room in our lives for the expression of genuinely free will. With spiritual progress this area of free will actually even grows and gets stronger. Karma sets many kinds of limits on our experience, but it is possible for us to move gradually from the world of karma to the world of love. Of course this demands a lot of inner work and its outer reflection. I wrote about this in the previous chapter and will return to it in more detail when I handle the cosmic Law of Love in chapter 12.

Pain is one of the ways that the universe draws your attention to the essential lessons, such as the connection of cause and effect. "The soup tastes the way you spice it; as you make your bed so you sleep in it; what goes around comes around." Different cultures have found many apt sayings to express this basic law, which could also be called the law of new possibility. That is, it offers the possibility of learning new things.

The Law of Karma is the way the universe ties together causes and effects.[18] When understood on a deeper level it is also the law of justice. Everyone gets what he deserves. The relationship of cause and effect has in the past been so distant that many people have failed to notice and realize this universal principle. Now the time lapse between cause and effect appears to have shortened, in other words if you "spit into the wind", the splat happens faster than before.

The Law of Karma can be seen to reveal an interesting connection with Newton's Law of Action/Reaction, also known as Newton's Third Law. This law, one of the basic laws of mechanics, says that if an object is affected with some force by another object, then at the same time that object must affect the other object with an equal but opposite force.

---

18   Some sources maintain that the continuum of time is an illusion, that all the lives are lived simultaneously, and that there is no difference between past, present and future. Nevertheless, since karma is transferred from one life to another, and since the karmic consequences become manifest in them, it is wise to think that the lives follow each other in order. See Hilarion, *Dark Robes, Dark Brothers*, pp. 27-28.

Universal Laws and Spiritual Progress

Balancing and Consciousness

Energies always strive to come into balance, on the material level as well as on higher levels. It is also good to notice that the Law of Karma is automatic, a lawfulness built into the nature of reality, in other words karma does not come from some council or judge. The consequences of an individual's actions travel with him in the various bodies in the form of a kind of vibrational charge, and the accumulation of karma is an entirely natural characteristic contained in reality itself. Positive actions increase the positive balance in a person's spiritual account and bring positive vibration to his being and light to his soul. Negative actions create their own kind of vibration and the corresponding consequences.[19]

An important karmic principle can be observed in human interactions: a kind of vicious cycle of predator and prey, a syndrome which, if not worked through, continues from life to life. The persecutor becomes in turn the victim, the oppressor the oppressed, and the prey becomes the predator. Here the Law of Opposite Expression meets the Law of Karma seamlessly. A good example of this are the slave owners of the southern states of the U.S.A., many of whom were born as dark-skinned objects of racial persecution in their next incarnation.

Another model can be found in the Middle East, especially between the Palestinians and the Israelis: they are born alternately from one people to the other until they finally learn that hatred, vengeance and other such negative expressions produce nothing but more of the same. Brotherhood, tolerance, and ultimately forgiveness and love must in the end come to bring peace between these peoples.

Hatred, resentment, insults, lack of forgiveness and other such negative models and emotions follow us – individuals as well as peoples – like sharks follow a boat unless they are confronted and resolved. Getting stuck in *samsara,* the wheel of rebirth, depends greatly on these footsteps from the past, which we always find in front of us un-

---

19   Hilarion, *Answers*, pp. 79-80.

til we take on our lessons in earnest. Confronting our karma always also involves confronting our lessons. Becoming bitter is not wise when karma stings.

In fact it is always good to maintain a healthy sense of proportion where karma is concerned. An apt Indian proverb says: I wept that I had no shoes until I saw a man with no legs. In some quarters it is said that the Law of Karma has ceased to operate. This illusory view may stem from the fact that in our times we encounter things more quickly. In the same way we could then say that the law of gravity has ceased to operate. The Law of Karma is the spiritual equivalent of the law of gravity, a kind of spiritual gravitational field, and as long as we are in a three-dimensional world, we are under the influence of time and space, gravity and karma. This inescapable lawfulness needs to be thoroughly understood.

In this context consciousness is both a causal and a liberating factor. An understanding of the causes behind things and of their consequences must penetrate our consciousness and all sides of our being before we truly begin to be liberated from the clutches of karma. The higher the level of consciousness that a person reaches, the less he is bound by the iron grip of time and the resistance of matter, inertia. The more time he has available (the nature of time is relative and is connected to consciousness), the greater are his chances of reversing karma in a wise manner. It is important to realize that negative karma can be redeemed by positive actions, for example by helping other people.

The enclosed model envelope illustrates this relationship of consciousness to the other factors in question, time, matter and karma.[20]

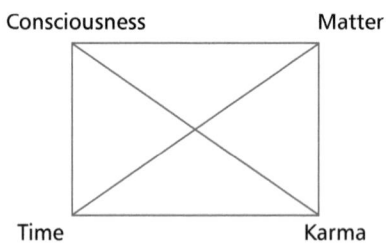

Consciousness — Matter

Time — Karma

---

20   Lehtiranta, *Astrologia ja Henkinen Tie*, pp. 34-35.

A good symbol of how karma operates is a boomerang. We could again use that already slightly hackneyed expression, "you get what you ask for." Hilarion tells us that every thought, emotion and action leaves a karmic residue, which very concretely clings to the being whose thoughts, emotions and actions are in question.

If the thought, emotion or action in question causes physical, emotional or mental suffering or limitation to another sentient being, this results in negative or limiting karma. However, it is important to remember in this connection that every positive thought, action or emotion creates expanding positive karma.

Within the created worlds there are many regions whose inhabitants could not even dream of performing any actions that would create negative karma. In this respect we, the inhabitants of our beautiful planet Earth, still have something to learn, and not so little, either.

Karmic Confrontations as Health Problems and Addictions

Some of the most typical things connected with confronting karma are various health problems. We could say that diseases are almost without exception karmic. Even as common a problem as ordinary flu relates to karmic causes, usually having to do with emotions of anger and irritation. A person gets a "cold" after he himself has been cold and unfeeling toward another person somewhat earlier, and after having allowed feelings of anger and irritation to become anchored in himself.[21] An excessive use of substances that weaken the body, such as refined sugar, is of course also often involved. This also predisposes the body to the flu. Another example is repeated throat infections, which are a karmic result of the person having attacked others verbally.

The backgrounds of health problems are quite complex, so very short answers do not do them full justice. For example, family kar-

---

21   Hilarion, *More Answers*, p. 52.

ma often plays a part in this, as does addiction. Abuse of the physical body in ways that have caused direct harm or chronic ailments, special mutations or other bodily problems for other people, often results in a need for karmic balancing in the next incarnation. The person then chooses karmic atonement for example through a limp, through a tendency to some weakness or even through drug addiction. These, then, are choices made before birth. They are coded into the individual's life plan.

Many people with a drug problem have been drug dealers in previous lives, and have exposed many people to drug addiction in, for example, the Chinese opium trade. Now they confront this problem in their own lives. I have pointed out this principle of the criminal and the victim earlier in this chapter as a vicious cycle of predator and prey where the roles just alternate from one life to the next – until someone severs that karmic cycle with the help of his own power, insight, forgiveness and love.

In this connection it is important to notice that the individuals who have overcome addiction, liberated themselves from it, and understood the lessons offered by it, are often the most creative, brilliant and strong individuals, who are able to learn much and of course also to teach others. The shadow self specialist, author and teacher Debbie Ford (1955-2013) was a perfect example of this.

In connection with addictions and similar problems it is good to remember the Bible's words: judge not that you be not judged. Through every inner and outer judgment a person attracts to himself the very thing that he judges or criticizes in others. It is great wisdom to avoid this kind of spiritual drag.

Where addictions are concerned, probably only about 30% of them relate to nutrition, alcohol, drugs, cigarettes or sugar. We can also be addicted to power, sex, controlling others, dramatizing things, exploiting others, being right, punctuality, and countless other ideas, people, behavioral models and emotions.[22]

---

22   LaVoie, *Return to Harmony*, p. 196.

I want to remind you that an unresolved karmic problem or lesson passes on automatically into the next lives and becomes even more severe. Compassion is the means through which full understanding of karma arises, since your love is a part of your existence and of your essential being. Hilarion states that love is actually the quickest and safest way to resolve karmic problems.

Gaining new perspectives and new understanding of these things is necessary. Even if you had nothing to do with a certain addiction, you can gain an understanding of its origin through intuition, spiritual impulse, regression into past lives, and some psychological method such as NLP, and ultimately see it with the eyes of the wisdom and forgiveness of the heart.

Of course we can always dismiss something by saying, "If it's their fate or karma to get into trouble, it's none of my business, and I'm not going to help!" All the same, a person's potential expands through compassion, inspiration, and helping other people, and he improves his possibility of attaining the so-called superconductive flow state, in which his karma lightens at the same time. (I will return to this state more exactly in chapter 5 in connection with the Law of Opposite Expression.) In other words, helping others really does speed up confronting and resolving one's own karma.

It is precisely for this reason that great deeds and helping others are much more than just altruism or something that looks good in a person's resume. In fact you help yourself on your life path. This is how the Laws of Karma and of Help meet each other in a good way.

At the same time it is of course good to notice and to understand that the positive and negative aspects of karma represent only a small part of a great jigsaw puzzle. Karma can be influenced in many ways by including for example a bit of playfulness, humor, new ideas, the influence of other beings and influence from many other sources which you cannot even imagine or describe. This is important to realize, because generally people understand karma as something hard, rigid, dense, tight and full of rules.

On the fundamental level karma can be understood simply as a cause-and-effect model of action, which is known for example as the interaction of matter and energy. It can also be seen through the relationships of friends and through human relationships in general, and understood as a means of learning from them, and it can be seen through an understanding of one's own life. Actually it is only through one's own direct **experience that a person can learn to know the full extent of the Law of Karma.** But he can also understand how karma can be faced and lightened in many ways without pain and suffering, and how many assumptions behind such things can be challenged. The Universal Laws as such are of course not challenged, since they simply make possible the way things work.

As a person's own potential begins to flow along with his spiritual progress, and as he from time to time reaches the superconductive state (where resistance is minimal and potentiality increases), the process of burning, changing, transforming and resolving karma begins in earnest. The longer an individual is in this superconductive state, the more choice he has as to what karma is burned and which direction he wants the karmic vector to take. This vector is connected to both the magnitude of the karma and its direction, to how much karma you are carrying with you and where you are directing it.

As a high state of consciousness gradually begins to become permanent in a person, a remarkable karmic change can take place. In the person's karmic vector, the factor that has risen to be the most important matter to work on, is usually the first to be resolved. For example during meditation or of breathing exercises, a person can reach a superconductive state even for long periods of time, and he can, within the space of a few microseconds, burn as much karma as was perhaps created over a year. Gradually the causal principle is undone and potentiality itself arises in a beautiful way. Having begun, the process then continues toward the greatest good, enlightenment, and other equivalent states that bring joy and even great ecstasy.

However, the truth at the core of karma is that it is neither positive nor negative, it is not a struggle to achieve balance, it just is: that there is cause and effect, and that through an understanding of this eternal principle, there is movement and change. This change leads a person inevitably to know himself better and to know better why he is here now.

The Law of Karma is unique in that through its own nature, through cause and effect, it covers many sides of existence, human relationships being very important among them. Because of this all the factors that affect the interrelationships of human beings are involved in confronting karma, whether these factors are conscious or unconscious, understood, or forced by other people, whether they were caused by physical matter, principles of energy, remote former lives or even by future lives. The central karmic interrelationship between you, other people and your world, and the various factors of your self-knowledge, proceed on an unconscious level. Therefore bringing them up to consciousness for example by working with the shadow self is recommended. I will return to this technique more precisely in connection with the Law of Opposite Expression in chapter 5.

The Karma of Nations: China and North Korea

Close to every good seed there is a seed of negativity, which is just waiting to be evolved, understood or liberated. This is true of human individuals, of communities and of nations as well. Countries are in fact a kind of karmic meeting and clearing bases, which call forth the important collective dimension of the Law of Karma and the karmic lessons of different countries and peoples. Hilarion has discussed this in his book *Nations*, which opens up new perspectives on the karma and the current challenges of some countries.

In the gradual evolution of countries certain attitudes and characteristics develop, and individuals who have a need to experience exactly these attitudes and characteristics, to develop or to experience these difficulties, are born in the countries in question. In this way they can learn a certain characteristic or to acquire certain experiences. In incarnating in the country in question their possibilities of acquiring these things are increased.

If they do not obtain these characteristics, which belong to their life plan, they are reborn until they have acquired their nourishment. In this way people often reincarnate several times, one life after the other, in the same country. In Finland, also, this is not very unusual. It is also possible to observe that many individuals whose planetary past is multicultural and who have been born in countless different countries and cultures, really have in fact internalized the lessons offered by particular countries and particular experiences.

Often the need to concentrate efforts in a certain region for a certain amount of time arises for the whole of humanity. When this kind of immense concentration is essential, a great number of souls, perhaps from different countries or different backgrounds, different lives, or from the same country, incarnate in this country in order to acquire the necessary lesson.

This explains the enormous explosion of energy that is now developing in China. Many people who have fought against democracy in the past are now incarnate in China. They have carried on this battle also within themselves and in relation to others and can now appreciate their experiences and see how they could help others to understand power by confronting and handling these lessons from many points of view.

There are also many of those who have stifled the attempts toward democracy in others, and who now want to make amends, as well as those who wish to balance the matter, and those who want to continue to stifle others, all working on these lessons and principles concerned with democracy, power and freedom.

The population size of China reveals what an enormous number of people need to work on these lessons. Historically China has had great power and authority to govern others in a feudal society and concentrating the power and energy of various rulers and emperors has been perceived as more important than human life. In this way China has become the place for learning these things anew.

The tendency of individuals toward distorted attitudes and toward controlling others and silencing the individual voice, is an important theme that humanity has been going through for the past 5000 years in many ways. Those who have not learned this lesson incarnate and come together in China at this time in order to understand it thoroughly. The matter comes up time and again in the activation of the democracy movement and its stifling by the government, as well as in the tensions between China and conquered Tibet.

This is how it is with every country. Every country has its own important lesson, just as we do as individuals. China's neighboring country North Korea is an especially important and topical example of this, and it is no wonder that these nations have a closer relationship with each other than closed North Korea has with any other country.

A very strong causal pattern is associated with that country, a pattern that involves the need to balance powerful karma. North Korea has evolved into a kind of karmic meeting base for those who have in their previous lives caused a great deal of negative karma on our planet. North Korea is now the region where these individuals confront themselves and their past through suffering, especially through starvation.

Who then are these people? Among them are many political leaders from the past, often influential individuals in the centers of power. They have now been forced to come into physical incarnation and to confront the fruits of their past in such a way that they can no longer cause harm to others by creating the kind of chaos that they did before. They are now obliged to confront difficulties both in their own souls and in their exterior world.

In this group are included, among others, political leaders of the American Civil War, leaders of Nazi Germany, and political leaders of Communist China. In other words, these individuals were born in North Korea in order to understand the consequences of their actions better and to work on them, and to confront their karma. This time they incarnated among the common people as agricultural workers and farmers.

One of their most powerful karmic lessons is an inner one: how can the balancing of karma happen for example with the help of a powerful experience of love, which at the same time would offer a great opportunity for progress? We can help them with the following exercise.

An Exercise: How to Help the North Koreans?

This is an opportune time to help people who are struggling with themselves and with their outer reality in North Korea. Begin the exercise by first imagining that you are inside a beautiful emerald-green cylinder. This cylinder of energy fills your entire being and has a diameter of perhaps 10 yards. Feel its protective, empowering and purifying energy and breathe it in.

Then think of something that you love, perhaps a person that you care about deeply. Imagine how you hug him or say loving words to him or how he talks to you lovingly. It does not necessarily have to be a human being. You might feel something similar for a pet, or a child might come up.

But whatever or whoever comes up, it is important that a deep and warm feeling of love is born in your heart. Allow the feeling to grow to where you can breathe it and observe that in connection with it there is an energy wave that expands out from you. Now it is moving a yard or two from your body and growing all the time. When the energy wave reaches the border of the emerald-green cylinder of light, you can send that energy directly to North Korea. Remember to load the energy with the purest, most loving feeling possible, and with the thought that it will find exactly the right targets in that country.

Feel and know that this love offers a real possibility, and with its help the North Koreans can aid the arising of changes in their country, in their lives, in their countrymen, and especially in their own political leaders that they might see their opportunity to expand their consciousness, to perceive reality more clearly and to build a better future for their country.

This possibility always exists in connection with the universal Law of Karma. There always exists a higher solution, which can resolve karma, and melt and change it, and at the same time make possible the creation of karmic balance to end a back-and-forth movement that has been going on for eons. At that point the thought and insight can be born that both the predator and the victim are one and that they both deserve love. Then in a sense you can hold both in the loving hands of your own God self, your own Christ energy.

This exercise connects the Law of Karma with the Law of Help, which we will return to more precisely in chapter 8. In this connection it is important to remember that the North Koreans also need a great deal of light and love. It is easy to judge and to scoff, that does not demand any effort or learned degrees, but loving is sometimes challenging if we think that in our opinion the object does not deserve it. It is again worth considering what the world needs now: it needs love and peace more painfully than ever before. Therefore it is worthwhile to do spiritual work to further these matters.

I will take up a couple more examples of the karmic background of nations. England carries heavy karma for the oppressive actions that the British Empire committed in the eighteenth and nineteenth centuries as it colonized various peoples and destroyed more than one tribe or ethnic group. All the actions that have caused suffering to other individuals or – as in this case – peoples, must be karmically confronted, and England is confronting this karma at the present. There has been an effort to remove a large part of the actions of the British Empire from the history books, but some scholars will always eventually bring the matter up.

Over the past few decades many of those who in their past lives were forced under the British iron fist, have been reborn in the former colonies and have emigrated from there to England with the help of its open doors policy, which the country has felt obligated to adopt. This for its part has also been a payment of the karmic debt. At the same time it has allowed the nation to attract to itself those elements and groups that can affect the karmic confrontation, which England has on its plate.[23]

---

23   Hilarion, *Answers*, p. 52.

The other side of the issue is that England has significantly furthered the spread of parliamentary government, the judicial system, and fair play on our planet. The mystic stone structure of Stonehenge has been a focus point through which the principle of fair play and honor in particular has flowed from another universe to our planet.[24] In this way England has also acquired good resources for balancing its karma.

Many people are interested in the situation and karma of Afghanistan. The country has been a battleground for centuries, and the situation shows no signs of easing even now. According to Hilarion the souls born into that country are without exception ones who have never learned to give up warfare and have not learned that there is only one way for people to live in peace: in the spirit of love and brotherhood among the entire human family. Life after life these souls who were born in Afghanistan have relied on war, conquest and plunder without ever giving thought to the despair and tragedy that they have brought to the regions and countries that they have conquered.[25]

But the wheel of karma has turned, and the country must pay a price for its own past. Karma cannot be escaped, in the end it has to be confronted and resolved. Afghanistan is going through this process right now.

There is reason to see natural catastrophes as discharges of collective karma. For example the tsunami in Japan in the spring of 2011 can be seen as a partial discharge of the karma that the country took upon itself during World War II. In this case the karma was created especially by the kamikaze, the suicide bombers who destroyed many human lives. In addition, this involved an unethical, distorted philosophy, to the effect that losing one's life in order to destroy others was somehow acceptable, even honorable. The truth is as far from this as can be. The same is of course true of the planners and perpetrators of the suicide attacks of our own time. They will confront the karmic consequences of their acts in the future.

---

24 Hilarion, *More Answers*, p. 129.
25 Hilarion, *More Answers*, pp. 69-70.

Nevertheless Hilarion also points out that in the Japanese catastrophe as well as in comparable earlier disasters, for example in Chile and Haiti, things could have been MUCH worse. The guides and helpers of humanity, among others, and the brothers and sisters of space, have significantly helped humanity in these situations, which have been known of well in advance on other levels of reality.

Saturn – the Lord of Karma

The important connection of the Law of Karma and the Law of Cycles can perhaps be best seen in spiritual astrology. The central karmic indicator in astrology is Saturn, which has an undeniably bad reputation among many aficionados of the discipline. Nevertheless, Saturn is the most important instructor in the heavens, who brings to his students the essential principles of responsibility and discipline, which are indispensable to genuine spiritual progress. This leaden planet is also the most central heavenly indicator of which matter is the essential one for a person to understand about himself.

The position of Saturn in a person's birth chart shows bluntly his life's most important lessons, the need to balance energies, and the extent of the karma meant to be confronted in that incarnation. The sign of the planet tells much about both the compulsory as well as the voluntarily undertaken karmic obstacles and limitations.[26]

The house position of Saturn suggests the part of life where at least some of the negative karma is to be confronted, and the aspects of the planet, that is, the angles of the planet to other planets, tell of the details of the karmic commitments.

Saturn brings not only important lessons and obstructions, but blessings as well: the refinement of spiritual qualities and character, the learning of self-discipline, the building up of strength, toughness, and purity, and the ability to bring things to a concrete level. When the life is examined toward its end with respect to those periods when

---

26   Hilarion, *Astrology Plus*, p. 63.

the individual learned the most at the fastest pace, it can be observed that Saturn has been active in his spiritual star chart during those periods. Since the purpose of rebirth is learning and spiritual progress, the impulses given by Saturn's vibrations can be considered the most beneficial in the long run.[27]

In the east the role of Saturn has in many contexts been understood more deeply and broadly than in western astrology. In the east Saturn has been seen as the planet of manifestation, enlightenment and in some cases awakening, the planet that aids in understanding transformation and in moving from one level of existence to another.

We will return to the important cusps of Saturn's seven-year cycles in chapter 6, in connection with the Law of Cycles.

Summary

✳ Karma is the law of cause and effect.

✳ Karma assumes free will.

✳ Karma is usually present in our close human relationships, and is also connected to physical matter, principles of energy, past lives and future lives.

✳ The full measure of the Law of Karma can only be known and felt through direct personal experience.

✳ It is a myth that karma creates a destiny that imprisons a human being.

✳ The eternal principle of karma includes movement and

---

27   Hilarion, *Answers*, pp. 97-98.

change. Such change inevitably leads a human being to know himself better and is the reason for your being here.

✳ The balancing of karma can happen in millions of different ways, not only through the patterns and habits that we are stuck in.

✳ In the so-called superconductive state an individual advances rapidly in liberating karma into pure potentiality.

✳ Love is the quickest and healthiest way to resolve karmic patterns.

✳ A connection to karma can be found in Newton's Third Law of Mechanics and in Ohm's Law of Electricity.

Literature:

Cooke, Maurice B. 1988: *The Mars Connection*. Marcus Books, Queensville, Ontario.
Hilarion 1979: *Seasons of the Spirit*. Marcus Books, Queensville, Ontario.
Hilarion 1980: *Astrology Plus*. Marcus Books, Queensville, Ontario.
Hilarion 1980: *Symbols*. Marcus Books, Agincourt, Ontario.
Hilarion 1981: *Dark Robes, Dark Brothers*. Marcus Books, Queensville, Ontario.
Hilarion 1981: *Other Kingdoms*. Marcus Books, Queensville, Ontario.
Hilarion 1983: *Answers*. Marcus Books, Queensville, Ontario.
Hilarion 1984: *Nations*. Marcus Books, Toronto.
Hilarion 1985: *More Answers*. Marcus Books, Queensville, Ontario.[28]
LaVoie, Nicole 1996: *Return to Harmony*. Sound Wave Energy Press, Pagosa Springs, Colorado.
Lehtiranta, Erkki 2008: *Astrologia ja Henkinen Tie*. Smiling Stars, Helsinki.

---

28   Some of these Hilarion books are available as e-books. See www.spiritualcompany.com.

4.

Permanence

"Everything that has reached a sufficient level
of permanence is alive because it contains
a God-spark. The Law of Permanence tells
of a living universe and of how the level of
permanence deepens with progress."

- Hilarion

THIS COSMIC LAW is very important in the total web of things, but at
the same time it is more difficult to bring to the personal level and
into personal inquiry than many of the other principles. The Law of
Permanence expresses the fact that there is a certain threshold of integration, unity or cohesion that every being must reach before it can
remain whole without the help of some kind of form or vehicle. In
addition, the slighter the level of integration of the being in question,
the denser the form it takes on must be in order to maintain its unity.[29]

This holds true for different realms of nature, for humanity, for
devas, for beings on a higher level on other celestial bodies, for planets, for stars and actually for solar systems, galaxies and even greater
wholes. The majestic character of the cosmos, and at the same time
our own long evolutionary path, opens up before us through this law.

---

29   Hilarion, *Vision*, pp. 16-17.

Let us take an example from the mineral kingdom. Stones, bits of sand and large boulders are all in a certain sense ensouled, because all expressions of form are necessary for the ultimate spiritual substance of the universe to be able to know itself.[30] This relates to the first law that we handled, the principle of manifestation, which we examined in chapter 1.

In comparison with the human soul the spiritual core being of stones and boulders is extremely primitive. Its grasp of being or of the idea of unity is truly so fragile that it needs a relatively concrete and dense stony or mineral body in order to stick together. If you crush a stone or melt a mineral to free the spiritual entity encased in it, it will immediately return into the "ocean of spirit" where it originated.[31]

There are of course different degrees of cohesion in the mineral kingdom. The so-called Mohs Scale of Hardness gives us some hints of this. On this scale, developed by Friedrich Mohs in 1822, talcum is the weakest and diamond the hardest mineral. A diamond can be compared with a spiritual master in an interesting way, because both allow light to travel through them with purity. In addition a diamond has a connection with a human being through carbon as well: because the human body contains so much carbon, its energy resembles the energy of a diamond more than that of any other mineral.[32]

From Being to Evolving

Hilarion reminds us in this connection that these primitive beings that inhabit the mineral kingdom are not expected to learn through this experience how to maintain themselves as a single integrated being without the help of a "mineral body". The basic lesson of the evo-

---

30 In the beginning of the 20th century the Indian scientist Jagadish Chandra Bose investigated the reactions of living and nonliving matter, using a great variety of stimuli. He demonstrated that at bottom there was not much difference between the reactions of nerve tissue and metals. Later the German scholar Karl Bonhöffer obtained similar results. These experiments open up two routes: either nothing is conscious (a fairly absurd idea) or else there is consciousness in everything. See Walters, *Superconsciousness*, p. 11.

31 Hilarion, *Vision*, p. 17.

32 Lehtiranta & Niemelä: *Kasvien viisaus, kivien muisti*, pp. 173-174.

lutionary stage connected with the mineral kingdom is simply the understanding that being exists. The evolutionary challenge is to remain in this "state of existing", of which the entity gets a taste while incarnate in the mineral kingdom.[33]

As you can see, this matter is not quite easy to understand and explain, because humanity has already long ago passed the evolutionary challenge in question. On our long path of pilgrimage we have nevertheless been incarnate in the mineral kingdom in the Himalayas in order to gain contact with the densest state of matter and to become accustomed to the vibration of the planet. According to Hilarion this stage lasted for more than 300 million years.

The different elements are all connected to the Law of Permanence in their own way. Even before the visit in the mineral kingdom, present-day humanity was a part of "the natural kingdom of air" on another planet so long ago that it makes no sense to even ponder the amount of time that has passed since then.[34] During this air stage we learned how to exist, but in addition to the lesson of existing, the lesson of beginning to evolve was impressed on our life stream.

The air kingdom is still present even on our own planet, and besides, it is very easy to find, if you just know how and where it is to be found. When you look at a cloudless sky away from the Sun with your eyes relaxed and unfocused, you cannot help noticing tiny particles that move like sparks in the air in different directions. These are particles of prana, the basic energy of the universe, and they undergo various changes of vibration as preparation for later experiences in denser bodies.[35]

An entity that has at one time reached permanence but then lost this characteristic, is drawn back into a kind of spiritual smelting foundry to be purified. Ultimately this purified essential being is sent back to different levels of existence but liberated from its previous unique characteristics. In this connection we can even speak of a

---

33   Hilarion, *Vision*, pp. 16-17.
34   Hilarion, *Other Kingdoms*, p. 36.
35   Hilarion, *Other Kingdoms*, p. 16.

new beginning without any benefit gained from previous learning experiences.[36]

In this way these primitive energy complexes learn to understand intuitively that existence and life have purpose, and that what is required of a spirit being is the desire to continue to exist. This may sound strange to the reader – how could anyone not desire to exist? However, with respect to the entire scale of spiritual evolution, it is extremely important to have an understanding of awakening the desire to exist, and along with it, the arising desire to evolve and unify. This scale begins from primitive levels, all the way from the mineral kingdom gradually toward more evolved expressions of life in the plant and animal kingdoms and in the higher forms of life. The chain is an unbroken one.

Water, Fire, and the Ocean of Spirit

The water element forms an important link in this chain, and so is involved in the examination of several of the spiritual laws. Water is necessary for life on this planet, and we are all born of water. Thus we have a natural biological union with water. Water acts as an excellent unifying element, which is strongly impacted by consciousness. Such wonderful researchers of water as Schauberger, Grander and Emoto have revealed many of the most secret characteristics of water with their experiments. In any case, the scientific view of water will have to become more diversified.

Water is no longer struggling to reach the level of existence, as are the previously mentioned prana particles of the air kingdom. Water is a sensitive but at the same time a powerful element, for it can travel through all fissures, to erode stone, and in this way to bring about great changes. In Taoism water is in fact considered the strongest element of all, even though at first sight it seems quite soft, even fragile. The water kingdom is a beautiful whole, uniting the physical and bio-

---

36   Hilarion, *The Master Plan*, p. 135.

logical principles. In union, these act as a wonderful magnet and can store the power of prana, the energy of life, and other things as well.

Water has nevertheless not reached a threshold of permanence that would make it into a *unified* whole. This is also true of the fire element and of the beings that ensoul it. They have come to study and to learn about the effects of fire, which are usually connected with different sides of negativity. Fire burns, but also purifies, which is of course well known to all of us, and at times necessary. Burnout is therefore a currently relevant symbol of the overheating of this element in humankind, as is the more prosaic "getting your fingers burned."

It is good to note the dynamism of water and fire in people's lives, for a great deal of creativity can be accessed through the harmonious union of emotional (water) and activating (fire) energies. In other words it is good to understand that these elements are also within ourselves, as for example astrology tells us. In Chinese thought they can be united with Yin and Yang, whose dynamics will be examined at more length in the next chapter.

The life forms of the plant kingdom of our planet are almost without exception below the threshold of permanence in the sense that when a plant or a tree dies, the spirit inhabiting it will inevitably return to the "ocean of spirit" where it originated. Here it is good to clarify that the ocean of spirit in question is not just a formless, undifferentiated, homogeneous mass of spiritual raw material. The material of the spiritual core being is namely differentiated into various degrees or vibrations, which extend through the entire scale from the most primitive and unconscious of self to the most complex and self-conscious levels.[37]

Let us ground this information in relation to the plant kingdom. Behind the evolution of the plant kingdom are the devas of each plant species. When some part is taken out of this mass of spiritual raw material, to ensoul a certain life form, and to learn about the manifestation of form, this part is not taken arbitrarily. It is carefully chosen out

---

37   Hilarion, Vision, pp. 17-18.

of the part that is best suited to learn with the help of the intended new learning period. The devas of the plant kingdom have been trained to distinguish from the soul material of our planet's aura precisely the part that is suited to the learning experience of the plant species in question. Placing an unsuitable part or vibration into a plant would not serve its purpose and could even hinder the evolution of the chosen spiritual material.[38]

Our Own Journey in the Realms of Nature

We ourselves have been a part of the plant kingdom in an early stage of our evolution, when we were passing through the various natural kingdoms in order to learn to know ourselves deeply. In the mineral kingdom the human soul group was still living in an undifferentiated state. Differentiation began to take place when the human soul group settled in gigantic plants that largely formed the origin of the current oil resources of the planet. Here we mean the giant ferns and similar plants. A great deal of the knowledge and wisdom of our ancestors is still stored in the present form of ferns, and these plants are energetically attuned to the naturalness of the past.[39]

A large part of the animal kingdom (especially the land animals) and all of humanity belong to that category on our planet, which has surpassed the threshold of permanence and thus can remain integrated even without the help of a physical body. The kinds of individual entities that ensoul entire beehives or anthills, are just at this threshold and are struggling to remain unified in a physical form. The swarm or community can in this context be seen as a unified whole, as a cooperating unit. At the same time they are struggling to learn unity and permanence on the level of soul or spirit. Here we also have an example of the Law of Reflection: the outer circumstances of the entity correspond precisely with the learning process that is taking place on the soul level.[40]

---

38   Hilarion, *Other Kingdoms*, p. 18.
39   Lehtiranta & Niemelä: *Kasvien viisaus, kivien muisti*, pp. 78-81.
40   Hilarion, *Vision*, p. 18.

A bee community tells us about uniting, about working for your own community together with the outside world, and about building. Perhaps a thousand or so bees are born and die daily in the average bee community. This continuous process of birth and death has its supreme purpose, unity, and sense of consciousness. The Law of Permanence is constantly present in our own sphere of experience, if only we know how to look and understand.

It is good to understand that all the warm-blooded animals of our planet originated in other parts of the galaxy and were brought here from there.[41] The views of Darwin and other researchers concerning natural selection and the nature of the evolution of life are very limited and will eventually end up as footnotes when the great panorama of life and the divine plan of progress is revealed to humanity in all its breadth.

Our own early contact with the animal kingdom is connected with the era of the various dinosaurs. At that time the life stream of humans divided into soul families that animated those huge beings. At that time we were studying the use of power and the control of energy from the point of view of the largest possible beings on the physical level, and in general studying, for the first time, how it felt to be in separate bodies that were able to move. This possibility was not offered by the plant kingdom.

The interest people have in dinosaurs has remained strong, in the same way that mountains with their snowy tops offer inspiration to so many of us. Our own planetary past sends reminders of itself to us through them. We have been here before, we have lived within the mineral, plant and animal kingdoms, and in this way obtained necessary, actually indispensable, knowledge and experience for our current stage of evolution.[42]

Through these evolutionary cycles humanity reached the degree of development where rebirth as individuals has become possible. Animals generally return to their group souls after death.

---

41 Hilarion, *Dark Robes, Dark Brothers*, p. 2.
42 Hilarion, The Master Plan, pp. 3-14.

In human life the Law of Permanence appears to conflict with the Law of Progress, which tells us that everything is in a state of constant change. This conflict is, however, a kind of optical illusion. Behind all forms there is change and transformation. For example the most valuable form of quartz, the amethyst, grows perhaps a centimeter or two in a million years. But it does grow, and at the same time its crystal structure remains the same. Its essential being, however, is behind the forms in the world of spirit.

A human body is also constantly in a state of change, and science tells us that in the space of approximately seven years almost all the cells of the body have been renewed. The different organs and systems of the body are nevertheless renewed in their own cycles and at their own speeds. For example the skin is renewed monthly, the cells of the eyes in two days, liver cells within the space of six weeks, and bone cells within three months.[43]

All the same there are some permanent factors in human structures, and they are significant from the point of view of the Law of Permanence. These include for example the permanent atom or seed atom, a kind of origin point of a human being, where all the experiences of the current life and of past lives are stored. I already wrote about this briefly in connection with the Law of Manifestation in chapter 1.

This eternal atom is usually found on the left side of the heart, and all the atoms of the physical body vibrate in harmony with it. The seed atom is something like a tuning fork that gives the keynote to the whole body. In this way it can be compared with for example a person's fundamental soul note, which holds him together. This basic note can be strengthened for example by listening to the music of Franz Schubert, which in general harmonizes a human being.

Permanence and Galactic Life

If we continue to examine the Law of Permanence from the point of view of other groups of beings, then the devas, whom we men-

---

43   Segal, *The Secret Language of Your Body.*

tioned earlier, and who are responsible for the welfare of for example the plant kingdom, are more or less at the same level as humanity in terms of their evolution, their understanding, and their permanence.

Their route is nevertheless quite different. These beings have the ability to work on unity with both higher beings as well as with the lower powers and beings that were mentioned earlier. In addition, the devas take care of for example the many challenges that arise with technology, and without the participation of these valuable beings there would be many more accidents and other such misfortunes in our world. For example airplanes have their own devas, who can be seen on the wings when the plane is in the air.[44]

When we begin to examine the kingdoms of nature that are above humanity in their evolution, we first encounter those civilizations outside of our planet which are able to maintain a three-dimensional form for a long time. However, they are able to change their energy into the fourth dimension, and this is important for them from the point of view of both growth and work. Since these beings know our world and our reality well, they also understand its difficulties. They have their own tasks, however, which partly include the study of humanity, and cooperation with us.

We ourselves are gradually reaching the level of permanence where a new dimension reveals itself to us. The cycle of evolution has speeded up tremendously in the recent centuries and decades, and we are thus, in our present incarnations, living in extremely important learning times. According to the estimate of Hilarion, the present cycle of rebirth will last another 300-350 years. After this we will most likely move to different evolutionary challenges. This will of course be decisively affected by our own free will, that immortal right of ours and the factor behind all true progress.

---

44 As I have previously written (*Tien päällä ja taivaan alla*, pp. 402-407), a mountain in Eastern Finland called Koli, and especially its quartzite, draws devas to itself. They come there from time to time to refresh themselves and to rest from their exertions. These beings come from all over Europe and also from inside the Earth, where a great deal of life exists, even though it is still unknown to people.

An important relationship of correspondence is to be found between the understanding of different dimensions and of unification. The beings that are working in the fourth dimension are, as a society, much more unified for example in regard to the understanding of the Universal Laws, and compared to us, they have a much deeper conception and experience, especially of the Law of Love, the Law of Karma, and the Law of Cycles. They are also better able to work with different frequencies. In the fifth dimension the universal principles have usually been well accepted and understood on all levels. The ability to move back and forth in the stream of time becomes very important with the ascent from the fourth dimension to the fifth. On the levels higher than these many other aspects begin to arise.[45]

On the levels higher than these there are found many galactic civilizations outside of our planet. These have reached an even higher integration and unification. They have completely accepted and understood the Universal Laws and apply them as a part of their lives. In this group are included the civilizations of the Pleiades, especially the life streams of the planets circling Alcyon, Merope and Electra, as well as the large beings originating in the center of our galaxy. These still resemble somewhat the humanoid form, though these beings function in many ways on myriad levels of spirituality without a physical body.

The life streams of the Pleiades are among the most important and valuable friends of humanity in our current phase. They have received the core teachings from the civilization of El Nath, whose beings have understood the universal principles and their connection with mathematics on a very high level.[46] A universal language has been constructed on the basis of their insights. The 12 cosmic laws that are introduced and studied in this book form a part of this language.

As we go to a higher level of evolution we come to groups of beings whose permanence and understanding are on a level that makes

---

45 In his classic book, *Gem Elixirs and Vibrational Healing, Vol. II*, Gurudas writes that the fourth dimension is the source of time, space and gravity, just as the fifth dimension is connected with electricity, the sixth with electromagnetism, and the seventh with consciousness (pp. 145-147).

46 Smulkis & Rubenfeld, *Starlight Elixirs and Cosmic Vibrational Healing*, p. 78 and p. 169.

it extremely difficult for them to take a three-dimensional form in which we could perceive them. In fact, they are basically energetic in nature. Their goal is to study, create and know on a very high level of existence.

On even higher levels there are beings with a multidimensional form, who ensoul stars, their planets and galaxies. Mother Earth is of course one of them. It is difficult for us to understand their size and their multiform being. For example most of the highest dimensions of our own planet are to be found inside the planet. Hilarion also mentions that the inner structure of Mother Earth is quite different from the way that science presently conceives of it.

There are also great creative beings on the high levels. In the motto of the first chapter Hilarion alludes to such entities, who have been responsible for the creation of our own planet, and he gives them the collective name Elohim. In the translations of the Bible the name has been rendered in the singular (which would have been Eloah), although the original text speaks explicitly of the plural, the Creators.

At this point it is good to return to the previously mentioned direct correlation between the general levels of dimensions and the levels of permanence. When working on the level of individual galaxies and united galaxies, we arrive at a level of universes, which is beyond our understanding, where certain other systems of Universal Laws come into the picture. These include the 12 cosmic laws that we cover here as a kind of sub laws.

Working with Mother Earth

If we return to earth, we can notice that all beings, from the smallest and least unified to the largest and most unified, have a significant effect on us people. The Earth truly is a living being, just as the minerals and the foods that we eat are alive (if we do not heat them to death). The fire and the water that are often needed, are alive as well. Thus we are in the midst of a living, miraculous universe. It is important to understand this, for it can create greater respect for the world around us. In addition, all the different levels of beings that we deal with – our galactic cousins, the Sun, Mother Earth, the deva organizations, the minerals etc. – can also learn from us. The movement of evolution is two-directional or multi-directional, and we, too, have something to give to the surrounding universe.

We are here to learn to know ourselves, and these other beings can help us in this task in a significant way. Thus it is worthwhile to ask good questions in the face of reality. Why has this crystal come into my life just now? Why am I so deeply attracted to water? What is the message of just that plant for me? What would be a good way for me to relate to Mother Earth? All these beings are alive, and their messages are not bound to time or place. The lessons given by them will not disappear when you have comprehended them, rather, the process in question is a living one. What you learn from the process and what you bring to it as your own contribution, is constantly changing and evolving. Your own contribution brings matters to the personal level and is the actual basis for understanding the Law of Permanence.

You can understand permanence on a deeper level by working with Mother Earth. It is impossible to see, on a detailed, scientific level, all the interrelationships between all the factors having to do with the different physical, chemical, emotional, animal, plant and other systems. What can you share with Mother Earth?[47] The most important thing you have in you is love: it makes you whole and permanent. The Law of Love makes it possible to see and to feel, with the eyes of your heart, the beauty of the world around you.

In this book we speak in many contexts of the importance of the Law of Love, and of how it is connected with all the other principles. For example in connection with the Law of Manifestation, the opening of the love streams and working with them, helps you to know yourself better without pain and suffering. In working with the Law of Reflection, when you consent to love what you see outside of your-

---

47   I will return to working with Mother Earth and to helping our planet more specifically in connection with the Law of Help in chapter 8.

self or what opposes you, you can more easily see it as a reflection of yourself. In connection with the Law of Karma you can notice how love changes karma, balances it and helps in resolving it on the highest level. In other words, unconditional love is the best and quickest way to meet and resolve karmic issues.

When the Law of Permanence and the Law of Love come together in your life, you can begin to understand the uniqueness that you yourself have created, and that has brought you to your present level of integration. And this is how the journey continues: as something began, so it tends to continue. The united energy of understanding the laws will take you to ever stronger unification, ever deeper integration and wholeness, and it will help you to have clearer insight into other natural kingdoms and other levels.

Exercise: Realizing Permanence

It is important to see the continuity of things, and to see that you yourself are a part of it. The following exercise illustrates this.

To begin, give your body the instruction to relax and breathe deeply into your belly. Feel how any unnecessary stress flows out of your being into Mother Earth, who knows how to transform it into constructive energy.

Then choose a part of your body, preferably a healthy and normally functioning part. It can be a fingernail, the hair, a certain part of the skin or perhaps an organ. Then see this part of your body in your mind. Feel as if you are touching this part or holding on to it. At the same time be very conscious of this part and now see it as quite large and see yourself as smaller than it. Then see yourself stepping into this part of your body.

Seek out one cell in this part of your body. The body is made up of individual units, each one unique and special in itself and by itself. As you study this particular cell, notice how it resembles a neighboring cell, but is still quite different, unique and special.

Now imagine that you step into the core of this cell, the control center called a nucleus. It does not matter whether you have read about it before or not. Go inside that core of the cell and notice that its inner world is full of colors, light and movement. There may also be feelings and even sounds – the sounds of various liquids, of various moving and changing materials. It is truly quite a marvelous factory.

You may want to go even deeper into the cell's core and begin to study and recognize the way it is made up of different elements. See the different minerals, see how the liquids move them about, how heat can melt some of them together and separate some others from each other. You see this as movement and breath. There is pulse and rhythm, and also the air aspect in a beautiful way. These things breathe your life with the help of oxygen and the release of carbon dioxide. And as you make yourself even smaller, you notice the very molecules and atoms in the cell's core.

You can make this journey as long or as limited as you like. Now notice how you have been looking at a part of yourself. In its own way this part represents the whole; it contains very much within itself.

Observe again from a higher level how this fits into the whole, and how this cell functions. See that you are one member of a society. You sit in this space, but at the same time you are a part of your community, your village or town, your country and your planet. You work together with others as one humankind, for common objectives and goals – for survival, learning and cooperation – in your own way.

Adopt an even broader perspective and see the solar system, with the earth and its human inhabitants that form a part of it. We are a part of that whole. As you live, breathe and work with the earth, in the same way the planets and the Sun itself pulsate, live and love. As you take yourself even further, you may get to see the whole galaxy and notice that there are also other points of light there, with nearly beehive-like entities swarming in them. They are massively intelligent beings, which are struggling to understand just as you are. In addition there are some who see you and our galaxy from far away. They are also intelligent and are easily able to travel here. Now you can see our whole galaxy and feel how you are a part of it.

When you return peacefully back into this space, you can understand and see yourself from a different perspective. So, return peacefully into your body and see this exercise as a kind of continuum. See how both the galactic entity and the tiny cell of your body with its components are a part of yourself and you are a part of them. When you send your understanding of love into the universe, it changes. See how it is one with you and how you yourself are a part of this mighty continuum.

If you gain a conception of this continuum, of your own permanence and of your own level of understanding and your ability to interact with these substances and beings, at the same time you begin to respect and to know that all your actions, from the least and most worldly to the most important and significant in your life, have an effect on these natural kingdoms. In this way you are beautifully woven together.

Now come back and observe your own physical body. Now you know on a deeper level, not only by seeing, but by feeling, sensing, tasting, on the level of sounds and everything else that you have met, that you are one with all of them, that you are a part of this world in a way that you may not have previously realized.

Including a cell in this meditation is significant in many senses. First, cells are central factors in our physical life. Another and slightly more mystical, but in no way lesser factor, is the fact that the universal principles are also coded into our cellular memory. They can be activated from there for example with the help of these types of exercises to become a part of living life.

Summary

✴ Everything that has reached the level of permanence is alive, because it contains the God spark

✴ The Law of Permanence is a very important principle in the totality of things, but it may be difficult to understand on the personal level.

✴ Working with beings living in lower dimensions helps those beings to learn and to stabilize permanence in themselves.

✴ The present level of permanence of human beings has been reached in a very short time.

✴ We have many distinctive characteristics in this continuum of permanence and we will soon enter a level of permanence, which leads into the next dimension.

✴ There is a relationship of correspondence between an understanding of the different dimensions and unification, as well as between dimensions and permanence.

✴ Things tend to continue as they began.

Literature:
Hilarion 1981: Other Kingdoms. Marcus Books, Queensville, Ontario.
Hilarion 1981: Dark Robes, Dark Brothers. Marcus Books, Queensville, Ontario.
Hilarion 1982: Vision. Marcus Books, Queensville, Ontario.
Lehtiranta, Erkki & Niemelä, Leena 2009: Kasvien viisaus, kivien muisti. Smiling Stars, Helsinki.
Lehtiranta, Erkki 2011: Tien päällä ja taivaan alla. Smiling Stars, Helsinki
Segal, Inna 2010: The Secret Language of Your Body. Atria Paperback, New York/ Beyond Words Publishing, Oregon.
Smulkis, Michael & Rubenfeld, Fred 1992: Starlight Elixirs and Cosmic Vibrational Healing. C.W. Daniel Company Ltd, Saffron Walden, Essex.
Walters, J. Donald 1996: Superconsciousness. A Guide to Meditation. Crystal Clarity Publishers, Nevada City, California.

5.

Opposite Expression

"When all sides of Divinity travel
through the various levels down into
the physical universe, at some point they
divide into positive and negative components."

- Hilarion

WE HAVE BEEN TAUGHT, since childhood, to examine the world
through different polarities and dualisms. There is day and night, light
and shadow, man and woman, good and evil, joy and sorrow, heaven
and earth, east and west, hot and cold, hetero and homo, life and death.
And of course the Beauty and the Beast, and Jekyll and Hyde. These
and many other similar pairs of opposites help us to understand ourselves and our true nature. However, this Law of Opposite Expression
is even much broader, for it also helps us to understand humanity as a
whole, the individuals, governments and politics that make it up, the
mechanisms of healing, and countless other things in our daily reality.

The Law of Opposite Expression helps us to understand for example the confusing situations that happen when seemingly opposite forces or factors occur close to each other. Such examples are to
be found near everyone's own environment, such as a bar or brothel
next to a church, or a meeting place of undeveloped souls near a New
Age center. Perhaps the most classic example is to be found in north-

ern Scotland, where Findhorn, a leading new age center, is located right next to an air force base for war planes.[48] In Amsterdam an old cathedral is located in the red light district.

In society the Law of Opposite Expression can be seen in countless connections, and it seems that the dualistic point of view has been necessary before the ascent to a higher level. The Berlin wall is a good example from recent history. A better understanding and application of this law is at present a central national project of Russia within the framework of the Universal Laws. The yellow ray of Russia brought with it two revolutions in the last century. Both revolutions (in the years 1917 and 1991) involved an immense pressure for change, as the old system was being replaced by the new. Most adults in Russia still remember clearly the Communist order and planned economy, which are in many respects the opposites of the present free market politics. Hopefully the Russians will in the end find a third possibility behind these two opposite expressions, one in which the best sides of the systems could be united and could present the world with a new kind of alternative.

In addition to Russia the Arab countries of the southern Mediterranean are just now going through the Law of Opposite Expression. It has been easy to notice this just by following the news about the so-called Arab Spring, that is, the waves of demonstrations and people's uprisings, which began with the Tunisian revolution in Dec.-Jan. 2010-2011.

A peculiar situation has prevailed between Israel and Palestine for a long time. This situation has united the Law of Karma and the Law of Opposite Expression with each other. Those born in these regions have a great tendency to incarnate on the side of the "enemy" in the next life. Only in this way will it ultimately be possible to get rid of this destructive vicious cycle of predator and victim. The domestic politics of the United States has for a long time been rigidly polarized. It does not have to be this way, however, for there is always a third possibility.

For example Fichte and Hegel, German philosophers of the Romantic era, wrote about the third possibility behind the thesis and its

---

48   Hilarion, *Vision*, p. 21.

antithesis, the synthesis, the reality that is formed through the thesis and the antithesis that is its opposite. For example for Hegel the antithesis of logic is nature, and their synthesis is spirit. In this way of thinking, the synthesis overrules the dualistic set-up.[49]

This matter can be illuminated if we examine the excesses of past lives, for example in regard to some characteristics or behavior patterns. Typically in the next life such an excess is rectified and balanced in such a way that it is difficult for the individual in question to express this characteristic or behavior pattern in the same way. Usually he is forced to experience its opposite, so that he might finally realize that traveling the middle path is the wisest way to get rid of confronting opposites in his own life. This process is illustrated by the simple drawing below.

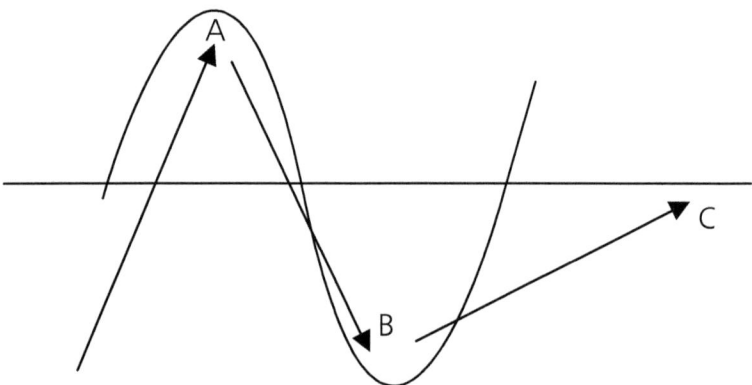

The process of balancing can also be seen when we observe an individual whose life includes a trait or a side that is overemphasized. This may involve any human factor of development, addiction, desire, and so on. In the drawing the overemphasis is shown by arrow A. Arrow B shows the bottom of the wave that usually occurs in the next incarnation in order to balance the situation. Arrow C displays the goal, the golden middle, to which the individual is being guided.

---

49 *Filosofian sanakirja*, p. 45, lines 72—73. In this connection it should be noted that for example Marxism has interpreted dialectics in a way that is suitable to its own purposes.

When the cosmic nature of the Law of Opposite Expression is examined, we can observe that at bottom every manifest thing originates in God's being. As all the sides of God's being travel through the different levels down into the physical universe, at some point they divide into positive and negative components. The nature of the "lower" worlds forces this dualism or the division into polarities because the levels at a lower vibration cannot support God manifesting in a unified form.[50]

From Duality to a Broader Vision

In our own reality this division has caused much pain, suffering, separation and problems both on the individual and the social level. All the same, we can lift our eyes and see that behind these often black-and-white, dualistic attitudes and points of view there is a higher perspective and a possibility of understanding matters more broadly. We can understand how they form a **spectrum,** how they unite and thus help us to awaken and to see the path that leads into our innermost being. Choosing the broader perspective can bring the individual many beautiful fruits of the tree of life, which he had never previously been able to taste

We can choose to move from the dualistic conception of reality to the integrating spectral conception, which can see behind the opposites and can realize the potentiality contained in their unity, which is more than the sum of their parts. This can be called moving from polarized thinking to multifaceted, or better yet, spectral thinking. Without it intuition begins to wilt.

Accepting the spectral thinking presented here is natural for a human being's intuitive nature as he reaches the understanding and the conception of reality of the fourth dimension. As we continue from here to even higher levels of vibration and evolution, we eventually arrive at the level where the energy of God can itself be felt. At this point we reach an understanding of All That Is, and of the fact that

---

50   Hilarion, *Vision*, p. 21.

this All includes all that is possible on all levels. This vision opens the heart energies and helps to understand love, knowledge and oneself, and to accept oneself and one's inner divinity without words, without verbalizing the matter and without mental understanding.

Polarities and dualism are created by thought. Of course thought also gives a purchase on reality and is useful in that sense. But at some point an individual may want to get rid of old thought processes and gain a direct simple intuitive understanding of the object that he is currently focusing on. Instead of reflecting on the object, he is now one with it, and thus gains the next evolutionary step.

At that point consciousness of the inner process brings forth a spectrum of possibilities, an amazing variety of life, energy and vibration. When you train yourself in this way internally, thought no longer divides things into polarities. You will gradually move very naturally toward a deeper understanding of how it is possible to be one with some object without needing to analyze or categorize.

In fact Hilarion suggests that in order to understand the Law of Opposite Expression better and to work with it on a deeper spiritual level we will be wise to make an inventory of concepts and to broaden our perspective by doing so. When we confront some dualistic factor, it is worthwhile to create a little distance from it and to study the polarity before us with the help of for example humor, that vitamin H so necessary to all of us. In this way the perspective expands, our opportunity to enjoy the full spectrum of life grows, and we no longer need to content ourselves with watered-down truth.

When we see both sides of the matter in a clear light, we can change the way we connect with them in our examination, and we can maintain both within ourselves without rejecting or denying them. This opens up an understanding of many things, not only of thought processes, but also of ourselves in order to reach exactly the goals that we desire.

The process can be compared with rising to the level of positive energy, where we may find health, wealth and success in some area, or reach some goal that is important to us. This often leads to the arising of all things seemingly forbidden and denied, because the person is ready to confront them in a new way. This relates to the need for unity and the desire to deal with both sides of matters, and to unite them with each other in an appropriate way within ourselves. In this way it is no longer necessary to project the matters in question onto external reality, as would happen if they were not dealt with.

Reality appears in a new light, since the individual has clarified his own consciousness by applying the cosmic principle wisely. This can be applied in many different contexts and in relation to many important themes. Both sides of these and of other similar themes can teach us important things, and it is good to distill knowledge and understanding out of both.

We can see many people around us who have chosen a negative growth path, one that is partly based precisely on a dualistic vision and dualistic thought patterns. We can accept and understand this as a truth in our surroundings and at the same time observe the blessing hidden in it: the freedom to choose to work with the darkness in us, or to reject it, saying, " I am not like that, it is just some other person in that situation; I am glad I am not like him". Each of us can reflect, in light of what has been presented above, which is the wiser and more useful starting point for spiritual progress and insight.

Denial and rejection simply postpone confronting and working with the matter. Accepting the matter, in this case our own shadow, even when it appears in our own reality, gives us the opportunity to work with the matter in our own life and also to help the collective consciousness to deal with it. We do not live only for ourselves.

The Law of Opposite Expression teaches us humans on a practical level how what we are working with is what we ourselves have created. In other words, when we encounter any of these external opposites or polarities, they reflect something within ourselves. Here the Law of Opposite Expression connects with the Law of Reflection, which tells us over and over again that the world looks like us.

This is sometimes difficult to see and to understand, since we are not always able to understand the cause-and-effect relationships of matters. This is true of the spiritual dimension of life, not only of its material dimension. Causality is discussed more closely in the third chapter of the book.

If the world appears black and white to us, this spiritual color blindness is a result of the wrong prescription in our spiritual eyeglasses, and of our unwillingness to see behind the deceptive curtain of dualism. The great Law of Symbols teaches each of us for example through the various symbols of the body, what we need to work with in ourselves.

At this time the traditional classic pairs of opposites yield more and more space to a higher and broader spectrum of possibilities in the consciousness and life of many people. This speaks of the nature of the universe: a higher possibility, a synthesis, always exists, but we have to awaken and realize it. In any case the Law of Opposites makes authentic choices possible, which is a precondition for the maximum expression of free will.

Shadow Work Evens out Opposites

A very useful thing to do in connection with the Law of Opposite Expression is to bring an understanding of the **shadow self** to our attention. The archetype of the shadow was an important part of the thought of the Swiss depth-psychologist Carl Gustav Jung in relation to the multilevel nature of our being. The shadow self is a composite made up of the forbidden, rejected and denied parts of the personality based on the sum of the present life and past lives, which speaks of our unfinished psychological, emotional and spiritual lessons, and which we confront daily, whether we want it or not.

However, this selfsame shadow is also an excellent source of information, understanding and knowledge, and working with it eventually brings us from denial to acceptance and from shadow to light and integration. Although the conscious self and the shadow self are separate, they are inevitably connected with each other in the same way that thought and feeling are in relation to each other.[51]

---

51   Jung, *Symbolit: Piilotajunnan kieli*, p. 118.

In his work *Aion* Jung writes that the shadow is a moral problem, which challenges the entire ego-personality, since no-one can become conscious of the shadow without considerable effort. Becoming conscious of it implies the presence of the dark aspects of the personality and a recognition of reality. According to Jung, this recognition is the fundamental condition for authentic self-knowledge, which is why it systematically encounters determined resistance.

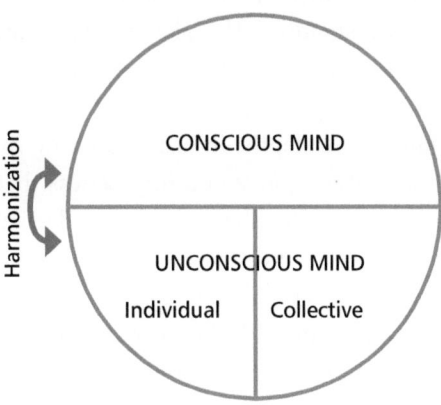

We have a clear even if unconscious tendency to project our shadow onto the external world, onto the things, circumstances and people that in one way or another irritate us, or that we even despise or hate. Nevertheless if we are able to, and dare to, bring up to the examination of our conscious mind those shadow elements hidden in our unconscious mind, we gain an excellent tool for shedding light on our own dark and denied side.

In the past few years much has been written about working with the shadow, and the reader is encouraged to acquaint himself with the thoughts of Debbie Ford, Deepak Chopra and Marianne Williamson on the subject (see the bibliography at the end of the chapter). As a method, Hilarion suggests that whenever you notice criticism, a desire to judge others and otherwise to bring negativity into the world, look and notice that there are reasons for this. It is easy to see the object of the criticism, the presumed or real fact, but when you notice the motive, the reason, that brought up this factor in yourself, you can progress from dualism a bit toward the foundation or the source of the matter: what caused this criticism in the first place.

With work on the shadow an individual's emotional body is gradually purified, and the energies are freed for the use of the higher tool, the mental body, which gives the individual a broader perspective and greater understanding. This also increases understanding of how expressing light depends on the ability to accept the dark areas in yourself, whatever they may be. In another context I have written that you must know your depths in order to know your heights.[52] It is only through acceptance, love and forgiveness that a person can consciously free himself of his shadow sides, and eventually an individual is able to see humankind's highest possibility, the possibility to love. At the same time it is possible to gain profound understanding of how others are struggling with their own shadow self.

All the creation of polarity that is connected with the Law of Opposite Expression really is in our own control, our own power and our own understanding, and in the end we ourselves will sooner or later clean it up. As we examine things looking backward, we can in most cases notice that these things and processes began within ourselves.

Thus, every time that we accept the purpose of the shadow self and at the same time undertake to work with it – that is, create some distance, notice the factual connection, see the truth that it contains, and then attempt to realize and work with the matter without denial – we are able to make great strides in our progress. In this way we progress from denial to acceptance and understanding, from denial and rejection to realization and insight. That is the path of wisdom, the Tao.

At the same time it is good to notice that it is important to work with the different aspects of the negative and positive emotions, since we can clarify and understand matters with their help. The main rea-

---

52   Lehtiranta, *Astrologia ja Henkinen Tie*, p. 233.

son is that our life is most powerfully impacted by our unconscious side, stored in the emotional body of most people, of both those on a spiritual Path and of those who are not at all spiritually awakened. Therefore it is good to begin by making clear which emotions are positive, which are negative. Later on we begin to understand that these can also be united, that anger sometimes also contains enthusiasm, and that where there is grief there is also sometimes embrace and love.

In working with the shadow self we can notice that in the end it is only energy. This is a new context: it is only undifferentiated energy, which we can develop as we want. Of course we can refuse to accept the reality that the shadow self presents us with. Still, we do not need to vent this energy in order to make progress. Rather, we need to understand that the energy brought forth by the pattern of denial holds us back in every way, since our emotional body simply broods on the matter.

This could be compared with a situation where you are asked not to think of pink elephants. No matter how hard you try, your thoughts will almost certainly return again exactly to – pink elephants. This is a symbolic example of how the emotional body functions: the emotional body is not limited by space and time and spends a great deal of unconscious energy on what a person denies or on what he does not want to work with.

As we do inner work with the Law of Opposite Expression, in the end we will inevitably notice that a thing and its opposite are one, they are aspects of our own being, and that we can find a way to express the thing from the point of view of this insight. With this, we are liberated from polarity-thinking. Without the filter of dualism we notice that the energy of God is more available.

At the same time we notice that we are making almost magical progress in some areas, or that we accept some different part of ourselves, or that we mysteriously draw to ourselves some person that we can work these matters with, and on whom we can project these aspects of ourselves in a constructive way. All this of course points to the cosmic Laws of Progress and Cycles, as we turn some cycle around and see it in a new light.

This law shows its effectiveness for example as you follow the media. Perhaps you are listening to the news and you say that this is good news and that other is bad news. Eventually you notice that the media try to make things as simple and clear as possible to sell more newspapers and magazines, more commercial radio time, more ads on television and so on. So if you delve into the matter more deeply in order to understand the entire spectrum of these things, you will be rewarded with insights into things that you had not previously realized. Various hidden agendas begin to reveal themselves, and even clever manipulation is brought into daylight. I will return to the matter more precisely in connection with the Law of Thought in chapter 7.

On a more general level, the gist of resolving most global problems and social questions resides in accepting these opposites within yourself, because you are society in miniature

The Opposite Zodiac Signs

It is sometimes said that opposites complement each other. This is also true, at least up to a point. A good example are the opposite signs familiar from astrology, i.e. signs of the horoscope that are located on opposite sides of the zodiac, such as Aries—Libra and Taurus—Scorpio. Here also the whole is usually more than the sum of its parts, and the opposite signs can learn many things from each other, traits and characteristics that are not strongly represented in oneself. For example Aries can learn balance and diplomacy from Libra, while Libra may learn decisiveness and dynamism from its fiery opposite.

Yin/Yang and the Inner Marriage

In history we can see that humanity has learned an enormous amount through understanding opposites, and this understanding exists in us deep in our cellular structures, in the purest form of energy. Most Chinese healing methods are based on this. They utilize the Yin/Yang-polarity, the receptive and the outward-directed energy, which are opposites and at the same time complementary. There is here a connection to ancient symbolism, but also for example to the way in which our cells function.

An important theme in the history of dualism and the opposites is the dynamism between the masculine and feminine factors, which is for its part expressed in the Yin/Yang design. Irrespective of our gender, all of us have both masculine and feminine hormones and characteristics, which are usually anchored in the classic equipment of one sex or the other.

Still, for true humanity, spiritual maturity and inner integrity, we need characteristics of both genders, and a good dynamic relationship between them. The Yin/Yang design illustrates this beautifully. It is impossible to say which of the polarities is inside, which outside, or which is up, which is down.  In this case these are inessential questions. Coming together, union, dynamism and fusion are the essential factors.

In this context we can speak of a kind of **inner marriage**, which exists between the masculine and feminine factors and which, when successful, is reflected in outer reality as well, in accordance with the cosmic Law of Reflection. We can again notice that the cosmic principles are present in our everyday reality and our ordinary life.

However, many men still deny and reject the existence in themselves of the softer feminine aspects, for example reserve, intuition, artistic talent. Similarly, many women deny their masculine side or consider its expression somehow unacceptable.[53]

One of the anatomical and physiological equivalents of the inner marriage is the dynamics and complementarity of the two hemispheres of the brain. In the west, the active hemisphere of the brain is usually the left one, which corresponds to the logical, verbal, mathematical and in general the measurable functions, while the passive

---

53 In this respect in Finland things are in a better way than in most other countries. One important reason for this is that many Finnish women have in their previous life been in a male body. Actually, they now have a good opportunity to understand things also from a masculine point of view. This is clearly visible in Finnish society.

hemisphere works with feelings, holistic, intuitive, artistic and evaluative factors in our life. Between these two hemispheres there is an important nerve called the corpus callosum, which when activated, begins to combine the characteristics of both hemispheres, such as the logical and the intuitive, the measuring and the evaluating sides. In this context we could also say that there are never two without a third – three is the charm.

Superconductivity and the Increase of Potentiality

The Law of Opposite Expression includes an interesting correlation with the laws of electricity, particularly with the trinity of voltage (tension), resistance and current. All beings have the potential to manifest things in many different ways. Sometimes the resistance is created specifically for bringing about two opposites. A condenser is a good example of this. It stores the charge as negative on one plate and as positive on the other. When we understand that this is simply pure voltage energy, which may collapse together and liberate a huge amount of charge, we can at the same time gain some understanding of ourselves, of how we often deliberately create a very specific resistance within ourselves in order to separate different sides of ourselves from each other.

This unique resistance exists mainly on the inner level. You experience it externally through symbols and through reflection as you draw people to yourself. Usually it is difficult for you to see this separation within yourself, but others see it in you easily and at depth. They may even say: "Look at how you separate these things in your life, why don't you unite them?", and move off shaking their head.

Still, resistance can gain a special significance when you finally begin to work with it. You can have **an inner experience of superconductivity** in this life as the previously separate factors unite, the resistance decreases and the potentiality increases. The Law of Opposite Expression influences your way of observing the tension and its potentiality, since the resistance acts as a mirror and brings forth the aspect that you are looking at and that reflects the potentiality onto yourself.

At a higher level of examination you begin to understand that potentiality often manifests as a pair of opposites and the real resistance is only in your consciousness until you realize that the opposites are one and the same. This can be helpful for example when you work with a person who is difficult for you. When you consent to love him the opposites begin to melt together and harmony returns to the relationship. The Law of Love works as a marvelous healer in this. As long as this is not understood and things remain as opposites, no great progress can be achieved; this is the nature of resistance.

The Law of Opposite Expression is reflected deeply into the nature of matter and physical forms. So many things in science have been developed to clarify these dipoles[54], polarities and opposites and to study how they can be worked with in an appropriate way. The wave/particle-dualism is only one way of examining this theme.

The law or principle of *resonance* is very close to the Law of Opposite Expression and is in fact an important corollary of it. The idea of resonance is present repeatedly on the physical level in energy transfer, as in sound frequency, when air is compressed and expanded so that sound can be transmitted from one person's mouth to the ear of another. In electricity, alternating current is an application of the same principle.[55]

This appears to be the nature of the three-dimensional world, but because of the inner nature of separation, there is a third and higher side, merging together, unity and core being. Superconductivity can be seen as a way of uniting the different sides: in the physical world there are many variations of matter and energy, which have not yet been discovered. It is a question of how to unite these opposites and how to work with this law of tension, resistance and current.

---

54 In physics we have the pair, or electrical dipole, of two differing electrical charges, a magnetic dipole of two magnetic poles, and a dipole molecule is the name of a molecule with two differently charged parts.
55 According to Hilarion resonance exists also without manifestations of matter or energy. The guiding core being of the principle of resonance can be called consciousness in its purest form.

Answers to these questions can be found, and I have alluded to some above. But we must understand that we have the possibility of choice as to how we examine these matters, how we accept them and learn from them. In general this is in direct relationship to changes in concepts. The underlying attitude is an essential factor in the matter.

Exercise: Meditation on Godlight

Sit comfortably in a chair, relax and breathe calmly and deeply into your belly. At the same time allow the higher sides of your being to become active. Then imagine, on the screen of your consciousness, a person whom you love deeply, and begin to send him/her pure, unconditional love as much as you can. Notice how he/she sees, feels, hears you as you perform this labor of love, and how his/her being brightens and strengthens with the help of the love you are sending. Continue for a few moments.

Now this person leaves the screen, and next you send love to a person that you have had some difficulties with. As you focus similar love on this person, you can see that love changes him/her as well. Your love can be a beautiful stream of love from your heart, a hug, perhaps a sound of some kind, perhaps just a pure loving feeling.

Then you let also this person go and there appears on your screen a person that you have had many difficulties with, and who perhaps feels to you like your opposite or your adversary. Now send him/her the same loving energy. Allow the same love, light and forgiveness, the same hug and sound to stream into him/her as well. And as this happens, you can see how this person also becomes whole, becomes radiant and more lovable. Send him/her this energy for a few moments, until it is streaming as evenly as with the first person.

Then imagine that a beautiful cone of light is shining from above onto the top of your head. At first this cone is streaming undifferentiated, perhaps pure white, light. As you look at the cone of light more closely, you step inside it and begin to feel its power, it begins to have a form and to dance within you.

As you dance in this cone of light, as you imagine it and feel it, at the same time consider which of the above ways to feel and to send your love was the easiest. As you recognize it, transfer it into this cone of light. You might see a hug in this light, or feel a wonderful love in it, or see how a beautiful light streams in and out of your heart with each breath. You are dancing as if above your head and enjoying this light of pure potentiality.

Now slip back gently and effortlessly into your physical body. Settle easily and calmly into your heart chakra and sit in your own body for a while. Perhaps you can now see an image of yourself in your heart, perhaps your own heart, or perhaps a light in the middle of your chest, or a spot of light between the vertebrae of your neck. It is important to continue to feel that you are in the light energy.

Now see yourself turned in such a way that you can reach forward and backward with your heart chakra. Reach back a moment in time with one hand and with the energy of love and potentiality ask for some negative aspect of your personality to come forth now. This may be a time when you struggled mightily or an event that contains grief and negative feeling, something difficult to accept.

But now see your other hand reach toward another time in your life, one that contained great light, a time of peace, love and companionship. If it is difficult to remember, reach up toward the light of potentiality and pull it down. Now see these two aspects, this beautiful positivity and this negativity, begin to swing around together deep within your heart center. You can imagine how this potential light is brought into a situation where you found yourself when you were younger or one from long ago, or into a situation where you were working with the negative aspect in question – and you will see it change.

Remember to breathe and to allow the light to flow into this situation as you breathe, integrating it and raising it into your consciousness in a new light. These two unite, and in this union there is revealed some energy, thought, idea, perception, universal law that you have not realized previously, some understanding about yourself that you have not known before. Now allow it to be with you in your heart.

We are here focusing on the heart center because it is an essential place in this balancing, when the matter is examined from the dualistic point of view: three chakras above, three below and the heart center in the middle. See that in this meeting there is simple peace without struggle. There is only light in it.

Then notice that a voice is heard from inside the light. You can imagine it to be the voice of Christ and allow it to be felt within yourself now. The message may sound different when you do the exercise again. It differs a little from past encouragement, but what it is, is inner acceptance, as if Christ said "You are loved" or "May God be with you" or "I forgive you" or something similar. When you allow this simple feeling to be born within you, see how it gradually melts and expands and travels up and down in the physical body. It changes into a feeling of light and love as it unites with the incoming energy and down into the core of the Earth, easy to breathe and to liberate.

We just asked you to do something fairly difficult. To change something that is basically energy or vibration into something more real that involves people, concepts and ideas, and then to change it back into vibration. But you can do this in your heart. In this way the heart resolves the dilemma of the opposites of suffering and joy, question and answer, masculine and feminine. The heart is single within you. It simply accepts and knows how. In this way you too can find your answer: by allowing the dualistic factors to unite with each other.

This is an experiential way of learning to know what the Law of Opposite Expression feels like internally. Recognizing its nature is easy: just look at humanity and its struggles. It is useful every now and then to send loving energy from your heart to people and their struggles, for then you will understand in your heart that they are a part of you, and you can at the same time gather lessons from them.

The same technique can be applied when you examine these daily events from the news or from human relationships that you hear about. In this way you will attain tranquility and understanding and then you will send Christ light around the thing in question.

Try to feel the presence of Christ energy as you work at the level of the heart and you will see that it is available continuously ever more and on levels that you did not even understand to exist. Day by day this energy increases on Earth. The Christ light is available to everyone for the resolution of the dilemma of dualism, to unite these opposites and to understand their ultimate purpose, and to see the real meaning of God's light – and once more to choose how you yourself will use this light.

Summary

✳ We can understand the true meaning of opposite expression only when in a dualistic situation we create some distance and perspective with the matter, for example with the help of humor. What is the third, harmonizing factor that is attempting to come forth?

✳ You can change dualistically polarized reactions into a larger spectral vision that does not get caught in black and white reactions.

✳ Resisting something acts as a mirror that reflects back to you the nature of the potentiality of that thing.

✳ An outer dualism is reflected from yourself and reminds you of the fact that you are working on something that you yourself created.

✳ The shadow self and the light self form a dualism within you.

✳ Both light and shadow always teach you something. The solution is in a thorough understanding of the matter.

✷ In order to know our heights we must also know our depths and our shadow side.

✷ Establishing the inner marriage, the uniting and harmonizing of the feminine and masculine traits and characteristics, helps in the integration of the personality, and is also reflected in your outer reality as increased harmony in your human relationships.

✷ Denial, resistance and suppression must give way to inner work and dealing with matters.

✷ With heart consciousness you can unite two seemingly extremely opposite factors, since that is the natural characteristic of your heart.

Literature:
Chopra, Deepak, Ford, Debbie & Williamson, Marianne 2010: *The Shadow Effect.* HarperCollins, New York.
Filosofian sanakirja 1999. WSOY, Porvoo – Helsinki – Juva.
Ford, Debbie 2002: *The Secret of The Shadow.* HarperCollins, New York.
Hilarion 1982: *Vision.* Marcus Books, Queensville, Ontario.
Jung, Carl Gustav 1964: *Man and His Symbols.* Doubleday, New York.
Lehtiranta, Erkki 2008: *Astrologia ja Henkinen Tie.* Smiling Stars, Helsinki.

6.

Cycles

" The Law of Cycles can be seen
to operate throughout the experience
of any given lifestream."

- Hilarion

ACCORDING TO THE DICTIONARY, cycles are recurring sequences, series or revolutions. However, they are also much else. Cycles are rhythms, they represent change in sequenced repetition and constancy, and sequenced repetition and constancy in change. The French have a saying: *plus ça change, plus c'est la même chose,* the more things change, the more they remain the same. Changes do not occur randomly, rather, behind them we can find lawfulness. One of the most central is the cosmic Law of Cycles. Without cycles our world would be in a constant state of chaos, and without cycles there would hardly be any life, at least not in the form familiar to us.

Originally the Greek word *kyklos* signified a circle. There are cycles everywhere in life, in its material expressions, as well as in time, and in various recurring events. A proverb tells us: what goes around comes around. This proverb contains a profound truth, and it relates to the cosmic Law of Cycles in our human world.

Many of the cycles of our lives are either so self-evident, or else so far outside of our consciousness, that we hardly give them any thought. Some cycles are short micro cycles, others long macro cycles, some are more regular, others less so. The breath and the heartbeat are typical of rhythms connected with the functions of the body. Most of the cycles of the human body are such that we are not even conscious of them, but they can be measured. Examples are the various metabolic cycles, cerebral frequencies, and biorhythms. The physical biorhythm is the most important of these.

A very interesting perspective on physical cycles is the meridian clock of Chinese medicine. Life energy arrives in the body through the meridians, which are located between the etheric body and the physical body. They are directly connected with the circulatory and nervous systems. The meridians, which are generally thought to number 14, connect the acupuncture points of the body, and flow through at least one internal organ and physiological system.[56] They take care of the organ and system in question, bring vitality and balance to the body, remove blockages, control the metabolism, and also greatly influence the speed and form of the changes that take place in the cell.

According to Chinese thought, the meridians have their own 24-hour cycle, in which each of the 12 main meridians has its own 2-hour peak phase. At that time the meridian in question is at its strongest, its pulses are the sharpest, and its energy absorption the most active. 12 hours later that meridian in turn has its resting phase. The next page picture shows the meridian clock and the flow of life energy in the meridians.

In the surrounding nature we can find enormously slow rhythms, such as the rhythms of the mineral kingdom, and also extremely fast cycles, for example ones that are connected with the functioning of our senses, and phenomena on the quantum level. They are, all the same, cyclic matters and processes. From the point of view of planetary life, among the most central natural cycles are the apparent revolution of the Sun in the sky, and the phases of the Moon, which

---

56   Each of the main meridians has a cyclical structure: each of them travels on both sides of the body. There are two additional special meridians: Du Mai or the governing meridian and Ren Mai, the central or fertility meridian.

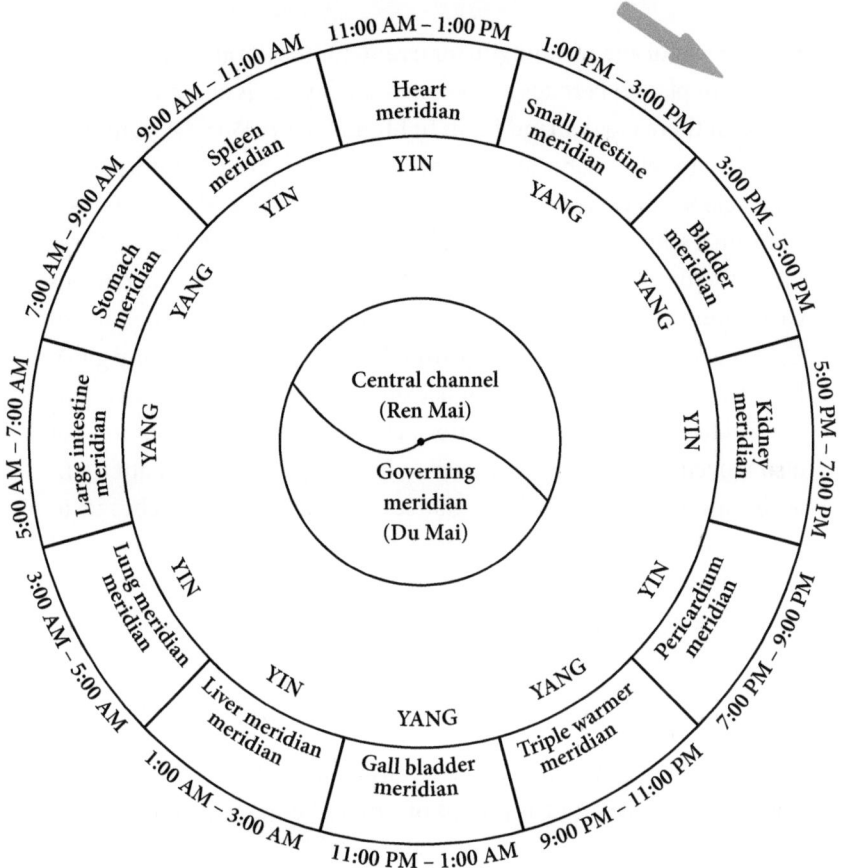

are determined by the mutual ring dance of the Sun and the Moon. Night and day, and the seasons, divide our lives clearly into phases, giving them predictability. In nature we can follow many other kinds of cycles as well, let's say for example the lemming years, or the seven-year cycles of some fish populations. And of course cycles reveal themselves in various guises in the great movements of history. After all, it is said that history repeats itself.

It is actually surprising that humanity has not yet realized the enormous database offered by various cycles, although it could in so many ways be useful and meaningful for us and for the life and well-being of the entire planet. Perhaps a new science of cycles is about to be born – at least there is a demand for it. In his book, *The World According to Cycles*, Samuel A. Schreiner Jr. offers good background information for a science of cycles. (See the bibliography at the end of the book.)

From a spiritual perspective, the great cosmic ballet of cycles provides the base, the foundation, and the rhythm for the current incarnation cycle of humanity. On a more general level, the Law of Cycles can be seen to operate through the experiences of any given lifestream, and as the temporal background structure for them. This law anchors us in time. Time does clearly have a cyclic nature, but also a cyclic quality, as Carl Gustav Jung expressed the matter.[57] In addition, the Law of Cycles organizes life itself, and it teaches us to understand the principles of repetition and of new possibilities, and in this way gives a clear temporal framework to everything we experience in our three-dimensional slice of reality.

The Cosmic Days and Nights of the Lifestreams

The different life forms on our planet all belong to their own lifestream. They can be considered as groups of similar beings, which have their origins in the same mass of "spiritual matter". This mass has been separated from the ocean of spirit or "the body of God", as some of the more religious texts express it. Thus the individuals that represent the same lifestream resemble each other in a way that makes them different from the individuals of another lifestream.[58] I already touched on this theme in connection with the Law of Permanence in chapter 4.

The Law of Cycles requires each lifestream to undergo a series of "outbreaths" or "days", and "inbreaths" or "nights". During the day phases each lifestream takes on the life form tailor-made for it in some

---

57 German Romanticism brought forth the concept of the *Zeitgeist*, which described the cultural and intellectual atmosphere of each period, the spirit of the time. The philosopher Hegel used this concept in his own philosophy of history.
58 Hilarion, *Vision*, pp. 22-23.

particular area of the universe that is appropriate for it. The lifestream usually progresses through some minor sub-cycles in order to learn the lessons that the chosen life form, its spiritual guides and the existing circumstances, determine for it.[59]

The lifestream called humanity is at present evolving on planet Earth through the process of reincarnation, in order to learn to understand, among other things, the true meaning of love, and to respect all life as sacred. This is a long process, which I described in a cursory manner in connection with the Law of Permanence.

At some point each lifestream withdraws into its night phase. During this time, that expression of cosmic life digests and classifies the experiences that it has just gone through, and integrates and balances them in order to prepare itself for the next outbreath, or day.[60] A clear analogy of this principle is found in nature's own rhythm, the alternation of day and night, and the changes of the seasons, in which summer represents the intense day phase, and winter the night phase at its most profound.

A clear allusion to humanity's own reincarnation cycle is of course also found in this. Life in this world is followed by a phase on more spiritual levels in one's own spiritual home, the so-called intermissive period. According to Hilarion, this is on average approximately one half the duration of physical life.[61] This cycle exists for the purpose of digesting the lived life and the experiences it has brought. Spiritually enlightened individuals use the time wisely for their benefit, studying in their own spiritual home, helping, teaching, and preparing with care for their next physical incarnation.

These days and nights of lifestreams were also included in the collective experiences of humanity in the collective periods spent in the mineral, vegetable, and animal kingdoms. We were digesting the

---

59   Hilarion, *Vision*, p. 23.
60   Hilarion, *Vision*, p. 23.
61   There are of course many variations of this, in both directions. For example a person who has committed suicide may live a life equal in length to the unlived years. An interesting presentation of the human incarnation cycle is Dr. Christopher M. Bache's book *Lifecycles – Reincarnation and the Web of Life* (1991, Paragon House, New York.)

teachings given by each natural kingdom before moving on to the next cycle of evolution. This is just what the other lifestreams do as well, after all, it is not wise to go seeking new experiences and teachings before the previous ones have been thoroughly integrated. This holds true also on the level of individual human life.

The most cosmic dimension of the Law of Cycles is perhaps found in ancient Indian literature, which tells of the days and nights of Brahma, the Creator-God, of the *Pralaya,* which leads to life withdrawing from material expression – and to reawakening perhaps thousands or millions of years later. This immense cycle belongs to the score of the Great Cosmic Musician. A certain Indian sage has expressed the matter in this way: the Eternal God releases the entire universe out of himself, plays with it, and pulls it back into himself. In other words, according to the mythology and wisdom tradition of India, the uni-

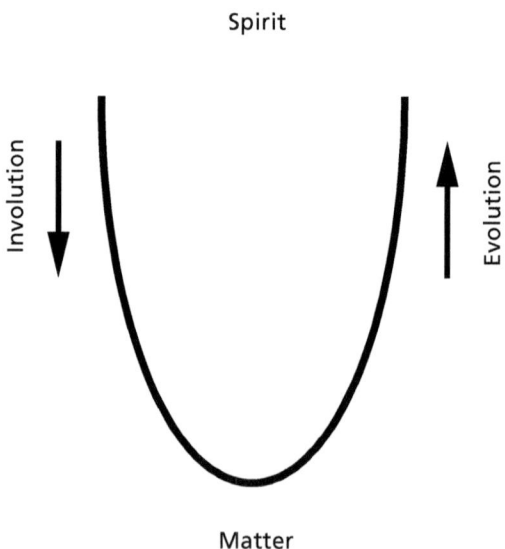

The Arc of involution and evolution.

verse adheres to its own slow cycle in the cosmic timetable. It has also been suggested that the universe inhales and exhales very slowly, expanding and contracting like our lungs. Here the dance of the cosmos and the breath of God are one.

Indian thought also relies on the existence of yugas, long evolutionary periods. These divide the human lifestream into the periods of gold, silver, copper, and the slowest, iron yugas. According to this point of view, the cycles serve evolution and improve its quality. Things are constantly progressing in some direction, not only in time but also in quality. Here the Law of Cycles connects with the Law of Evolution, with the concepts of evolution and involution. Many thinkers add to this view the teleological concept of evolution, where evolution has not only a direction but also a purpose and a goal. This is a familiar view, for example from the thought of Aristotle.

Basics of Cycles: How to Ride the Cycles?

How then to work with the Law of Cycles? This also can be approached from a purely intellectual point of view, calculating different rhythms and in this way gaining some understanding of them. However, we are offered another way, where the central tool is our miraculous **biocomputer,** the heart, which can in its own way understand the cyclic nature of life, and at the same time help you to feel it in your own being.

It is namely very important to gain personal experience of cycles, otherwise they remain only an intellectual pastime, which gives us neither much joy nor benefit. With the help of the heart you can recognize some of the cycles in yourself, not so much to understand the point at which the cycle is, and where it is again going to be, but in relation to where you *yourself* are. This helps you to understand how to act in an appropriate way in relation to the Law of Cycles.

Thus, when you notice some energy-wave which seems to throw you off the tracks in some way, to change you in one way or another, or to teach you something that you feel you are not yet ready for, that is a good time to look into your inner being and note where you are just now. No need to look at biorhythms or astrological transits and progressions, you only need to accept that experience, the pure present moment, and to be consciously present.

What is essential in relation to cycles is to recognize them and to accept their existence. For there are many who do not believe in them, even though matters may be right under their nose or biting them in the ankle. Various recurring patterns and phases, which seem to be swinging different variations of energy back and forth, are natural to existence, to our lives, and to all the things that you see in abundance around you. The cycles of life apply even to things that appear to be permanent and final: good examples are the Rock of Gibraltar and the Sun, which also live and change in their own slow cycles.

Central to each cycle is the fact that it brings with it **change** from one state to another. Understanding change and living in accordance with it gives more life-wisdom, resisting it brings difficulties. The phenomena you experience, such as light, sound, warmth, nervous impulses, and other similar things, are also cycles. It is just that they occur very fast, in a millionth or a billionth of a second. Telepathy and intuition are also connected with cycles on subtler levels.

In all these there is alternation of the active and passive phases of the cycle, as in the resting and the activation phase of the synapses in neurological impulses.

The resonance phenomenon is a part of cycles. Wherever there are waves, there are also cycles, as in the case of sound waves and light waves. For example, the receptive mechanisms of your eyes vibrate differently depending on which color stimulates them in its turn. What is in question is a resonance between the stimulant and the receptive mechanism. I already wrote about this in connection with the previous law, the Law of Opposite Expression, in chapter 5. You can take advantage of resonance as you work with the larger, longer cycles in your life. When you do, notice that you begin to resonate with the cycle and thus are able to pluck information from it.

Universal Laws and Spiritual Progress

Different Forms of Cycles

Cycles are truly not linear. There are an infinite number of themes and variations on themes, within which cycles are born. Most of the cycles that occur in nature are spiral in nature. This can be seen in many of the forms and processes of nature, from snails to galaxies. Spirals are formed from the interaction of two forces, an inner and an outer, and in the three-dimensional world spiral structures tend to become either larger or smaller. A spiral in itself is a naïve reminder of the habit of viewing cycles in a two-dimensional form.

The spiral appears to be the general wave cycle as we slowly transition from the Piscean Age into the Aquarian Age. This spiral cycle is now in an expanding phase, until it will again contract during immensely long periods, and once more begin to grow after hundreds of thousands of years.

A cycle can in many ways be compared to a sine wave or a circle, which is the origin of its name. A sine wave travels through minor variations to the peak of energy, information, vibration etc., and back to the bottom again. Usually we work with a cycle connected with a sine wave by adjusting to it, and by knowing and feeling it within ourselves.

A circle is usually connected with cycles that begin anew in a new place, a new time, and in a new way. A sine wave and a circle are very similar in that they are determined by the same mathematical principles. An incarnation cycle – and we will return to this in a bit – appears to be circular, while a general evolutionary cycle is more like a sine wave.

These are not the only cycles that we encounter. Sometimes there are very dramatic changes, which could be called *hysteresis*. What this means is a characteristic of some system, such that it slows down the reaction to changes, or prevents the system from returning to its original state. The old saying "two steps back, three steps forward" might express this principle. This can be seen in many political and economic cycles. For example, in economics, hysteresis usually means that once unemployment has gone up, it does not easily return to its original base.

How then can we work with cycles on all levels, and learn to adapt to them? In connection with every aspect of the Law of Cycles, we should pay attention to at least three factors:

- accept their existence
- find the state that resonates with the cycle
- as you begin to resonate, notice how its sympathetic response arises as if as a sign of how you are progressing.

This holds true for cycles of the Moon, and the cycles of markets and the economy, just as much as for the great evolutionary rhythms of humanity, and the incarnation cycle as well.

The Incarnation Cycle

We can gain an enormous amount of information, experience and emotional understanding through the incarnation cycle. Through a certain continuity and uniformity, being reborn offers us the possibility of reflecting on the various sides of our own nature, of refining them, of obtaining new characteristics, and at the same time freeing ourselves from others.

Change and permanence meet in this process in a way that is more than interesting. In the cycles of the wheel of karma, we can move between greater and lesser knowledge in a conscious way. As we incarnate in matter, our consciousness shrinks from what it is when we are on the spiritual level between physical incarnations, during the so-called intermissive period. In the world of resistant matter we can nevertheless raise up out of ourselves the best and the highest, or else sink into the darkest and basest energy, if we so wish. The Law of Karma is a powerful background force in this, and its rules are built into the circumstances of our lives, whether we realize it or not. In this context we should clarify that the same situation pertains to cycles as to the Law of Karma, the law of cause and effect – you do not notice them, if you are not able to observe them. Living in a human body demands a special spiritual wakefulness and presence for it to give us its best.

In the cycles connected with reincarnation the question is not about breaking or changing some cycle, but rather about observing it and resonating with it. An interesting matter connected with this is the fact that the resonance can easily combine waves from different cycles, or from your own way of being, your particular energy, in such a way that the cycle itself is strengthened. Because of the strengthened cycle, understanding expands, experience and consciousness are deepened, and together they help you to draw the best out of yourself.

The reincarnation cycle is a very complex, and partly a very obscure, matter, and it is not possible to consider, in this context, all the factors that are connected with it. It is nevertheless good to remember that reincarnation is never a "solo gig", but rather orchestral music in the metaphysical and karmic sense of the word. Every Earth life is carefully planned, and for every life a wise soul design is prepared on the basis also of previous experiences, karma, and lessons learned. This appears to contain both a positive and a negative variant.[62] When an individual follows the positive life plan, life becomes easier, and greater possibilities arise. In that case the karma does not have to be confronted through pain and suffering, but through helping others, through love and service.

Some people want to get away from this challenging world of matter to some other world, perhaps to the starry heavens. However, here you must make sure that this wish does not contain escapism, a flight from reality. And in any case, why leave in the middle of the battle, since the unfinished lessons will inevitably sooner or later come knocking on our door? It is better to "see all the cards".

In the three-dimensional world, the principle of reincarnation is very valuable. As we gradually move to a higher dimension, we are ever better able to understand those of our choices that relate to rein-

---

62   This was often emphasized by my first spiritual teacher, Tyyne Matilainen, the founder of the correspondence school Kirjeopisto Via. See the article *"Opettajani Tyyne Matilainen – hengen pioneeri ja uuden ajan airut"*, Uusi Safiiri 1/2011, pp. 34—39.

carnation. In a sense, we are able to live our lives simultaneously with former incarnations, and also to guide our energies more consciously into the next life, wherever we may live it. Perhaps the cycle will continue for us in other life spheres on other planets, where we ourselves can initiate the incarnation cycle for primitive life forms, and with it, help them to know themselves. This is how we, also, have learned, through a very long journey, to know our own being, its breadth and its relationship to the Creator of Love.

Through innumerable incarnations, we can learn to understand our own cycles, and strengthen our ability to unite energy, love and information, and finally, our own unique God-nature. In this way we can eventually also guide and help other life forms on their chosen path.

Heavenly Lights and Breath of Mother Earth

Let us return once more to experiencing cycles in our own life environment. The daily rhythm is of course the easiest to experience, but it is not very difficult to observe matters connected with the Moon cycle, since they are in direct relationship to the physical biorhythm of approximately 28 days. A woman's menstrual cycle is very close to the cycle of the Moon's revolutions.

In this, the Moon's gravity influences your bodily fluids, and at the same time reminds you, on a subtler level, of your cells, of what they are, and of the fact of their existence. Additionally, your bodily fluids symbolize your emotional life. It is important to understand that in the evolution of our species, we will soon become especially sensitized to the Moon cycle. Our ancestors knew instinctively how to follow and utilize this cycle, and contemporary people will become ever more conscious of it. This can be seen in people's conversations, as well as in the ever-increasing literature on the topic.

It is good to observe the rhythms of the Moon and its effects, especially at the two culmination points of the Moon cycle: at the new moon phase and at the full moon. These alternate at approximately two weeks. These culmination points are important from the point of view of our self-knowledge, since the regions of our minds symbolized by the Sun and the Moon, the conscious and the unconscious mind, also meet at those times.

At the time of the new moon they come together in the sky, in other words, they align with each other from our perspective. At this time the two regions of the mind are also aligned, and our instincts and intuition awaken and open to new ideas and insights.

An even better barometer of the harmony – or the lack of harmony – between the conscious and the unconscious mind, is formed by that other culmination point, the full moon, when the heavenly bodies are, from our perspective, furthest apart from each other, at the opposite sides of the zodiac. If, during the full moon, we experience a restless mind or sleep disturbances, there is usually an unresolved tension or conflict between the two regions of the mind, which attempts to come forth in order to find resolution.

This is actually an excellent time for meditation, since only when the monkey mind is silenced, are we able to clarify the mental disharmony in question. For some people, the full moon state triggers much more serious matters, such as addictions, mental problems or violent behavior, as many people in the healing professions or the police force know so well. In light of this experience, it is quite surprising that many people still maintain a skeptical attitude toward the influence of the Moon on the human mind.

In the example offered by the Moon cycle, there is a great meeting ground of the Law of Cycles, the Law of Thought (which includes the contents of the unconscious mind as well), and the Law of Reflection, and it is worthwhile to observe closely the culmination points of the mutual cycles of the Sun and the Moon.

In addition to the phases of the Moon, it is wise to define more precisely the views on, and the experience of, the yearly cycle, which is strongly connected with the annual breathing cycle and the energy currents of Mother Earth, the movements of energy within the meridian system of our planet. To be specific, the energies flow along planetary ley lines, which connect all the power points of the planet. Additionally, these energies have an energy cycle that resembles the movement of energy in an individual's meridian system. As our planet's energies flow along the ley lines, they travel in one direction from the summer solstice to the winter solstice, and then reverse their direction.

This energy rhythm forms the annual breathing cycle of Mother Earth. What is in question is ancient wisdom, which is again coming forth. The summer solstice, which occurs toward the end of June in the northern hemisphere, is like a moment of holding one's breath between two breaths. When the planet exhales, the breath travels through the balance point of the autumn equinox, at which time the balance between full lungs and empty lungs is reached.

When the exhalation is complete and the lungs are empty, we come to the winter solstice toward the end of December. It is the deepest period of silence and peace, which is symbolized by so many things at that time: a profound peace in nature, the hibernation of some animals, the withdrawing of some people into their own inner being, etc. Then the planetary breath begins again with an inhalation, which travels through the balance point of the spring equinox to the culmination point where the cycle began a year ago: to the summer solstice.

The amount of sunlight is at its most dramatic at the solstices. At the end of June the days are at their longest, and at the end of December at their shortest, in our hemisphere. The moments of greatest potential also occur at the solstices, but the periods of greatest expression and activity are at the times of the equinoxes, when the greatest amount of energy is available.

The Long Planetary Cycles

A cycle that is longer than the monthly and yearly cycles of the Moon and the Sun, but one that is still understandable through experience, is the cycle based on the movements of the karmic planet, Saturn. I already wrote about this leaden planet in the previous chapter, and now is the time to take a closer look at the cyclic nature of Saturn, which is familiar to many people through their own experiences, through confronting many important life lessons. These often bring to the fore patience and self-discipline, those cardinal Saturnian virtues, which are connected in many ways on the individual level to the cosmic Law of Cycles. A person who is not able to wait patiently for the ripening of spiritual fruits, is often left without their blessings.

The Law of Cycles is also fundamentally connected, through Saturn, with another cosmic law, namely the Law of Karma. It is precisely karma that binds a human being to the wheel of rebirth, and which also appears on the scene to be confronted through the cyclic rhythms. Spiritual astrology gives many clues to this. The interconnectedness of these laws in astrology can perhaps best be seen in the seven-year cycles of Saturn, where a part of an individual's karma returns to be confronted, clarified, and – hopefully – to be learned from, and to be rectified.

Saturn, i.e. Khronos, or the Father Time of Antiquity, is the most important task master of the heavens, whose lessons are worth listening to carefully on the spiritual Path, as I already wrote earlier in this book. The better we have learned and digested the lessons of the cycles we have previously confronted, the better prepared we will be to confront the lessons of future cycles. In my opinion, this is nowhere as true as in precisely the cycles of Saturn. Our worldly way becomes easier when we recognize the heavenly signposts.[63]

The approximately 29.5-year revolution of Saturn in the zodiac is neatly divided into four subcycles of 7 – 7.5 years each. The rhythm of these subcycles in human life is coded into the picture on the next page.

Experiencing the longer planetary cycles is not always easy. For example, it is not easy to daily feel the slow rhythms that are connected with a great change in our cosmic sphere. Right now, the point of the

---

63   Lehtiranta & Stenberg, *Astrologiset syklit ja elämänhallinta*, p. 8.

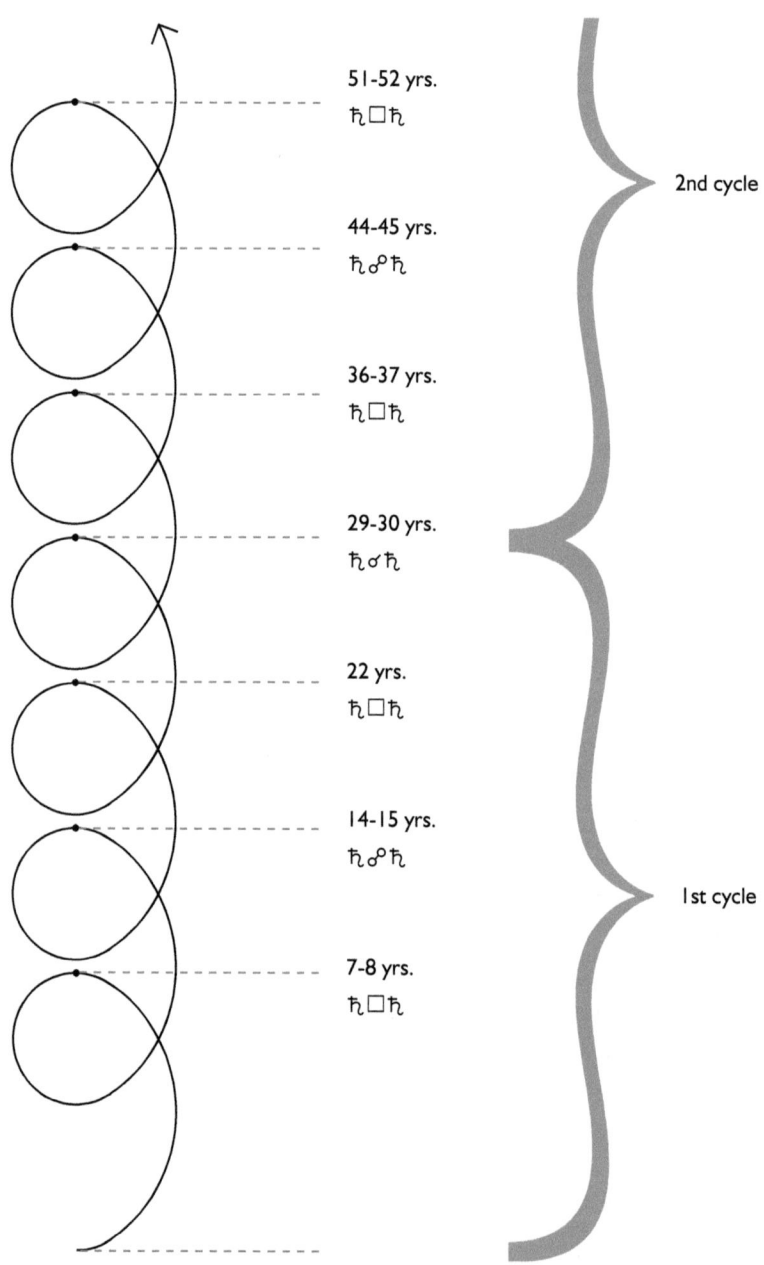

51-52 yrs.
♄ □ ♄

44-45 yrs.
♄ ☍ ♄

36-37 yrs.
♄ □ ♄

29-30 yrs.
♄ ☌ ♄

22 yrs.
♄ □ ♄

14-15 yrs.
♄ ☍ ♄

7-8 yrs.
♄ □ ♄

2nd cycle

1st cycle

Universal Laws and Spiritual Progress

spring equinox[64] is gradually moving in the sky from the sign of Pisces to the sign of Aquarius. This is what is in question in connection with the Age of Aquarius, and I alluded to this earlier, in connection with the spiral cycles.

What is in question is the ending a very important cycle, and the beginning of the next one on our planet. The location of the spring equinox moves very gradually in the zodiac, about one degree in 72 years, and it revolves around the entire zodiac in approximately 25,920 years. This great planetary, or Platonic, year is divided into 12 subcycles, or planetary months, of about 2160 years each.[65] As a new planetary month changes, new matters and currents are poured into our planet and into humanity. In general, in the great economic, political, and social cycles, the systems and institutions that no longer resonate with the Aquarian Age, will be the first to change dramatically.

The Aquarian Age is the stepping forward of a synthesis of spirituality and science, and of brotherhood. Its first rays can already be seen in our spiritual sky.

The change of the planetary month is also synchronized in an interesting way with the end of the Mayan calendar, which has been the object of a lot of buzz and hullaballoo in recent years. In my opinion, the discussion has been fraught with a lot of unnecessary drama, and various ethically questionable theories, with unclear motivation. In addition, these views often fail to remember that what is in question in the Aquarian Age, as well as in the turn of the Mayan calendar, is largely the free will of humanity, our readiness to be receptive to the new currents, or to retreat and to resist them. Both routes are open, otherwise free will would not exist.

---

64 Because of the precession of the Earth's axis, the point of the spring equinox does not always occur in the same constellation; instead it reverses in relation to the constellations approximately one degree in 72 years.
65 Lehtiranta & Stenberg, *Astrologiset syklit ja elämänhallinta*, p. 10.

Meditation: The Cycle of Existence

Relax and breathe deeply. Imagine that you have a great emerald in front of you. Enter into it and notice that you are a part of it. As you exhale, the emerald grows larger and larger, until you can no longer see its edges. You are tranquil inside this magnificent light. Feel how the energy waves of the emerald travel through you.

The waves move very slowly, like waves or ripples in the ocean, and you can feel and experience them. But you are safe within this emerald light, and you are able to experience the waves at any speed whatever. Imagine that the waves begin to move faster and faster, until their cycle moves through you and affects you at the deepest level: the waves shape the processes of your body and affect your nerves and your thought patterns, and influence what you see and hear.

Then notice that these waves of emerald light are moving more and more slowly, until they are finally the great patterns of your whole life: the cycles of your birth, your maturing, your education, your aging, and finally your passing away. Your own cycles are magnificent in you.

Next see the great cycle of all your incarnations and see how this energy that you share with others, unifies to form the magnificent wave of all humanity in this emerald green light. It moves gradually and slowly together, as if all your bodies and minds were one, and all were in the same place at the same time, without crowding, but full of a radiant ecstasy of leaping forward, and full of expressions of great inner joy.

Feel this inwardly and notice how you have taken into your being some of the most authentic qualities of the emerald light. Concentrate on this beautiful light as it now moves through all humanity, and at the same time, you can understand the experience of cyclicity deeply. You can see the change that it brings, how it brings joy, and gives people everything that they have yearned for and waited for, for a very long time. You can jump for joy with other people and hear the thunder. All this feels wonderful, and creates a sense of oneness, all this in everyone together, and at the same time in yourself.

Universal Laws and Spiritual Progress

Now relax out of these thoughts. If you want, you can from time to time return to this emerald within you. It is important to notice, and to understand, that if you sometimes experience fear and struggle in connection with the cycles, find its source, free yourself of it, and understand how it keeps its hold on you, and how it appears, and in what sphere of life. Notice also that in the cycle itself there is something that you receive with pleasure, that strengthens you, and that you can enjoy. In this way you can flow with the cycle and add to it these qualities – and enjoy the cycle on many levels.

Summary

✳ A cycle expresses and represents change.

✳ What you leave behind you, you will find before you through cycles.

✳ A cycle is an energy wave, an energy pattern that is built of individual elements. These can move in resonance in different ways.

✳ Energy is always made up of consciousness.

✳ Repetitive movement is fundamental to the nature of existence and life.

✳ Cycles occur within the framework of time, space, matter, and energy.

✳ There is a limitless number of variations within which cycles can occur.

✴ Cycles that occur in nature tend to be spirals that continuously become either larger or smaller.

✴ On the physical level the most important cycles for us are the ones, which occur with a very rapid rate of change.

✴ The life cycles confront you with things. You express your uniqueness with your free will in the way you respond to these things.

✴ Your free will defines what you feel about a thing that the cycles confront you with, how you understand it, how you receive the information it represents, and how you work with that information.

✴ When you feel a wave of energy brought by a cycle, you are required to respond to it in some way.

✴ Cycles can lead to an opposite expression if you pay attention only to their peaks and valleys, and ignore the spectrum, which results from seeing a cycle as a wave.

✴ In connection with the Law of Cycles, it is not so important to understand where the cycle was, or where it will appear next, but rather where **you** are. You yourself are the focal point of cycles.

✴ You can gather information from a cycle by resonating with it. Then you can flow with the cycle and move within it in many ways.

✴ When a cycle that you have already dealt with returns, it brings with it additional information in a pleasant, humorous, and joyful way. A returning cycle whose lesson you have not learned, returns in even harsher form.

✴ Your reaction to a returning cycle functions as an indicator of your own evolution.

✴ Resolving karma is not so much a matter of breaking or changing a cycle, but rather of understanding it and resonating with it.

Literature:
Hilarion 1982: *Vision*. Marcus Books, Queensville, Ontario.
Lehtiranta, Erkki & Niemelä, Leena 2007: *Suomen luonnon valkoista magiaa*. Smiling Stars, Helsinki.
Lehtiranta, Erkki & Stenberg, Sven 2010: *Astrologiset syklit ja elämänhallinta*. Smiling Stars, Helsinki.
Schreiner, Samuel Agnew 2009: *The World According to Cycles*. Skyhorse Publishing, New York.

7.

Thought

At the beginning of the experiment
represented by the planet Earth,
the creative thought energies —
those which literally called the solar
system into being— came from a group
of very powerful beings, known
in some texts as the Elohim.

- Hilarion

THOUGHT IS A CENTRAL FACTOR in human life. It is in fact said that thought is the beginning of all things. It precedes speech, it is also the precursor of act and activity, even if we do not always believe this. Language is the central instrument of our mind, and in connection with thought we can speak of thought-acts, which then tend to become concrete in our actions and choices. In fact, our entire life is in some sense an expression of our thoughts.

The Law of Thought is in this sense the great law of creation. In the Bible we can read: "In the beginning was the Word, and the Word was with God, and the Word was God." I doubt if we damage the concept if we change "Word" to "Thought". In my own opinion, this entire manifest universe is a great Thought of God, in other words, in everything, there is God, this cosmic Thought. The Creator thinks, and worlds form. Finally the Divine arises in us as, well, – thinking.

Ancient wisdom expresses this as follows: God sleeps in stone, dreams in plants, moves in animals, and awakens and becomes conscious of himself in humans.

Thoughts Shape Our Reality

Although the power of thought is one of the greatest forces in the world, it is also one of the least well understood characteristics of humans. Someone may of course say that we can all see that the world is full of wonderful thoughts and thinkers. To be sure, but in general, the power of thought has not been realized and understood correctly, or it would not be misused so much! The power of thought is, in fact, incredible, and it is not wise to underestimate it. Rather, we should learn to use, and to channel, this valuable energy in an appropriate and wise way.

An American, Dr. Ken McFarland, has said that 2% of people really think, 3% believe they think, and the other 95% would rather die

---

The Manipulative Thoughts of the Media

Good news is no news has long been a saying that has crippled the information media and above all their target audience. Of course difficult things and injustices should be talked and written about, but positive factors should also be noted sufficiently, for example the ordinary heroism and goodness that people also demonstrate in our time. I remember that years ago I saw a tabloid called Positive News in London, and I wish that more of this type might be created in various parts of the world. People long for hope and good positive examples and ways of solving problems in order to have the strength to meet the challenges of daily life and the current turbulence of the planet.

In this connection we can ask how the media could better, more efficiently and above all more consciously serve the welfare and the spiritual progress of humanity, and further the solving of problems. It is possible to speak and write about spiritual matters with objectivity and appeal. The influence of the media on the collective consciousness and their responsibility for its formation are great. We should not underestimate or avoid this responsibility.

than think. This provocative view may not hold true all the way, but still, it gives us – something to think about.

In addition, our thoughts are strongly bound up with our emotions and our will. Our thoughts shape the circumstances of our lives in an incredibly powerful way and are present everywhere. They "stick" to the walls, and to the rest of our own environment, they are present in the aura of hotel rooms and other public spaces.

The invisibility of thoughts is thus a kind of optical illusion, for they become visible everywhere in our environment. For example, computers, windows, eyeglasses and cars are the fruits of long pondering and many questions, born to respond to the needs of humanity. These needs have then taken on the form of thoughts, and been realized as plans, acts, and achievements.   .

After all, we are thinking all the time, in other words, we do not have to obtain this basic skill as such, but improving the quality of our thinking is, on the contrary, both laborious and necessary. How challenging this task is, may become clear if I ask you RIGHT NOW to think a really original, high-level, true thought. What comes to mind? Most likely some familiar, safe ideas, rather than original, creative ones!

I do not wish in any way to disparage your ability to think with this thought game, I only wish to emphasize the importance of improving it. Comfort-loving indolence has already long ago been noted to be one of the most serious obstacles to spiritual progress. This is also connected with our way of thinking: why fix it if it isn't even broken? In this way we may get on the misleading path of least resistance, where thoughts follow the familiar patterns, habits, customs, and beliefs that billions of others also observe.

Everyone who thinks with his own brains, understand the dangers that lurk here. There are some who would like to see people remain on their knees, in their own corrals, as easily controlled masses, peaceful and well-behaved, and at least not too demanding. Still, when the lamp of independent thought is once lit, it is not easily put out, and a person begins to be conscious of the models and mechanisms with-

Universal Laws and Spiritual Progress

in the structures of community and society which have been used to steer people in the direction of uniformity and spiritual hibernation.

Thought awakens along with the thinker. When your consciousness is alert and capable of discernment, you awaken to see even the many subtle sides of mental manipulation, for example in the media.

You do not need to give up television or unsubscribe to newspapers or opt out of the social media, but you are no longer their prisoner, but rather an alert observer and – when necessary – an opinion maker and activator of fresh new ideas. Concentrating on the essential is one of the important lessons of our time. When we become capable of that, the result may be a whole new kind of fireworks of ideas.

Thought Shapes History and Yourself

Besides being such an important and ordinary tool for us, thought is also a great force that shapes history. As Victor Hugo wrote, no army can resist an idea whose time has come. Thoughts have an influence on the collective level as well. If we think thoughts on a larger scale and collectively, they become culture, which is one of the activating forces of all humankind. Ideas also give birth to ideologies, which may be destructive, constructive or perhaps neutral.

In history massive thoughts like "an eye for an eye, a tooth for a tooth", Hammurabi's cruel law, and the much more humane and spiritual so-called golden rule, "do unto others as you would have them do unto you", have for millennia traveled along with humanity, coloring the collective experience and the understanding of the principles of life for people.

Some of the power-thoughts of our time have been for example Martin Luther King's "I have a dream" and Obama's "Yes we can!" Charismatic leaders touch unspoken collective feelings with their compact slogans, and in this way give a voice to many people.

The magical power of thought is one of the most powerful creative forces in the world. A person who controls his thoughts and the movements of his mind is close to this power and can do much good for himself as well as for his environment.

I suggest that you think at least 100 good, wholesome thoughts every day. Repeat these positive affirmations and they will start to become forces that shape reality. See what the world needs and construct your world in the direction of these needs. If you feel that the world needs more love – as it sure does! – increase the love energy of your thoughts. Call in love from the inexhaustible stores of the universe with your thoughts. In this way you will also learn the refreshing grammar of love and compassion.

In the following you have some mantras for daily use and various needs. They have been collected in accordance with the principles of the logical positive thinking taught by Kirjeopisto Via, a Finnish spiritual correspondence school.

The basics of the teaching were formed largely during the years 1955–1957, long before the American wave of positive thinking!

- I am joyous, happy and optimistic!
- I am spiritually balanced and calm!
- I am inwardly humble in the right kind of way!
- I am authenticity!
- I am Love that grows and gains strength!
- My mind is like calm water!
- I control my thoughts better and better!
- I am opening to new positive insights!
- My creativity increases and my health improves in the space between my thoughts!
- May the best come true!
- I remember everything necessary!
- I have an abundance of divine energy and will!
- I am learning to understand the spiritual laws better and better!
- I am learning to bring spirituality into my daily life better and better!
- I am anchoring light, wisdom and love into myself!
- My wise thoughts improve my health!
- My body is becoming more relaxed, youthful and flexible!

- I am receiving the gift of a healthy person's restorative sleep!
- May divine joy of life fill me completely right now!
- May divine love fill me completely right now!
- May divine peace fill me completely right now!
- May divine patience fill me completely right now!
- May divine will fill me completely right now!
- I harmonize all sides of my being!
- My sense of humor is warm and inoffensive!

What you think, repeat and study is what you energize and attract to yourself, and it begins to open up for you. This holds true for these mantras as well. So you see that mantras can be used for many different purposes. If you repeat these or similar affirmations that you have created for your own purposes, try to avoid using mindless, mechanical repetition. Give yourself to the thought and to the energy in it, make it emotional if necessary, and if you like, connect a colorful and lively mental image to it, either from the past or from a positive future. In this way you will unite these in a power triangle of thought, imagination and emotion.

Remember that loving thoughts lead inevitably to loving speech and loving deeds. Here the Law of Thought comes together with the Law of Love and the Law of Speech. A meeting of three Universal Laws and their conscious use is a very powerful thing.

A little rhymed song with simple, positive words is a good habit every morning and evening, for example when taking a shower. A song like this, with its rhymes, anchors the positive thought energies deep into the structures of the unconscious mind and into the memory banks. It is like a deposit with good interest. In addition, when the thought is spoken aloud, or in this case sung aloud, it really gains wings and ultimately has a powerful effect on the physical level as well. And this has nothing to do with your singing voice – even if you are off key, you are on the energy. I will continue this consideration in connection with the Law of Speech in chapter 10.

Thought Is not Self-Evident

I think my thoughts onto paper, and you in turn read them right now. We are both working with the cosmic Law of Thought, each in our own way. One of our peculiar features, though, is that we hardly ever reflect on our own thinking – even if we think a lot otherwise. However, it is quite difficult for thought to understand thought, in other words, we would have to get outside of our thinking in order to understand it. Even then, we should perhaps, paradoxically, return again to the process of thinking itself.

Thought is not at all self-evident, for it has many dimensions. Telepathy is one of the forms of thought, and it has already for a long time been so common among spiritually awakened people that it is no longer actually considered questionable. Thoughts really are "in the air", as is so aptly said. We are in telepathic contact with innumerable people, even if we ourselves do not know it or notice it.

Thus we can understand that thoughts move on their own frequencies from the consciousness of one thinker to the consciousness of others. In fact, we share many thoughts even on a global level, and these make up our collective, planetary consciousness. Peter Russell's classic book, *The Global Brain* (Routledge & Kegan Paul, London, 1982) is an important first entry in understanding global collective consciousness.

Lynne McTaggart's book, *The Intention Experiment* (FreePress, New York, 2007), opens fascinating perspectives on the positive possibilities of intentional thought, and especially of guided collective thought. Among others, the works of Deepak Chopra, Gregg Braden, Ervin Laszlo, and Danah Zohar deserve our attention as well.

We may of course fear the blossoming of telepathic abilities into full flower, which has not by any means occurred in the present stage of human evolution. Nevertheless, we have at some earlier times been much more open in this respect and have seen ourselves through the mind's eye of other people. In this way, we found out a lot about ourselves and our true nature, which frightened many at the same time.

When our telepathic abilities really become active again, even our deepest thoughts will be open to our fellow humans, in other words, our thoughts will become visible as a kind of "mental clothing". Thus, knowing the cosmic Law of Thought helps us to prepare for this challenge, and for a great opportunity to evolve and to grow, at the same time.

All this pertains especially to Finnish people, since according to Hilarion, the cosmic Law of Thought is currently the most central of the cosmic laws for Finns. I already wrote about this in connection with the Law of Reflection. It is then not surprising that for example the university of higher thought, Kirjeopisto Via, was founded in Finland. In addition, the Finnish people read a lot, and illuminate their own thinking in this way. In Finland they have good opportunities to discover and develop the many applications that relate to improving their thinking and building a better tomorrow precisely with thoughts. What kind of future do you want to live in? Because that begins right NOW, and you influence it right now with your thoughts and your beliefs!

Our thoughts are the scaffolding of our future, and our happiness – or its opposite – depends in the end on them. Actually, every thought is an order made to the universe. As a common saying has it, "you get what you ask for". But not everyone understands that this is specifically connected with the Law of Thought.

In addition, every thought returns to the thinker himself, in other words, it is as if we nourish ourselves with our own thoughts. From this point of view, it is important to understand the mechanisms and the laws of our thought processes.

The Multifaceted Thought Process

Master Hilarion tells us that thought is a process between the subtle bodies and the physical body. The mental body, the emotional body, and the etheric body all make their contribution to the thought process. The central energy stream of the process travels first from the mental body, the seat of our thoughts and mental images, to the etheric body, and from there onward to our physical vehicle. In a secondary manner, thought energy streams from both the mental and the emotional bodies to the etheric body, and from there onward to the physical vehicle. Thirdly – and this is the most difficult for most people to understand – thought energy streams directly from the emotional body to the physical body.

The mental body and the emotional body are very closely connected, and are in a reciprocal relation to each other, since every thought triggers a certain emotional reaction pattern, which then influences a certain energy center, or chakra. For example friendly, compassionate, loving thoughts are felt in the heart chakra, and they make you feel especially good, while thoughts based on fear trigger lower emotional patterns, which get stuck around the third chakra, or solar plexus. There they have an effect on the digestive system, on respiration, and on the heart. A martyrdom-addiction is one possible result from this.

Every thought sends messages to the entire nervous system and affects every cell and organ of the physical body. The greatest trap of any mental or emotional imbalance is getting stuck on past memory patterns, or on constant future plans and worries, so that the person is not completely here in the present moment. With this package then comes constant comparison, judgment, discontent and over-analysis.

The mind is never at rest when it's overactive. Just like explosive, overexcited emotions, the mind also needs the right kind of nourishment, practice, and rest, in order to stay in balance. The continuous offers of consumer goods and of overexcited media fare is nowadays, especially through television, the internet and the social media, the most depleting factor, not only for our mental, but also for our emotional body as well as for our physical well-being.

In the interaction of the subtle bodies mentioned above, at first the energy streaming into the physical body is relatively undifferentiated. It begins to change in the physical body with the help of soul energy frequencies, and the frequencies created in this process define the way in which the energies are filtered into the higher chakras, for example into the centers above the head and into the seventh chakra at the top of the head.

In this mutual interaction of the subtle bodies and the chakras, in the filtering process, and in the mutual networking of the frequencies, the frequency levels gradually become lower. Finally, in the interaction of the etheric body, and especially in the interaction of the brain, the vagus nerve, and the spine, the cells are in a constant state of change, moving, transforming, discharging, or moving back and forth between a resonant and an unresonant state. This creates frequencies, and our experience interprets these frequencies as thoughts.

From Quantity to Quality, from Logic to Intuition

We can understand that this is a very profound, and partly a very complicated, process, which nevertheless tells us that our thinking does not actually take place in our brains, as materialistic science assumes, but rather, our brains interpret the information of the frequencies as thoughts. The brain is a computer that is programmed by consciousness. But if we can accept the process of transformation that is connected with this way of thinking and accept the fact that we have the capacity to utilize it in many ways, this will help us to understand that we have so far used only a fraction of our potential.

Nowadays scientists say that on average, we use perhaps 12% of our mental capacity. What does the remaining potential of 88% contain, if with the help of our current capacity we are able to send people to the Moon, to study our genetic inheritance, and to create dazzling art? Surely magnificent things, which we can realize by clarifying, developing, and above all, improving the quality of our thinking. Emptying the mental trash is essential in this process.

Miracles start to happen when the quantity of our thinking changes ever more into quality. As the space between two thoughts grows, it is possible to experience the beauty and meaning of the eternal present moment in all its glory. Only your thoughts come between you and reality. It is also possible to have a profound personal experience of the fact that you are not your thoughts – you have thoughts, but you are the eternal, divine, calm and peaceful consciousness behind your thoughts, the consciousness which is also a part of divine consciousness. Nobody can take this knowledge, this insight, this understanding away from you. This consciousness is also the factor behind the Universal Laws, and it observes itself through its own evolution. The evolution of consciousness is the true spiritual evolution. Consciousness in itself is connected to the seventh dimension.[66]

We have been taught to reason. Well and good. In the West, the use of linear thinking has been practically built into our thought processes. This means certain ways of gathering and organizing facts, numbers, information, and some other things connected with the thought process. In this way, the rules of logic can be applied in a way that leads to certain desired results. However, since a computer does all this so much better and faster than we can, it would be worth our while to study other ways of developing our thinking skills.

What we have become over the years and decades speaks of our addictive relationship with the thought process, because it seems to work. The traditional logical thought process helps us to cope with daily life, and sometimes causes us to feel that what we have created is sufficient and enough. Why then create something more? This is of course a thought addiction that impedes progress, one of the most difficult dependencies of our times. It is based on an over-dependence on the logical side of the mind, which usually leads to being overly analytical, and attempting to find a solution to everything – often at the expense of intuition and the wisdom of the heart.

For if our goal is spiritual awakening, understanding life and love, enlightenment, and expressing our own unique potential, we notice sooner or later that though logic has its place in all this, we cannot depend on it completely in relation to most of the answers we get, the things we understand, and finally to the central purposes of our life.

---

66   See Gurudas: *Gem Elixirs and Vibrational Healing, Vol. II*, p. 147.

Our higher capacity opens as our telepathic ability and our intuitive knowledge and understanding open. This includes many means and levels, and one of these is a spontaneous holistic understanding of something or some aggregate of things. Logic has nothing to do with this. The reality of a deep inner knowledge opens up in the blink of an eye. Making it logical may be a long process – if it is necessary at all.

Telepathy is also of interest to researchers. Sometime in the nineties, I was watching conversations between Nobel laureates in science. One of these involved the Nobel laureate in medicine for that year, who was asked what his greatest dream was now that the most respected prize in science had been achieved by him. The French scientist said that he would still like to prove telepathy. The interviewer became embarrassed and thought that this was witty Gallic humor. But no, the Nobel laureate was quite serious, and added at the end, "it's just so damned hard to prove!"

Thought Vibrates, Mind Opens

Every thought is also an electromagnetic vibration, which vibrates with its own frequency according to its quality, its content and its nature. Beautiful, pure and noble thoughts vibrate at high frequencies, dark and negative thoughts at low frequencies. For example "joy", "love", "peace", "tenderness", and other positive concepts contain in themselves an uplifting power, so it is possible to use them as such, when dark clouds crowd in on our inner sky.

Thought is energy in the same way as electricity, light or warmth. We only need to learn to control this form of energy, since an untamed mind often fights against reality. An unsatisfied and unclarified monkey-mind worries about the future and also clings to the past, repeating it over and over again in an inner dialogue. In other words, when we could have handled some matter, even a painful one, thoroughly and once for all, the uncalmed monkey-mind gets stuck and repeats it perhaps 500, 5,000 or 50,000 times! Does this self-inflicted suffering make any sense? It does not.

Control of the mind succeeds best by calming the mind. An excellent tool for this is a regular meditation practice. Different meditation techniques are excellent for clearing various confusions and troubles of mind, in other words, for changing the quantity of thoughts into quality of thoughts. At the same time a person can act as the observer of his own thoughts, without needing to react to them or analyze them as they appear on the screen of consciousness.

It is said that the mind resembles a parachute in its function: **it works best when it is open.** But too much stimulation taxes the mind as stress and may cause a short circuit in the sensitive synapses and meridians, which are the psychic energy channels of our body.

With meditation, the mind begins to balance itself, when the person notices that he is the observer rather than the reactor as various thoughts arise. Some of them are not necessarily your own at all, but rather they come from the collective thought material of humanity's mass consciousness, which is a kind of mental recycled material around our planet. A great deal of this material is founded on old, fear-based limiting thought patterns, beliefs and programs. It is not worth your while to allow them to attach themselves to you any more. In a state of calmness and clarity it is easy to make the correct evaluations and corrections in relation to these materials.

Among some excellent guides for clearing the mind are for example Byron Katie's *Loving What Is - Four Questions That Can Change Your Life* (Harmony Books, New York, 2002), and Eckhart Tolle's *The Power of*

Byron Katie's Method of Four Questions

Whenever your mind starts to make trouble and criticize your fellow beings, try the following method of four questions:
- Is it (your thought, your assertion) true?
- Can you absolutely know that it is true?
- How do you react, what happens, when you believe that thought?
- Who would you be without the thought?

Then turn the thought around to its opposite in various ways and you will notice that the criticism says more about you than about the object of your criticism.

More information:
www.thework.com

Now (Namaste Publishing & New World Library, Novato, California, 1999). They give practical, tested tools for recognizing and working with the mind's mechanisms. As an undisciplined master the monkey mind is a troublesome fellow, as a calm servant it is a good working partner in the spiritual growth and evolution of a person. Mind takes its measure of us – and vice versa.

Brain Frequencies and the Unconscious Mind

Some psychologists have come to the conclusion that a person thinks on average 13–15 thoughts a minute, which comes to nearly 1000 thoughts an hour and perhaps 15,000 thoughts in 24 hours. Some others believe that this number is even greater, as much as 30–40,000. So all of these are orders made to the universe, and not often very wise ones.

The number of thoughts is of course quite individual. One person's consciousness is a swarm of thought children, while another might well keep only two or three thoughts in his consciousness, or perhaps even only one, but that one all the better. The number of thoughts is no guarantee of quality, rather the contrary. Often a person who is able to concentrate well on a few thoughts and to go to the depths and heights of them so to speak, can achieve wonderful results. Many philosophers and scientists are good examples of this.

Our thinking is closely connected with our brain activity. A general rule of thumb is that as brain activity slows down the number of thoughts decreases. Beta frequency (the basic frequency of brain waves in this state is 13–25 pulses or Hertz per second) is the usual brain pulse in daily activities, in the use of logic, and similar activities. The slower alpha frequency (8–12 Hz) on the other hand is a state of relaxed concentration and alertness, which is often called the optimum state for learning. According to some studies, for example listening to the slow movements of Baroque music takes a person into this frequency band.

However, perhaps the most profound thoughts, ideas and insights are found when a person gets to the theta frequencies (circa 3,5–7,8

Hz) for example in deep meditative experiences. In connection with these people have attained among other things an increased ability to handle stress, mental and emotional renewal, effortless visualization, elimination of blocks to artistic creativity, automatic creative solutions to problems, an ability to access their own inner source of original ideas, raised levels of intuition, an increased sense of emotional balance, and a feeling of being "in the flow", when a person feels he is in the right place at the right time. This can also be called the superconductive state, where resistance is minimal and potentiality maximal.[67]

In these slow brain states we arrive at the interesting boundary of the conscious and the unconscious mind, which is the magnificent terrain of our creativity. The inspiration which appears suddenly and often unexpectedly from the unconscious mind is the cause of many of the best ideas of scientists, philosophers, and artists.

Our unconscious mind is an enormous database and memory bank, like a computer, but with memory capacity that is immensely greater than that of any manmade computer. The unconscious mind also has stored in it past meetings and experiences with the souls that are again involved in our current life plan. This explains the commonly observed fact of people meeting for the first time but feeling a strange spiritual kinship. Love at first sight is a good example of this.

What is most essential from the point of view of the Law of Thought are the central principles and lawfulnesses of the unconscious mind. I have observed four of them.

First, **the conscious mind acts, and the unconscious reacts.** It is as if the conscious mind functioned as the one that places the orders, and the unconscious mind is the receiver of the orders that have been couched in the form of ideas. The unconscious then throws them in-

---

67   The American Ph.D. and composer Jeffrey Thompson has made many significant recordings of precise frequencies where he has utilized scientific results about brain frequencies and the capacity of sounds to activate those frequencies in our brain activity. Among these are *Brainwave Suite* and *Meditative Ocean: Timeless Pacific Surf with Theta Brainwaves*. The theta frequency can bring on a feeling of a deeper connection with all life. It has been described as a state of unity, ecstasy and miracle.

to our sphere of experience in the future. I have called this the mail order–principle.[68]

Also, **the unconscious mind loves rhymes and repetition.** For example the effectiveness of the repetition of mantras is related to this. Rhymed sentences stick well to the unconscious mind, and from there rise back to the conscious mind. This is worth taking advantage of, for example in connection with studying, as many studies have shown. Often the nonsense rhymes learned in childhood come to mind even in very old age, when everything else seems to have been forgotten.

The arithmetic of the unconscious mind is something like this: one, two, three, four, MANY! Thus, when you repeat positive things, for example with the help of mantras, finally the unconscious in you experiences a joyful flooding: it is as if things overflow their bounds in a good way, and that hidden part of the mind then reflects these things and characteristics strongly into our daily life. A good barometer of this is when suddenly, out of the clear blue sky, your mind is flooded with many good, uplifting thoughts, which for example heal your self-image. After all, that image is mainly precisely in your unconscious mind! That is when the message of your good thoughts has gotten through.

The principle of resonance is present in many Universal Laws, and it is connected as a kind of corollary particularly to the Law of Opposite Expression, as I wrote in chapter 5. There is a strong resonance relationship between the conscious and the unconscious mind, and when your thoughts and beliefs are in harmony between these two areas, your thoughts have a strong sounding board, and they are listened to with a sensitive ear. For then your entire being resonates in relation to the thoughts that you express.

An essential part of the unconscious mind and of understanding the Law of Thought are also our beliefs, and other mental programs, some of which are hiding in the unconscious. In the end we must free ourselves of old belief systems and duality-based models, which

---

68   Lehtiranta: *Tien päällä ja taivaan alla*, pp. 433-435.

have been built on fear and control. Examples of such outdated models might be:

Poverty is spirituality.

Suffer, suffer, the brighter will be your crown in heaven!

The fear of God is the beginning of wisdom.

Women are lesser beings than men.

The universe is a cold machine.

Owning things makes you happy.

I am my title, my status, and my role.

The more I consume, the better I am.

Often these and similar models go back to our childhood or our youth. Recognizing this programming is a good starting point for undoing them.

Thoughts build and characterize the thinker's aura, which then functions as a kind of filter, drawing to itself thought materials from the outside world, which correspond to the individual's own thought patterns. The more beautiful the aura, the more beautiful the person's thoughts! We could also express this by saying that good thoughts seek out similar company, negative thoughts likewise. Besides, what we think about others, they tend to think about us.

The relationship of thought to speech was already mentioned at the beginning of the chapter. It is wise to understand this relationship and to notice that positive thoughts generally lead to positive speech, which in turn conditions and strengthens the throat chakra, the higher energy center of self-expression. Negative, sharp, and offensive language on the contrary damages that chakra. I will return to this thought again in connection with the Law of Speech in chapter 9.

It is important to send other people good, blessing, uplifting thoughts. In this way you can become a great invisible source of blessings to your environment and your neighbors. In the current turbulent times, the world needs for example a great many thoughts of peace. When people take the time to think of peace, for example by participating in regular meditations for peace, the thought accumulations for peace begin to gain strength, to spread, and to peak. Sometimes the concept of critical mass is mentioned. This also works on the level of thought.[69]

These meditations for peace are held throughout the planet, for example on the 21st of March, June, September, and December, at 7:00 PM local time. At those times we are close to the four annual culmination points of the relationship of our planet to the Sun. They are the equinoxes and the solstices, which I already wrote about in chapter 6.

The Mind Imagines, but How?

The imagination is the twin sister of thought. We can say that the mind thinks, but it can make pictures as well. The difference between a thought and a mental image is minimal. It is also said that the imagination easily overrides the will. If for no other reason, it is important to keep our imagination as positive and constructive as possible. It is another thing that is a good servant but a bad master.

The imagination was originally given to humanity from a very high quarter. In fact, it was given in order to guarantee the continuing evolution of humanity, for with the imagination a person can see the next evolutionary step ahead, and at the same time create the guidelines of his own future.

Just as it is important to control our thoughts, so it is important to control the imagination. No doubt we all have experience of situations where we did not control our imagination, but rather it controlled us. Do some come to mind? In the following exercise (given by Hilarion in *Symbols*, channeled by Maurice B. Cooke)[70] you have a chance to try out your "muscle condition" where the control of your thoughts and your imagination is concerned.

---

69 When like-minded people unite the power of their thought and their imagination, the results can be immense. One of the most beautiful examples of this is "the silent minute" from the time of World War II. When the Big Ben struck 9:00 PM, every listener of the BBC was asked to remain silent and to pray for peace for one minute. Millions of people did this every evening, which may have shortened the war by a couple of years. See Wellesley Tudor Pole, *My Dear Alexias*.
70 Hilarion, *Symbols*, p. 78.

A Spiritual Muscle Exercise for Thoughts and the Imagination

To begin, relax, and for a while breathe deeply into the belly. Then close your eyes and try consciously to calm your mind. For example, try the following method: observe the space between two consecutive thoughts, and "stretch" this space out longer and longer. Next visualize a screen in front of your eyes, as if you were sitting in the first row of a movie theater before the beginning of the show, and focus all your attention on this screen.

When the screen has become sufficiently bright and clear before you, allow the number seven to travel across the screen from right to left, so that it eventually disappears behind the left edge. As it disappears slowly from view, the number six comes onto the screen in the same way from the right, and travels in the same way on the screen and then disappears to the left.

Next come the numbers five, four, three, two, and one, in that order. All the time, focus all your attention on these numbers, in whatever form that they appear, and with each number, slow down its speed.

Finally, when the number one moves out of sight behind the left edge, allow a zero to appear from the right side. Allow it to move very slowly on the screen of your consciousness, let it become slower and slower, and when it arrives in the center of the screen, have it stop there – and keep it stationary in the middle of the screen.

Remember to focus all your attention on this number, without allowing any thoughts to come to mind.

Now the number zero is stationary in the middle of the screen. Look at it as an observer, do not evaluate or compare it to anything. Do not allow other thoughts to enter the screen. If one attempts to crawl in from an edge, push it back and keep it away. Then return to the role of the calm observer.

Here the number zero symbolizes the absence of thoughts. Keep your attention focused on this number as long as you can. With practice, you can eventually lengthen your concentration to five minutes. At that time, you will notice something important: your ego or your being has in no way been diminished or shrunk because your thoughts have stopped. YOU ARE NOT YOUR THOUGHTS!

What else can you learn from an exercise like this? At least the fact that you are able to control your thought process with the help of your will. You can also achieve a mental state where you can open to information from other sources – for example from your guides and spiritual teachers. If you want to take advantage of this technique in order to gain such information from higher sources, it may be good for you to begin by imagining that the zero in the middle of your consciousness is like a gate to another dimension, an opening through which your teachers can allow you to see pictures as answers to your questions.

In that case, as you look at the zero, first allow it to change into a kind of trans-dimensional gate, then formulate a simple, clear and direct question, and then just remain waiting for what will appear inside the circle. The first thing that appears is the answer from your guides and helpers. The first thing is ALWAYS the answer.

Too many people allow the rational mind to jump in with its judgments, its comparisons, and its rejections. For example, someone may think that his own consciousness has sent this answer, these pictures, or whatever. But this is not the case.

All the same, a word of warning is appropriate here: avoid questions that concern your own personal future. Your own teachers and guides have certain limitations in relation to what they can tell you about your own future. Often in connection with these questions, they step aside, and allow your own desires and wishes to influence the image that is created.

All this may at first blush sound a bit mystical, but I have, over decades, been able to witness that this technique, and other similar ones, work well. You just have to use them intensively, with enthusiasm and faith, and then you will be able to charge the thoughts and images that you repeat with a great deal of positive energy.

A creative imagination is actually one of our most essential mental muscles. When someone visualizes a circumstance, a situation, and a goal that he wants to reach, what is actually happening? He is literally creating a thought form in the all-encompassing ether of space, a thought form, which then begins to attract to itself exactly the goal and situation that he visualized in his mind. This interaction and correlation between the physical and the higher levels takes place automatically, according to spiritual natural laws. "What you think and keep constantly in your mind, that you attract to yourself." This is of course a double-edged sword, which can be utilized both for good and for its opposite.

Summary:

✳ Energy follows every thought.

✳ Every thought is an order made to the universe.

✳ Thoughts are the precursors of action: thought – deed; thought – speech.

✳ "Sow a thought and reap an act; sow an act and reap a habit; sow a habit and reap a character; sow a character and reap a destiny." - W. M. Thackeray.

✳ Thoughts are a dynamo that turns the wheels of destiny.

✳ Thoughts are choices.

✳ Every thought strives to fulfill its own content.

✳ Every thought returns to the thinker himself.

* The thoughts of a spiritual seeker gain strength and return quickly to their sender.

* Every thought loves similar company, that is, thoughts with similar content and similar frequency create thought forms.

* Every thought is an electromagnetic oscillation, which vibrates with its own frequency according to its content, quality, and nature.

* Every person is measured by his thoughts.

* Every thought is a tool, a good one or a poor one.

* A thought precedes and controls all material manifestation.

* The sum total of our thoughts, our beliefs, and our mental images creates our reality.

* It is worthwhile to contemplate the relationship of thought and reality.

Literature:
Aivanhov, Omraam Mikhaël 1988: *The Powers of Thought*. Editions Prosveta, Fréjus Cedex.
Dryden, Gordon & Vos, Jeannette 1999: *Learning Revolution*. The Learning Web, Torrance, Canada.
Gavand, Dada 2006: *Intelligence Beyond Thought*. Exoloding the Mechanism of Mind. Dada Center Publications, Mumbai.
Gurudas 1986: *Gem Elixirs and Vibrational Healing*, Vol. II. Cassandra Press, San Rafael, California.
Hilarion 1979: *Symbols*. Marcus Books, Queensville, Ontario.
Katie, Byron 2002: *Loving What Is. Four questions that can change your life*. Harmony Books, New York.
Lehtiranta, Erkki 2011: *Tien päällä ja taivaan alla*. Smiling Stars, Helsinki.
Tolle, Eckhart 1999: *The Power of Now*. Namaste Publishing & New World Library, Novato, California.
Tudor Pole, Wellesley 1979: *My Dear Alexias. Extracts from the Letters of Wellesley Tudor Pole to Rosamond Lehmann*. Neville Spearman Ltd, St. Helier.

8.

Help

"Knock and it shall be opened,
ask and it shall be given."
However, the nature of the help is not always
what the petitioner expects.

- Hilarion

COUNTLESS PEOPLE HAVE SEEN this familiar quote from the Bible without understanding that it contains great wisdom and spiritual lawfulness, which penetrates all the created worlds. This law demands without exception that a more evolved being offer his help to one on a lower evolutionary level, if he **asks** for it. Therefore it is important to remember that whenever difficulties appear, help is always available. The petitioner needs only to ask for his spiritual guides, his helpers, his angelic friends, or the Masters of Light to come to his aid, and it is certain to be given.[71]

All the same, in this context it is good to keep in mind that the nature of the help is not always what the petitioner wishes or expects. The beings on a higher level are able to see more broadly, and at the same time, they observe the spiritual and karmic conditions of the situation. Thus they can in each instance see the most appropriate

---

71   Hilarion, *Vision*, p. 26.

way to give their help so that it meets the person's true needs. The help they give also includes maximum respect for our own free will. The help is in no way forced on us, it is rather given the opportunity to enter our life.

Just as your own guides and helpers are obligated to offer their help when you ask for it, so you also must feel a similar responsibility toward your fellow human beings, especially toward those who ask for your help, and who are as yet unable to see the spiritual vistas that have opened up for you. If you refuse your help, you yourself will also be denied help from higher levels. When you help others, you are always also helping – yourself. Here also it is good to remember respect for free will.

The Law of Help is one of the most practical of the Universal Laws. We can employ it daily in our own lives. Besides, the ability to help grows with helping. This law is often in direct connection with the Law of Love. Love very often activates the desire to help one's fellow men, nature, and even the entire planet. Good examples of this are the Nobel laureates Albert Schweitzer and Mother Teresa. Schweitzer abandoned his career as perhaps the most renowned Bach organist of his time and went to the rain forests of Africa as a doctor. Mother Teresa for her part spent the better part of her life in the slums of Kolkata (formerly Calcutta), helping the poor.[72]

Helping is Interrelationship

It is possible to give and to receive help in many ways: consciously, unconsciously, sometimes in a very subtle way, or even by sending energy. The scale is very extensive. A purpose of the Law of Help is to show you more of your own being. Help is usually based on an interrelationship of beings, but it is also very important to **learn to help yourself** as well. As Benjamin Franklin said: "God helps him who helps himself."

---

72   In my opinion one of Mother Teresa's most luminous statements is this: "Do something beautiful for God every day."

The most beneficial contacts are the ones where the vibrational characteristics of the helper are so different from those of the recipient that they cause a significant raising of the vibrational level of the recipient. In general the more evolved being is able to offer more, and to effect a change in the vibration. But of course this can happen also when we are in interrelationship with animals or plants.

In the helping process something is transferred between the giver and the recipient. It may be pure energy, it may be something specifically requested, it may be vibrational characteristics, a raising of intelligence, opportunities, or other similar things.

Of course it is possible to effect a vibrational change even with a method as simple as a smile, or by sending good feelings or happy energy to someone. This is worthy of consideration, since this also is vibrational interrelating between you and another being. We are all vibrational beings and are able to resonate with each other in countless different ways.

The Law of Help seems to work best when a person is glad to take on the interrelationship that comes with it, and also to put some effort into it. In this way he can both give and receive. It is a mutual activity. A corollary of the Law of Help is that the more conscious the help that is given or received, the greater the vibrational change, the evolution, and the help. To put it a bit more prosaically: **unrequested help does not in general work very well, requested help is certain to work.**

In other words, it is no use teaching a cow to grow its own food, in its present stage of evolution it is not capable of this, so feeding it is still the best idea.

A request for help opens a gate through which beings can transfer help in the form of energy, information, or something else, from one level to another. Have you ever given thought to how much help you have received during your life in the form of guidance, ideas, messages, symbols, vibrational effects, and energy, from your spiritual guides, your helpers, your angelic friends, from spiritual masters, from your soul, and from other beings of higher vibrational levels? If this opens to you even slightly, might there be reason to be thankful?

So, say THANK YOU! Giving thanks maintains the positive energy channels in good condition now and in the future.

You have actually requested this kind of help already before coming to the physical level. In fact you have asked for help knowing that it would arrive, even if you were not conscious of that. Guides are often with you for your entire life, or perhaps for a period of 20-30 years. That is a long commitment in Earth terms. The gist of the matter is that if you had not requested help clearly enough, your guides and helpers would not have committed themselves to you for such a long time.

When you begin to understand the power of asking for help, you will also realize that what is in question is an actual **contract** between a giver and a receiver. Get acquainted with both sides, and you will know what is appropriate in giving and in receiving help. If you have only been in the status of receiving help, it is difficult to know how to give help, and of course vice versa.

If you ask for something more tremendous, and need the help of your guides, your helpers, and even some more worldly help, then be prepared to also help others in your own way. You will realize that the help you give reflects the situation in which you yourself are in need of help.

In this way you might for example find a volunteer work, bring help, caring and love into the lives of others and help them in one way or another on their own journey. This in turn raises to the surface everything that has prevented you from helping others and prevented the energy of help from flowing through you. Sometimes it is a question of the other person not wanting your help or not wanting to ask for it. There may be many reasons for this. The karmic path of the individual will nevertheless open to him a greater understanding: help is a kind of **stepping stone** on which energy travels simultaneously between many beings.

Miracles of Help

The mutual dependency, connection and union that are a part of help remind us of the union with God. You begin to understand better and more deeply that you are not alone, that you are one with others. You can for example recall a situation where you asked for help, and it actually came. You then understood that it actually arrived as if from the angels, from God, or from some other very beautiful source, which at that time you perhaps called coincidence. Whatever it may have been, you knew deep within yourself that you were helped, that you were not alone, that someone heard your prayer. This is very simple and childlike and is in many ways connected with the Law of Love. You are loved – and you truly deserve love and help. You only have to ask.

On a deeper level a feeling of emptiness, loneliness, or an inability to receive love is in direct relationship with the individual's unwillingness to ask for love, help, and guidance. It may be difficult to break these patterns of negativity and rejection, because they often have their roots from long ago in childhood or in past lives. But breaking these patterns is important on the path to light and healing.

If there is a situation where you are not sure whether the help you are offering would be accepted, you can always ask: "Do you want some help?" or "Do you want me to help you?" These questions usually resolve the situation.

When you yourself ask for help, you may notice that it does not always come in the way that you had requested. I already wrote about this principle in the beginning of the chapter. The help may be different and unexpected; it may even be more beautiful than you had expected. If you trust that the vibration of the help that you have requested is sufficiently clear, powerful, and high, you can also trust that the help that flows to you from the higher levels knows the right route and arrives to you in exactly the appropriate way and at exactly the right time.

You guides understand and are conscious of the appropriate way and time, which you yourself do not necessarily know. For example you may ask for a very particular form of help, which cannot be delivered in the way you wish, or within the time frame that you wish. This in no way means that your request has been rejected. Even in this case your guides and helpers will give you at least some part of the help on some level and in some time frame, usually as soon as possible.

For example when you pray for something, you at the same time activate a vibration that can be very powerful and that may resonate and continue for a long time. According to the Law of Speech, when you say your prayer out loud, it becomes even more real, clear, and powerful. Therefore it is useful to pray and to ask for help out loud. When you pray for someone else, perhaps the best thing that you can ask for him on a general level is clarity, the ability for him to see things in as many-sided a way as possible. Your prayer and affirmation becomes especially powerful if you make it into a rhyming couplet. I will return to this theme in the next chapter, when I take up the cosmic Law of Speech.

When you activate energy, it is important for it to be such as to magnetize, draw to yourself precisely the energies that are possible within the bounds of the spiritual laws. Consciousness is a very important factor in working with the Law of Help, since with its aid the things connected with your request actually come true.

You may also observe that when you ask for something with sincerity and true intention and give the higher powers a certain amount of leeway in fulfilling your wish, at the same time some obstacles, negations, rejection and struggle arise in your consciousness. If you ask for clarity, help, and energy in order to confront and work on the challenges that have come up, that also will be granted.

A request for help brings about a kind of energy vortex. When it is born in some form of intermediate material, for example on the etheric level, that vortex draws the material in question into itself. In other words, an energy vortex always draws something into itself. Consciousness determines how this something becomes resonant on the same frequency with the petitioner. When you realize how the process works and are able to expand your consciousness in relation to it, help will function better and more rapidly.

You may notice in connection with this law that there are beings that want to help simply for karmic reasons. There is nothing wrong with this, as long as you understand that there are also karmic limitations involved in the picture. The angelic kingdom offers its help to humans only if the help is appropriate and – what is even more important – if it helps the person to find something new within himself without interfering with his free will.

You can accomplish much with the angels' willingness to help, if you just open up to them. Even if you do not open, they will nevertheless help, but in ways that allow you to easily ignore their presence. They perform their work invisibly or contrive for it to seem accidental. Still, when you do ask for their help, they bring much more energy to it. The angels enjoy working with people on the physical level who are able to manifest something through the help that they give.

When you ask for help, at the same time it is good to ask for the help to come in an appropriate way, for it to be for your best from the highest point of view, for it to be useful for others as well, and for it not to be harmful for anyone. This is the **cosmoethical** way of acting, which is practiced in the higher levels. Thus the help is given in the best available way, since the petitioner's motives are as pure and as altruistic as possible.

Meditation: Simulating the Helping Process

When preparing to help other beings, it is always useful to go through the entire helping process within yourself. That is the purpose of this exercise.

To begin, relax, and breathe deeply and calmly into your belly. Then see, on the screen of your consciousness, an image of yourself. Imagine that you are looking at yourself in a mirror. If necessary, allow the being in the mirror to become larger, smaller, older or younger. See him with different clothes or without clothes. Play with the image for a few minutes, until you feel that you are a totally separate being from the one in the mirror.

Then allow that being to be in interrelationship with the world. He may for example be working with someone whom you see to be in trouble and whom you would like to help. Then see your double in interrelationship with that person and notice how that feels in your body. Try out different things and see how your double helps that other person in many ways.

Then notice what is happening in yourself. You may feel better physically, or feel a sense of lightness or warmth, or a deeper sense of life or presence, or some other good feeling in yourself. Perhaps that feeling will come up when you do certain things. That feeling may be a good indicator for what to try when you are later working with that person on the physical plane.

And vice versa: if you feel heavier or colder or more limited, or if the situation brings up a sense of struggle in you, then perhaps it is best not to act with the person in the way you have visualized. These are obvious feelings that you can use to your advantage in your helping work.

Remember that an aim for synthesis will help you and when you include your intuition, you prepare the way for real and necessary help. The help does not occur only on the physical level, or only by using the voice and the mind, but also with whatever help your and the other person's guides, helpers and teachers bring to the matter in such a way that the help will continue to manifest.

Then, when you are later working with that person on the physical level, it may be necessary to get more information from him about what should be done next. At that point, return quickly to the state of non-attachment where you were earlier, and where your double is again available to you. Your double may give you some information, or you may get a certain feeling, or you may simply receive intuitive knowledge about the right word to say or the right way to act.

This exercise can be developed in many ways. But it is important for you to be present in it with your whole being. That is how you will get the best results.

You are in this world also to learn to help others and to discover how that feels. If you have a genuine desire and motivation to help people to express their potential better and more easily, it is wise to follow the path of helping and to expand it. But, do not do it out of a sense of guilt.

Also, do not lose sight of the basic motivation and commitment: not that you should learn to help every person, no matter what the price, but rather that you might learn from the experience of helping, and you would like to continue working with it and get something valuable for yourself from it.

Mutuality in Helping

Our spiritual guides arrange opportunities for us to help and to serve more or less every day. They steer people to us who are in need of exactly what we can give them. It may be a warm word, a smile, a shoulder to lean on for a moment, or for example some practical task or hint. It is good to remain alert about such things, since the opportunity may arrive only once. Even minor help may be great in value, for it may revive the recipient's faith in humans and humankind.

Here we can again mention that genuine coincidences are truly unusual events – in reality they do not exist. The fact is that we are often led to people and situations where we can help. We may hear a snatch of conversation and know the right way to help, or know what to say, and moreover, to do it in such a way that it does not help only others, but ourselves as well.

Actually, in a situation such as this, we may manage to drop some old habits and to change our way of behaving with other people and know how to ask exactly the right question. You can offer your help in these situations in a tactful way: "I know something about these things, would you like to hear about it?" In this way we are not forcing our help on people.

This is important, because it is not a question of whether you are willing to help, but of whether you are willing to ask first. There is a time to speak and a time to be silent. This is something we need to learn on our journey.

Examine some helping situation within yourself: what did you learn from it, and what did you perhaps ask for, what were you unwilling to receive, to ask for, or to understand? Working sincerely in

Universal Laws and Spiritual Progress

this way with the Law of Help and its genuine spirit will expand your consciousness.

This works in both directions. In fact the mutuality of the Law of Help is perhaps its most important and its most delightful characteristic. By helping, you further the process of expanding and transforming your consciousness, and you become more conscious of who and what you yourself are.

It is good to become aware of the fact that the other person may become dependent on you in the helping process. In this case you must do everything you can to encourage him to look into the matter more deeply and to question his need for help, himself. Helping must never become manipulative in either direction. You can try to show the person that in reality what he needs is love. Perhaps your help is needed to show him how to find the love that he needs. In this way he will probably be able to find a clear direction in his life.

A sense of guilt can also prevent an ability to help or to receive help. In fact, a sense of guilt can in many ways destroy a person's ability to ask for help or to receive it. What is often in question in this case is rejected love. Internalizing three simple ideas can help to free yourself of a sense of guilt: I can make mistakes, I can ask for help, and I can start over.

Devas as Our Helpers

There are factors in requesting and in receiving help, which have hardly been understood by humanity. Without knowing it, we are actually completely dependent on help that we receive from the invisible world, not only from our guides, our helpers and our teachers, but also from many other quarters. Our survival is largely dependent on them.

We have invisible helpers on the wings of airplanes (I already wrote about this earlier), in atomic plants, in many underground systems, in cars, in various vehicles and technological devices, to mention just a few. The only task of these devas is to prevent these devices from exploding, from their killing people, and from causing other destruction.

We do not understand or notice their presence, but they do not care about that. They do their job simply for the love of people, and in order to help us. Sometimes they are overshadowed in this work by another being, an angel that has created them. But beings such as the devas on the wings of airplanes, nevertheless function on their own, independently of the angelic powers that coordinate them.

It would be only right and proper to give these airplane devas your warmest thanks on your next plane trip, and to send them some love and also a bit of energy fuel for their blessed work.

The other galactic races send us their help mainly through invisible energies and streamings, and they do not usually make their help obvious. These more evolved beings of the higher light planes understand the basic idea of help very well: help must be given in an appropriate way.

They have learned during their own journey that rough interference in things is not appropriate. As humankind gradually learns to know galactic life and these lifestreams, and to welcome their help consciously, they will be able to give ever more of elevating influences and energy streams to us. Meanwhile this help streams in particular to the more conscious individuals who are able to attune to the higher frequencies.

Helping and Serving the Earth with Joy

Mother Earth needs our help sorely. Every one of us knows what humanity has done to this beautiful planet, how it has been wounded in so many ways. But wounds can and must be healed. People have been allowed to destroy the planet only in order that humanity might awaken from its winter hibernation, and see the results of that destruction, and learn to understand the real nature of Mother Earth as a living and feeling being. Our planet is an irreplaceably valuable living library, which is what the inhabitants of the Pleiades call it.[73]

---

73   See Barbara Marciniak, *Earth: Pleiadian Keys to the Living Library*. Bear & Company, Inc., Santa Fe, 1995.

Universal Laws and Spiritual Progress

People have gradually begun to understand and to value the great beauty of the planet, to become better acquainted with it in person, and to protect it from ecological catastrophes. We belong to one of the first generations that have the possibility of seeing our planet as an ecological system with its own circulatory system (the waters), its own nervous system (the ley lines), and many other structures, which can be compared to the structures of human individuals. The hermetic axiom makes its appearance again: as in the small, so in the great.

We can do countless things for the benefit of our planet's problems. After all, the problems are constantly before us in the media. But we seldom hear them talk about sending love to Mother Earth. All the same, this is one of the most powerful things that you can do for our planet wherever you are, at any time, and in your very own way. Every tree, bush, stone and stump, every lake, river, and ocean bay, deserves our love, as does the road under us and the starry sky above us. Do we limit our love to only a few human relationships, or perhaps to our pet, our car, or our boat?

In a group, the act of sending love to our planet and to its nature is even more powerful. Various meditations, rituals, and ceremonies are familiar, and have already been used by our ancestors. It is time for us to take them into use again, and at the same time to bring them up to date for our time and its needs. Notice at the same time how Mother Earth answers our messages of love.

One of the finest ways to help Mother Earth is having a sense of community, for example the founding of communities where the Universal Laws are known and practiced. Master Hilarion has given good guidance for founding such communities in his book *Vision*, to which I have referred several times.

Helping could in many cases be compared with serving, and another name for this law could in fact be the Law of Service. A kind of **line of demarcation** is here drawn between **service to oneself and one's ego, and service to others.** Our knowledge grows and changes into wisdom, love grows and expands gradually into unconditional, universal Christ-love. Our willpower gains strength and finally becomes unshakeable – all this will happen so that humanity can ever better help those individuals who are blinded by the illusion of matter and by selfishness, but who are seeking glimpses of light and a true direction for their lives.

Whom Have You Helped and What Have You Learned?

I have already earlier used this illuminating story by Master Hilarion about how an individual leaves his physical body after so-called death and moves into his emotional body. In this subtle body, he arrives in a tunnel of light, hears heavenly music, and meets people or other beings who act as his guides to the higher planes. Halfway to those heavenly meadows, to the Land of Golden Light, he meets a high representative of the angelic forces, who asks him: "What have you learned and whom have you helped?"[74]

In that state of being we all understand the language of angels and also answer truthfully what we have learned on our journey, and how we have offered a helping hand to others. If we are able to answer that we have served our fellow humans and humankind and the Higher Purpose with the means that we have had available to us, we can see a magnificent sight: a beautiful smile on the angel's face.[75]

There are many invisible ways to help people, and one of them is sending positive, constructive, loving thoughts. In chapter 7 I wrote extensively about the power of thought and its possible use as an instrument of light. Thoughts, especially if they are repeated and strengthened, remain alive and are reflected in our outer perimeter, our aura, where they inevitably influence our environment through their own quality, their power, and their light.

Your own example can also be of great help to others. The world is currently in sore need of positive examples as role models. Every

---

74   Hilarion, *Seasons of The Spirit*, p. 82.
75   Lehtiranta, *Tien päällä ja taivaan alla*,ap. 457.

one of us is a walking advertisement board, and our example is certainly followed. So then, leave a beautiful energy trace wherever you travel, if for no other reason than that you will travel on those same paths again.

You should not be naïve where helping is concerned. Many hands will reach out toward you, if you travel for example in Asia. Many appeal to you by their poverty and misery, some have a young child in their lap – one that is sometimes rented for the day for the purpose of begging. We should nevertheless see what can genuinely help them, where the real suffering is, and how it could be alleviated in the wisest possible way.

We have come to the conclusion that what works best is to help the people in developing countries specifically through enduring structures. For example orphanages, and support for education, are these kinds of forms that can be of long-term, real help. Best of all is if you yourself can watch over the destination of the aid and ensure its use for its intended purpose. But do not expect any thanks from the world. Helping is already its own reward.

Usually the best help is helping people to help themselves. It is good to remind ourselves again of the old story that asks which is more important, giving a man a fish, or teaching him how to fish. Of course it is natural to answer an immediate need and emergency, but beyond that, it is good to ponder the wisdom of that fish story.

In helping, your attitude, your motives, and your own energy, are especially important. Do I help joyfully and wholeheartedly, or with a frown and reluctantly? We can again point out the close connection between helping and serving. The following questions by Dan Millman may for their part shed light on the matter:

- What does serving mean in relation to you?
- Where can I find my own field of service?
- Whom or what should we serve?
- How can we serve ever more and ever better?
- What are the current blocks to my service work, and how do I intend to overcome them?

- What is service, as examined from a higher point of view?
- Do I serve when it suits me?
- Do I serve when it does not suit me?

These and similar questions clarify our course on the path of help and service, which may at times be full of potholes. There are situations where you would truly like to help, but your help is not accepted. This rejection may leave psychological scars, but it is best to take care of those as fast as possible.

Serving with joy and without any expectation of reciprocal gifts, or gratitude from the world, is a wonderful way of utilizing the uplifting, purifying energy of joy! Joy is a high emotional energy, and when it is combined with warm, inoffensive humor, it is an incomparable way of lightening the atmosphere and elevating the mood. It could well be called important spiritual work. For example the comedians of the golden age of silent movies, such as Charlie Chaplin, brought joy, and through it, hope for the future, to people who were struggling in the dark depths of the Great Depression. These days for example the Dalai Lama shares warm joy and heartfelt warmth with millions of people.

Joy makes it possible for us not only to serve and to help, but also to overcome the obsolete idea of growth through suffering, which belongs to the energies of the past. Sharing and extending joy is in fact a very important way of serving the Lord of Love. Thus it is important to anchor ever more of the energy of joy into our own lives and into our surroundings.

Summary

✳ If help is asked for, it should be given.

✳ What is done should be appropriate to the situation in order to be helpful.

✳ The ultimate appraisal of the appropriateness of help belongs to the recipient, not the giver.

✳ A purpose of helping is at the same time to reveal more of the nature of your own being.

✳ A good way to learn about the process of giving is to consciously offer your help to others.

✳ A purpose of helping is also to remind you of the fact that you are not alone, that you are one with others.

✳ Helping is primarily an interrelating of beings, and it can further spiritual evolution or physical healing.

✳ You can help others by the power of your example.

✳ Helping works best if those involved have the understanding to welcome it consciously, and to participate in the interrelationship.

✳ Help that is not asked for does not generally work well. Remember the principle of free will.

✳ Prayer is a particularly powerful form of asking for help, because it brings consciousness and choice into the picture with it.

✳ Ask for help that is appropriate for you.

✳ Sometimes you have to decide whether giving help is worth the trouble.

✳ Rejecting help results from a belief that you do not deserve love or help; therefore you do not ask for either one.

✳ Asking for help opens the door also to the blockages, the negation, and the struggle that is connected with the help. Pray for clarity, help and energy for conquering these difficulties.

✳ At times helping may lead to an addictive syndrome where the recipient of the help is completely dependent on the giver of the help.

✳ A sense of guilt can block a person in relation to helping and destroy his ability to ask for or to receive help in many ways.

✳ A sense of guilt generally implies a denial of love.

✳ In order to liberate yourself of guilt, remember these three things: I can make mistakes, I can ask for help, and I can begin anew.

✳ Manipulation in connection with giving or receiving help leads to a blurring of consciousness, and to misunderstandings in such a way that the entire energy of the situation is blocked.

✳ Helping is an agreement made with your own guides.

Literature:

Hilarion 1980: *Seasons of The Spirit*. Marcus Books. Queensville, Ontario.
Hilarion 1982: *Vision*. Marcus Books. Queensville, Ontario.
Lehtiranta, Erkki 2011: *Tien päällä ja taivaan alla*. Smiling Stars, Helsinki.
Marciniak, Barbara 1995: *Earth: Pleiadian Keys to the Living Library*. Bear & Company, Inc., Santa Fe.
Millman, Dan 1999: *The Twelve Gateways to Personal Growth*. Time Warner Company, New York.

Universal Laws and Spiritual Progress

9.

Speech

"Until the tongue has lost its power to wound,
it cannot speak the truths of the spirit."

- Hilarion

MANY THINGS THAT I already wrote about in the chapter on the cosmic Law of Thought can be applied to the Law of Speech as well. Thought and speech are in many respects parallel functions, and a person who controls his thoughts well has come far in the most important thing, the control of his own self.

Speech is the continuation of thought and functions as its transformer and strengthener, allowing entrance to many levels where thought alone could not penetrate. In speech, thought is accompanied by sound frequencies, the movement of sound waves, and the dance of air molecules. This is why speech has a stronger effect on the physical level than does thought, which mainly operates on higher frequency levels.[76]

In addition, speech is a great occult tool. At the end of the 19th century Master Hilarion dictated a book, *Light on the Path* (1888 George Redway, London), to the English theosophist Mabel Collins, and it is from this book that we get the motto for this chapter: "Until the tongue has lost its ability to wound, it cannot speak the truths of the

---

76   The quality of thought of course influences the level on which the thought operates.

spirit." Repeated negative speech blocks the throat chakra, the center for higher self-expression and creativity. At this point the speaking of higher truths does in fact become impossible.

The Importance of Right Speech

All this is entirely lawful. These days, when people are fairly civilized, we do not usually wound others with swords or other such weapons any more. The wounding most often takes place mentally, through thought and speech, and insulting, critical speech is one of the most central ways of wounding and doing harm to our fellow human beings. Then speech shows its bloody teeth.

Therefore we still have a lot to clean up in our own thoughts and speech, in order not to harm our fellow beings – and thus ourselves. For thoughts and words do return back to ourselves. It is good to understand and remember these spiritual laws, which are independent of our opinions or of our acceptance or rejection of them.

In light of this, when you speak ill of others, eventually you will have to "eat your words". In addition, negative thoughts and spoken words produce mental karma, which the individual will in time have to confront.

Right speech – which was wisely emphasized by the historical Buddha – is a part of our ethical being. We have for a long time already had freedom of thought and speech. They are our civil rights, but have we given thought to the **responsibility** involved in our thought and speech? For truly, they have a karmic echo.

Speech is a two-way street in important respects: there is a speaker and a receiver, or receivers. Both have a responsibility in the communication situation, just as non-offensiveness and non-offendedness are mutually connected. It is not wise to be insulting, but it is also not obligatory to feel insulted, even if this is sometimes really difficult. "Be silent when offended", is a stern but profound principle on the spiritual path.

A good question to ask in this connection is: who is it in me that is offended, is it my own eternal being, my higher Self, or is it my ego whose toes have been stepped on?

Universal Laws and Spiritual Progress

The same principle holds in speech as in thought: quantity is no substitute for quality. An overabundance of speech stresses the hearer's ears, and besides, **the least knowledge often has the most voice.** On the other hand, the wise person may speak less often, but will focus on the content rather than the number of words. Such economy often gives the words more weight. It is also good to be economical with your promises, because your street credibility will evaporate if you constantly promise things that you then cannot keep. Every promise is a kind of contract or commitment. A man's word is his bond.

It is good to ask three questions also in connection with speech: WHAT, HOW, and WHEN? If you do not pay enough attention to the middle one, you may allow some pretty ugly frogs to escape from your mouth, and you will not be able to stuff them back in there, no matter how hard you try. Good intentions must here be combined with appropriate means and the right timing.

Tripwires of Speech

It is said that silence is golden. That is a very wise thought, for in the silence of the mind and the heart we can hear the voice of God. An hour of silence with the God of Love can teach us much more than an entire human lifetime spent in loose talk and chatter. For example, in the mystery school of Pythagoras about 2500 years ago, every student was required to keep silence for years before the more profound spiritual truths were revealed to him. Was this done just to harass him? No! For in silence a person learns to hear and to know his own thoughts and the movements of his mind. When these are under control, he is also able to speak what is Good, True, and Beautiful.[77]

One abuse of the Law of Speech is speaking ill of others, and gossiping, which is not only useless, but also deeply harmful. It is a doping material to be avoided, especially on the spiritual path. What hap-

---

77   I am here alluding to central ideas of Plato's *Doctrine of Ideas*. Plato was one of Hilarion's better-known incarnations.

pens in connection with calumny and gossip? A great thought form is built, which is then given extra energy, and which is then sent spiritually to burden the victim, the object of the gossip. The receiver of this negative energy package may even feel heart pain or other such sensations as a result.

Naturally this results in heavy karma for all those who participated in the activity. In other words, it is not a question of a harmless pastime during a coffee break at the office or some such situation, far from it. The fact is that when a person utters out loud a negative thought about a fellow human being, its consequences may be far reaching. First of all, negative and critical words uttered out loud create a tight dark ring around the speaker's throat chakra. This ring acts as a block or limitation, which prevents other, higher thoughts and ideas from entering his own mental world.[78] There is in this a clear connection to the way in which the thoughts that we have shape our aura. I already dealt with this theme in connection with the Law of Thought in chapter 7.

Clairvoyants can often see a dark or dark red field covering the area of the throat chakra of a person who is inclined to be negative and critical. Within this field there can even be lightning-like energies, which indicate that the person tends to strike out like lightning with his words. An individual who has this kind of coloration in his throat chakra cannot, finally, speak spiritual truths, as was mentioned at the beginning of the chapter. Besides, the abuse of speech can cause karma that the person will later have to confront in the form of repeated throat infections, since karma has a tendency to return to the place where it originated.

Supportive and Loving Speech - The Nectar of Sounds

A study conducted in the United States tells us that on average children receive six negative comments for every positive, supportive and

---

78   Hilarion, *Other Kingdoms*, p. 31.

encouraging one.[79] Nevertheless American culture is on the whole quite supportive. Comments like "You're not allowed to do that" or "Don't you know how to do that?" cause deep problems, because they eventually sink into the unconscious mind, and continue their harmful, undermining influence from there. Negative feelings often arise from criticism that we received in our childhood or youth. **The emotional memory traces of words are long.**

Have you ever attempted to consciously refrain for a day from speaking insultingly, or from criticizing others with your speech? If this is easy, try it for a week. If that is easy, try a month.

On the other hand, loving speech is one of the best ways to help other people, and it is often an indication that the important channel between the throat chakra and the heart chakra is open.[80] Then there is warmth in the person's speech, even if he had to broach difficult matters, for example concerning his work or his human relationships. The heart is reflected in its own way in the tone of voice that is used, not only in the words. In our times, where cold winds sometimes blow, words that are "warmed" with positive feeling and good will are a true balm, and healing for the soul, in more senses than one. Every one of us remembers how much supportive and loving words have helped us on our journey.

An open and transfigured throat chakra opens the way to higher inspiration. Because of the good evolution of this chakra, humankind has over the centuries received streams of immortal poetry and distinguished prose from great creative individuals. These are still able to move readers to tears. But an evolved throat chakra has equally made possible the expression of simple yet durable spiritual truths. They are as likely to have come from the mouth of a great visionary as from that of a little child.[81]

It is actually impossible to overestimate the value of the right words and right speech. We have in our thoughts and in our speech the

---

79   Dryden & Voss, *Learning Revolution*, p. 232.
80   In vibrational healing for example flower essences made from cosmos flower and passion flowaer open both of these chakras and create a connection between them.
81   Hilarion, *Other Kingdoms*, p. 31.

power to create, to preserve and to destroy. In this there is an allusion to the three divine aspects of the Hindu pantheon, Brahma, Vishnu and Shiva.

Master Hilarion has said that the greatest harm in the world at this time is caused by the indifference arising from a careless use of words.[82] The tongue is an instrument of the mind, and even though it is said that a person says whatever happens to slip out, behind that "happening" there are always our thoughts, negative and confused ones, or else clear, constructive and loving ones – or something in between. In the end nobody else sets words in our mouth or pushes them out; we ourselves are completely responsible for them. Our consciousness is strongly reflected in our speech, and in this sense our speech is also a reflection of our character.

Speech Can Bring About Change

A person who watches his words and speaks only out of altruistic purposes in order to convey love energy through his tongue, is fast on the road to taking the first steps toward preparation for initiation. On a practical level we can in many ways polish our verbal expression and bring good energy streams into the world through our words. An American acquaintance of mine, a music producer, long ago taught me a technique, which he himself had proved to work in practice, when creative solutions were needed, for example in lengthy recording sessions. From time to time he had to bring up some difficult matter, a slightly off-key note for example, in a situation where the singer might already be just about at the end of his tether.

In this situation the producer would first say two good things ("What an impressive interpretation" etc.), and then take up the matter that he wanted to improve, and finally end with one more positive comment. It may not be a good idea to make this a rigid model of behavior, but rather to keep the idea in mind. In any case it is im-

---

82   Charlton, *Master Hilarion*, p. 24.

portant to remember not to end a conversation on a negative note, as that tends to resonate for a long time.

David J. Schwartz has presented a similar model that he calls the **art of praise.** It is based on six principles:

- Tell people that they look good.
- Say something pleasant about their family.
- Make a note of their accomplishments.
- Admire their possessions.
- Acknowledge their ideas.
- Praise them for trying even if they fail.[83]

Speech is actually a very powerful tool for changing the world and other people. It reminds us of what a natural power we have at our disposal. We are here to do different things in life, and to influence our environment in a positive way, and we have in our spiritual toolkit an incomparable speech apparatus. With this tool we can strengthen love, further peace and harmony, and encourage other people to grow into better people than they are now. Wishing nothing but the best for others is a good example of this practice. And once more: what you wish for others, that you wish for yourself as well.

Empowering Effects of Song

Song is one of the parallel phenomena of speech, and we are not even yet able to say with any certainty, which was born first. In any case, in singing, speech is combined with melodic and rhythmic elements that it does not usually contain. For example, rap exists amusingly in a no-man's-land, since it is a kind of speech-song. In a sense, melody gives the message of song wings, which can take it around the whole planet in a few days, or at most a few weeks, in this era of technological progress.

---

83 Schwartz, *The Magic of Thinking Success.*

No matter what type of music is in question, we should pay particular attention to the text of songs. It has long been known that our unconscious mind "grabs on" to repetitive choruses and rhymes, as I already mentioned in chapter 7 in connection with the Law of Thought. This is of course true for both positive and negative lyrics. Everyone knows how the hits of the day are repeated and shouted out in the streets, in the coffee houses, and in the karaoke bars.

Negative lyrics can become like slogans that attract to themselves exactly the things that are mentioned in the texts: suffering, betrayal, drunkenness. It is more meaningful to create healing and positive lyrics that generate faith in life in the audience. Of course they need not be like religious hymns, or naïve ditties. There is always a place and a market for beautiful melodies and clever lyrics.

While you are waiting for those, you can make up your own songs, and build yourself up in the direction that you desire, according to the musical orders that you send to your unconscious mind. Note that in this also there are clear, practical laws whose power and functioning it is worth your while to test. Making up little songs is one of the best ways to apply the Law of Speech effectively to improving your life and your spiritual progress.

You do not need a workshop of song-making for this, only some ordinary courage, humor, and creativity. I am sure you know who the most creative people in the world are: children of course, since they are not burdened by the overdeveloped monkey-mind of adults, or by the opinion that it is not "appropriate" for adults to become like children again, even for a moment (even though it is recommended in the Bible, no less.) On the other hand, your unconscious mind expects new songs, chants, and why not even hymns, from you.

Rhymed couplets are the most effective, as I already wrote in the previous chapter in connection with prayers and affirmations. So then, when you know what you want, form the thing into a song, and you will have results even sooner perhaps than you could have believed!

Here are a couple of examples of such couplets:

- May my third eye be open and bright, and may my spirit be full of insight.
- I remember whatever I need to, and even better than I used to.

No need to be Shakespeare or John Lennon, just be yourself and see what you need, and what you can reach for, with these kinds of simple but powerful techniques. Thoughts are effective, and when pronounced out loud, they are even more effective, and when formed into songs or mantra melodies, they reach their peak effectiveness. The power of many of the most popular mantras is also partly based on this. Besides, creating your own mantras tailor things specifically for yourself. The fine-tuned ear of the universe will catch your wishes, your needs, and your intentions beautifully when it hears them pronounced or sung out loud. You can always develop your own versions of them, I have just given a few suggestions for them here.

As for myself, I use this technique of singing and sending my orders to the universe every morning in the shower, and of course at other times, too. I have striven to combine fun and profit by for example adding some positive mental images, good feelings, and pleasurable expectations to the orders. In this way things have started to "rain" into my life.

When the power of song is examined from a broader perspective, it is good to remember for example the "singing revolution" of the Baltic nations. For example in Estonia, in connection with the dissolution of the Soviet Union in 1991, huge crowds of people gathered on the choral stage in Tallinn and elsewhere, to sing patriotic songs that aroused the national spirit. The full effect of these will only be understood later on. When we sing or chant positive things together, their creative power is usually multiplied manyfold.

Magic of Speech and Chemistry of Bodies

A chapter unto themselves are the various mantras, sounds, and vowels that relate to working with the chakras. Quite a lot has been written about these, and different vowels as well as different frequencies have been proposed for the chakras. The matter is not altogether simple, and it is good to avoid "truths" that have been carved in granite. The general principle is that the lower frequencies combine with the lower chakras and the higher with the higher. Also, robust people often need the lower sounds, while the smaller need the higher. What is important is that by testing out, and experimenting with, the sound scale, you find the frequencies that resonate best with yourself. I have written about this kind of sound work in my Finnish book *The Higher Octaves of Music*.

Hilarion gives us the hint that in connection with the chakras it is possible to experiment with for example the old Tantric syllables: *lah, vah, rah, yah, hah, ah,* and *om.* On this esoteric sound path we start out from the root chakra and rise to the crown chakra at the top of the head. For example, when you are in some way dealing with the connection of the root chakra and Mother Earth, that is, with the basic matters of survival and sexuality, you can try out the first two syllables lah and vah. It is good to sing these syllables on a low note, which resonates with the region of the body that corresponds to this chakra. In this kind of sound work it is important to always maintain energies, thoughts and images that are connected with health, well-being, and love. In this way the effect reaches the chemistry of the body better.

If you sing these syllables in order from the bottom to the top, sometimes this can result in a powerful rising of kundalini energy[84] in your body, which may bring about useful astral travel, the opening of the crown chakra, and in general, an overall stimulation of the higher chakras. If some problems manifest, for example in connection with astral travel, it is good to sing the syllables from top to bottom. You are allowed to, and in fact should, use common sense in connection

---

84   By *kundalini* we mean the coiled serpent fire energy, the great energy reserve at the base of the spine, which rises safely toward the crown chakra at the top of the head as spiritual progress takes place. When it arrives at the crown chakra the kundalini energy produces enlightenment. See for example David Pond, *Western Seeker, Eastern Paths* (2003, Llewellyn Publications, St. Paul, Minn.)

with these types of exercises. A refining of character and of ethical standards should always accompany their practice.

Of course we do not need to go on Eastern travels in order to obtain help from the effects of voice and speech. The general principle is that all words have their own power and effect, and the power that they exert on you personally is an important starting point. When you speak words that have built up a positive energy in your mind, you can achieve considerable results.

In this we can utilize the possibilities of technology. First record some of these positive words, and perhaps some sentences created from them, and then play them back to yourself, erasing the fundamental frequency of your voice and some of its higher frequencies. This is easily done with the frequency controller of modern technology. The result can be sound energy that could cause significant changes on the cellular level and on the health of your body.

For example, experiment with some highly charged affirmation, such as: **I am of the inner light of Christ. I am a pure and perfect channel, and light is my guide,** or some of the mantras given in connection with the Law of Thought. These kinds of affirmations can bring magnificently charged positive energy into your being. You will obtain a powerful tool for your health when you filter out of them frequencies lower than approximately 390 Hertz, and also those higher than 11,000 Hertz. You might hold on to the loudspeaker as you listen to your filtered voice. As you listen to this sound material more or less daily, it may bring interesting health effects to your body.

What is in question is neither an electrical nor an electromagnetic phenomenon, but rather one that is connected to speech as such. Words seem to have a different effect when you erase from them the characteristics that make them appear to be separate from you. Instead you are left with the core of the words, an energy feeling that is usually connected with the intonation and the variations in the voice, and which is often perceived in the middle frequencies of speech. This research can be developed in many ways, as scientists all over the world are doing.

You can also use your own name in these exercises and methods. The energy of speech can trigger connections to different organs, meridians, and other physical systems of the body that have a great significance for the whole. This energy can often also trigger past memories or ideas that are connected with a certain organ or system. If we take the kidneys as an example, they have a direct connection with fears. Ideas that become speech, which affects you by increasing your fears have a direct effect on your kidneys. And of course when speech is able to free you from your fears and brings with it a feeling of inner caring, love, and a deeper concern for your body, it expresses radiant loving energy and brings some of that into the kidneys.

Researchers and the Speaking Voice

It is interesting to see that such pioneers of sound therapy as Alfred Tomatis, Sharry Edwards, and Nicole LaVoie give a great deal of weight to the speaking voice and its frequencies. According to them it seems to reveal a great deal about us humans. It is possible to find, in the frequencies that are missing from the speaking voice, connections to the periodic table of the elements, and for example mineral deficiencies. In other words, the speaking voice can truly be a key to health problems and their care.[85] The American sound therapist Sharry Edwards has obtained good therapeutic results when she has sung or played missing low frequencies for people. With this, healing has taken place even in diseases that have been classified as "incurable".

The French Alfred Tomatis (1920-2001) has been considered one of the most notable pioneers of sound and music therapy of the last century. His central insights were presented at the French Academy of Science already in the 1950's. Tomatis has been called the Sherlock of the ear, the Einstein of sound, and Mr. Mozart.[86] He did research on the collective "ethnic ear" of different nationalities, among other

---

85 The connection of the speaking voice with a person's character is worth studying.
86 Tomatis' autobiography, *The Conscious Ear* (Station Hill Press, New York, 1991) tells of his marvelous journey into the realm of sounds.

things. The auditory spectrum of the citizens of each country is dominated by a certain frequency range, a sort of favorite frequency, which is also reflected in the speech and hearing of the people. This sensitization to sounds is culturally, not biologically, determined.

According to Tomatis, the sensitized range of the German ear is 100 – 3000 Hz, that of the Slavs 100 – 8000, in other words, much more extensive. Because of this extensive frequency range the Slavs are able to learn foreign languages easily. The corresponding range of the English is 2000 – 12000 Hz, of Americans 750 – 3000 Hz, of the French 1000 – 2000 Hz, and of the Italians 2000 – 4000 Hz. These discoveries of Tomatis' may explain why the French often have difficulties with understanding the speech of Englishmen, but not of Americans. The peak frequency of American speech is found at approximately 1500 Hz, which is close to the fundamental frequency of the French. This is why the French learn the English language more easily from American than from English teachers.[87] What you do not hear you cannot repeat.

These are interesting scientific and technical aspects of the Law of Speech. It is to be expected that in the near future many new discoveries will be made in the area of the frequencies of the speaking voice, and in general around the effects of frequencies. In this connection Hilarion mentions the frequency 728 Hz, which has very interesting powers to dispel negative thought forms. These may relate to viruses, bacteria, and harmful micro-organisms through which these negative thought forms tend to anchor their most debilitating energies into the human body. The exact frequency in question (which is close to the f-note) is very useful as a general healing factor.

Humming Meditation:

The following meditation is connected with the voice, with a deeper consciousness of it, and with its real power within yourself. You can

---

87   Lehtiranta, *Musiikin korkeammat oktaavit*, pp. 146-149.

use this energy of the creative power of the voice simultaneously with almost any other meditation or guided visualization.

It is again good to relax your body and to breathe deeply into the belly. At the same time visualize a beautiful emerald green field around you, which gradually changes into a cylinder that reaches both into the Earth's core and into the heights of heaven.

Then imagine that you are in one of your favorite places in nature, a place with many plants. It is a warm day, and a gentle rain is falling on the ground. You can perhaps see and feel the plant devas all around you and know how both the devas and the plants receive nourishment and strength from the rain.

Besides receiving nourishment, the plants also receive a connection with you. It is mainly unconscious, but nevertheless full of positive feeling, and unconscious ideas and moods. If you open up this connection more consciously, you yourself may also be able to receive positive healing energies from the drizzle of rain.

Now imagine the gentle sound of the rain, as the little drops fall on leaves and on the ground around you. (If needed, you can also listen to the sound of rain from a nature recording, or just use your own creative imagination.) You will notice that the sounds seem to change slightly, and that they seem to have an effect on you at the level of the heart.

Then begin to hum softly. Begin with an inner hum that slowly becomes audible and gradually grows in volume. Feel the vibrations in yourself, and experience how they loosen and release your inner tensions, which are now free to be neutralized by Mother Earth.

Continue humming and allow it to come forth in a natural way along with the breath. If there is an occasional break in your breath, pause for a moment, then breathe in deeply, and continue humming.

Feel how the energy of the space around you changes slightly as you hum. It need not be a melodic hum, you can just open your mouth a bit and sing an ah-sound, or you can try a deeper throat sound. Allow all these vibrations to touch you, and also experience the feelings created by other sounds in the environment. Then allow your voice to grow a little stronger so that you can become more conscious of it.

Universal Laws and Spiritual Progress

Then imagine that you hear a humming sound from somewhere very high in the air, somewhere at cloud level. That humming sound causes the rain to fall on the ground. When the rain hits the ground, the plants, the flowers, the trees, the bushes and all their roots begin to suck in this energy, as if they were sucking in your humming, and drawing it deep into their being. It nourishes them and is changed within them.

Thanks to their chlorophyll, they produce green energy, the energy of life, out of this beautiful water. Life rushes forth at once: seeds germinate, plants drink this energy in, become conscious of it, grow stronger, and push deeper roots into the ground. At the same time a great dance is taking place. Tiny beings, tiny sparks of light, are dancing around each plant in a spiral, faster and faster, and they, too, are humming.

As they suck this light and this energy into themselves, they begin to notice the sound coming from you and from the other people who may be in the room. So now those light-beings want to dance near you for a moment. Those sparks of light in the spiral are now dancing around you. They enjoy their dance for a moment, and then go out through the windows, through the walls, and back into the plants.

As you are humming, imagine for a moment that your feet are like roots in the ground, that you are drawing in power from this beautiful humming energy field, and that your branches, your arms, are pulling this energy in from the Earth and from the sky. Suddenly, not only are you one with these beings, but your energy is theirs, and their energy is yours. An exchange of energy is taking place between you, and they are receiving your love just as you are receiving their love.

Now visualize a favorite flower or plant. This plant is now with you, and you are sharing your love with it as well. As your love deepens, allow the humming to become softer and gentler, and gradually make it an inner humming again. As even that begins to die down, all that remains is a sense of life, of energy, and of being nourished. The rain washes away everything that blocks that feeling.

Now out of the ground right under your feet there begins to flow a beautiful, continuous, nourishing energy, which says simply: "You are here, and that is good. I welcome you into my body, I welcome your life. I share myself with you with love, with pleasure and joy." This is the message to you from Mother Earth, from your soul, from God, all together, at all times.

Finally, be conscious of the richness of nature, and of all the beautiful sounds that the rain created. Give thanks and smile.

Summary

✳ Speech has a stronger effect on the physical level than thought alone.

✳ Speech draws energy to it and has an effect on your throat chakra.

✳ Using right and wise speech is ethical. Take conscious responsibility for what you say.

✳ Speech must be based in love in order to have positive results.

✳ Speaking ill of others, and malicious gossip, have deep karmic effects.

✳ Learn to speak and to be silent at the right times. Your speech may cause the wheels of karma to turn.

✳ Create your own songs and mantras, and with them order good things into your life.

Literature:

Charlton, Hilda 1989: *Master Hilarion*. Golden Quest, Woodstock, New York.
Collins, Mabel 1888: *Light on the Path*. George Redway, London.
Dryden, Gordon & Vos, Jeannette 1999: *Learning Revolution*. The Learning Web, Torrance, Canada.
Hilarion 1982: *Vision*. Marcus Books, Queensville, Ontario.
Lehtiranta, Erkki 2004: *Musiikin korkeammat oktaavit*. Dialogia, Helsinki.
Pond, David 2003: *Western Seeker, Eastern Paths*. Llewellyn Publications, St. Paul, Minn.
Schwartz, David J. 1987: *The Magic of Thinking Success*. Melvin Powers, North Hollywood, California.

10.

Symbols

"Humanity's guides utilize wonderful
symbolic schemes for the passing
of information to souls in incarnation.
Life on earth is literally alive with signs, symbols,
allegories and portents for those whose eyes
are opened enough to perceive them."

- Hilarion

SYMBOLS FORM PERHAPS the greatest wisdom library of humanity, but we have not yet learned to use it very effectively. Nevertheless, there are symbols everywhere in our lives, even in forms whose symbolic function we have completely forgotten. I mean for example letters and numerals: what are they at bottom other than symbols? And what an immense amount of information we are able to transmit and to receive with their help! Even all the chapters of this book are written and numbered with symbols.

Even something as mundane and common as a symbol drawn on a piece of paper reflects much more than the symbolic meaning of a word. This principle can be illuminated with the help of Tibetan prayer mills. In them words, that is, symbols, have been used to anchor and to transmit the energies, the love, and the spiritual understanding of many people. When prayer mills are twirled clockwise everywhere in the Himalayas, the radiance from them is not only symbolic, but rather, a part of the energies coded into these writings flows inevitably into the world.

This example is in itself an important symbol of how to work with symbols. When the energy of a symbol is activated in some way, and it is used and coordinated deliberately, we begin to understand the power hidden in it. Symbols have more power and more extensive influence than has been understood up to now. A symbol creates an authentic energy pattern, a real flow, and an authentic connection that extends far beyond mere symbolism. Symbols can also form a bridge or a connection between individuals and also between cultures. When we understand each other's symbol languages, we will also understand each other better.

Thus, reality is full of information coded into various symbol languages. In addition to letters and numerals, for example musical notes, colors, traffic signals, hand signals, individual and collective archetypes, logos, flags, rituals, works of art in their own way, and many other things, are symbols – or at least they can be used also as symbols. Among hand signals come to mind the well-known peace symbol used by hippies and anti-war demonstrators, and the victory symbol introduced by Winston Churchill. Symbols send us messages in our dreams and come into our meditations. We are never "safe" from them anywhere.

The Symbolism of Art

In art symbolism is present everywhere, after all, art in itself is a symbol of the unlimited nature of human creativity. The symbolism of art is of course intensified in the movement called symbolism, which began at the end of the 19th century in France and Belgium. Symbolism is also widely present in the rich language and metaphors of poetry, and in notable works of painting and architecture. In music, for example, the four initial notes of Beethoven's 5th symphony (da-da-da-daah) symbolize fate knocking at the door, as the composer knew he was growing deaf.

And what about animals, plants, or stones? Stars and constellations? The grammar of the human body? All these also have an immense amount of symbolic material, which is sometimes overt, sometimes hidden. In any case, many learned books have been written about these symbol codes and their various meanings.

It is said in the Bible that man is the image of God. I doubt if we will be offending the holy book if we say that man is the symbol of God. In us the Godhead awakens to know itself, as I already noted in the introduction to this book.

Our Guides Communicate through Symbols

On an unconscious level all people know that the events of their lives have cycles of meaning that extend far beyond the everyday. Every one of us can become aware of these deeper meanings by being awake to his intuition and following the whispers of his inner voice, for example as some symbol appears repeatedly in his life. This may be a wild animal, a combination of numbers or letters, or similar things. In this way we can learn to understand the cosmic Law of Symbols through our daily life. I will give many examples of this in what follows.

Very often our own spiritual guides, our unconscious side and the entire universe are in one way or another manifesting these symbols in order to increase our understanding of ourselves and of the nature of reality. As our ability to read the language of symbols increases, we are ever more able to find spiritual signposts on our journey.

Our guides never waste an opportunity to give us these hints, which really CAN be connected to such ordinary things as for example numbers, or series of numbers, letters, animals, or natural phenomena that we see.[88] It is not difficult for them to cause appropriate symbols to come our way, since they are able to manipulate the three-dimensional world from the higher dimensions. This is how they operate every day.

We can also see symbolic dimensions in world events, natural catastrophes, and why not in the economic crisis of the euro zone.[89] Very often combinations of the Law of Symbols and the Law of Reflection

---

88 Hilarion, *Symbols*, pp. 86-87.
89 For example we may well ask whether the best currency for the euro zone is the euro, or might it after all be love.

Universal Laws and Spiritual Progress

can be seen in them. Of course great natural catastrophes usually also include a karmic dimension. In this way the great law book of the universe opens up from numerous different places, if only we have enough zeal for study and a lack of preconceptions. There is no danger of running out of things to research.

Thus, symbols penetrate our entire reality from the microcosm to the macrocosm, from tiny flowers and pebbles to the immense world of stars and galaxies. Nature itself is a magnificent symbol: after all, Mother Earth with all her symbols is our greater home, and the symbolism of the starry skies is immeasurable. In addition, the stars are constantly sending us information with their light.

Besides us human beings, animals also use the language of symbols. This is obvious for example in their ritual dances and mating calls, and in other matters that pertain to coupling and to finding a mate. The animal world offers us many wonderful and powerful symbols, for example the butterfly emerging from its cocoon, the snake shedding its skin, or the legendary phoenix bird. These are all ancient symbols of spiritual transformation and rebirth, and have energized and inspired many cultures, epochs, and artists.

In particular, the guides use wild animals to send us messages. If a relative is about to pass to the higher dimensions, the guides may want to prepare the person for this, and for example arrange for a dead raven to be placed by his jogging trail. Guides often use the person's belief system, which is well known to them, as an aid in this.[90] A friend of mine told me that just before a family member died, a fox ran across her front yard. The family of this relative came from a part of the country where there was a belief that when a wild animal runs across your yard, it is bringing just such a message.

Animal symbols, for example in the form of power animals, are very significant. In connection with these it is always good to ask what it is that people project of themselves into these animals. There is always more to things than what the eye can see or the ear can hear!

---

90   Hilarion, *Symbols*, p. 87.

These kinds of events can of course always be dismissed as coincidences. I remember very well where I was on 9/11/2001, when the world changed along with the terrorist attack on the United States. I was just beginning a lecture in a small Finnish town when the news arrived. But I was not altogether surprised, since a week earlier a raven had crashed into our window, and in the morning it lay dead in front of the window with its wings spread out, like an airplane. The window had broken in the crash.

That event was etched clearly in our minds, and we were immediately conscious that some symbolic message was in question: a raven, a death, and a glass window. Nevertheless we did not have the feeling that a family member was about to pass, but rather that there was an attempt to transmit something else from the spiritual levels. When news of the destruction of the glass-covered Twin Towers arrived, things clicked into place right away. In this connection it is good to remember that great catastrophes like this are of course known beforehand in other dimensions[91], and there is an attempt to prepare people to receive the news in advance. But this is not done in any obvious way, but rather through these types of symbolic means.

The Rich Symbols of the Plant Kingdom

Profound symbolism is also found in the plant and mineral kingdoms. Some of the characteristics that developed in some plant species during the evolutionary cycles do not have much evolutionary meaning, but rather exist simply to distinguish them from other plant species. In addition, the doctrine of signatures of Paracelsus, which I already mentioned in this book in connection with the Law of Manifestation, is an inseparable part of spiritual botany. Nature offers innumerable examples of this doctrine, some of them obvious, others more profound.

According to Paracelsus, the handwriting of the Creator is visible in nature – for example in the forms and characteristics of plants – if

---

91   They can be observed in the ionosphere, among other places.

only people have eyes to see these matters. In other words, there are resemblance-hints that help practitioners of natural healing to understand the effects of plants. If some part of a plant, typically the flower, but also some other part, resembles an organ or system of the human body, it most likely also heals it. This knowledge is often used in fytotherapy, but also in flower therapy and in shamanism, among other things.

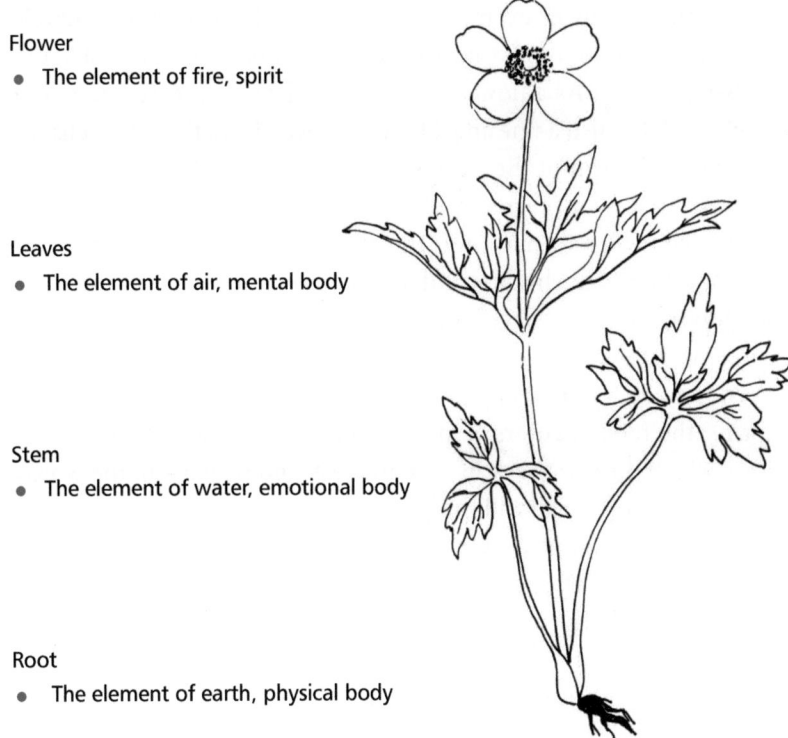

Flower
- The element of fire, spirit

Leaves
- The element of air, mental body

Stem
- The element of water, emotional body

Root
- The element of earth, physical body

There are immense numbers of classic examples of Paracelsus' doctrine of signatures. A walnut resembles the brain closely, with its two halves and its cortical folds, and it is considered a good "brain nut", which for example enriches micro-doses of silver out of the ground, and silver is very important for the nervous system. Now we know that walnuts help in developing more than three dozen neurotransmitters, which further the functioning of the brain. In addition, as a flower essence Walnut (in the Bach flower essences) is an excellent stress reducer. And of course stress is often mental in origin and is thus greatly connected with our brain function. According to some opinions, letting go of unnecessary stress lengthens our life expectancy by ten percent.

Another excellent example is Angelica archangelica, an umbrella-shaped plant of the far north, whose flowers greatly resemble the nervous system. As a flower essence this plant is an excellent nerve balm, and it is also a fine angel flower, as even its Latin name tells us.

The symbolism of the rose is also moving, and it suggests in an interesting way the corresponding symbolism of sweet and salt water, which I will return to later. The rose species represent, along with the lotus flower, the highest and most evolved expression of the plant kingdom, and roses have since ancient times been connected with love. Worldly love is symbolized by the plant's thorns, which have been literally felt by many in their sensitive being. But the luscious forms, the radiant colors, and the fragrance of roses refer to higher love, which does not seek its own interest, and which – in the words of Brother Paul – bears all things.

The lotus flower has in various cultures been connected with spirituality, purity, perfect beauty, resurrection, and enlightenment. The crown chakra at the top of the head is often called the thousand-petaled lotus, which symbolizes spiritual revelation. In bud, the flower is a symbol of human potentiality. In mandalas, the lotus is a common symbol of meditation. The journey of the lotus through mud and water into the light is a beautiful symbol of human growth and progress, where the individual must travel to higher levels of consciousness by working through uncontrolled emotional life, which is symbolized by muddy waters.

In the history of humankind, the lotus has evolved along with the crown chakra. This plant also acts as a bridge between many levels

Universal Laws and Spiritual Progress

of the water and air kingdoms, as well as between the energies of the earth and the sky. Its important symbolism is connected with unifying different energy levels.[92]

A tomato has four chambers, and it is usually red. The same characteristics are found in the heart. The red coloring agent in the tomato, lycopene, which belongs to the group of carotenoids, has been shown to protect against cardiovascular diseases, according to research. Kidney beans resemble kidneys closely, and are healing and strengthening for them, while celery and rhubarb resemble bones and strengthen them. Bones contain 23% sodium, as do these plants. If there is not enough sodium in a diet, the body takes it from the bones, which then become weak.

And what about carrots? The "annual rings" revealed in a cut carrot resemble the eye with its pupil, its iris, and its radiating lines. Science has shown that eating carrots strengthens the circulation and the functioning of the eye. Nor is this all, for the roots of most types of carrots look like the rods and cones at the nerve endings of the eye, which lead to the midbrain.

As a flower essence the uncultivated form of the carrot, the wild carrot (Daucus carota) strengthens these rods and cones. In addition, the essence helps with nearsightedness, which often occurs when the mental body of the individual has difficulties in focusing on larger issues. The carrot essence helps in seeing auras and also develops our telepathic gifts.[93]

Along with all this botanical knowledge it is worthwhile to study for example how a plant creates its flowers, where it grows and prospers, what is the typical way in which each plant species carries nutrients for its needs, etc. As you think about such questions and in general spend time with plants, you are no longer working with their outer forms, but with their inner and symbolic meanings.

---

92 Gurudas, Flower Essences and Vibrational Healing, p. 171. As a flower essence the lotus is a kind of philosopher's stone of the plant kingdom, which treats people on many different levels. At the same time it enhances the effects of other essences. Also the flower essence combinations produced by Smiling Stars include some lotus.
93 Gurudas, Flower Essences and Vibrational Healing, p. 199.

Trees also speak to us through their symbolism. A holy tree in Finland is the juniper, the elegant birch in our home yard is a beloved symbol for us, we can feel profound peace under the branches of a spruce tree in the depths of the woods, and in the hum of great forests we hear the symphony of nature, as Sibelius heard it.

The symbolism of trees can also be read through their general form. The evergreens typically have a triangular form, while the deciduous trees often have a leafy structure that resembles a circle or an oval. A triangle suggests the symbolism of spirituality, while a circle is one of the symbols of earthiness, practicality, and even of fertility.[94] The apple tree is a good example of this.

Hilarion gives us good hints on this.[95] The beings that are experiencing reality in the evergreen, the spirits of the trees, are by nature very committed and devoted. Thus, these trees give people the spiritual comfort that many so sorely need. Often people do feel peaceful and balanced in the proximity of evergreen trees, for example in a pine forest.

In addition, many people have noticed that especially the big evergreen trees have a marvelously calming effect on the subtle bodies of people when they are in the aura of these trees. The aura of the tree usually reaches as far as its branches. The effect is even stronger if you have your back against a tree and are facing north.

If on the other hand an individual needs to ground himself and to bring himself back to ordinary reality after for example a powerful meditation or an out-of-body experience, it is best to find his way under a fruit tree. Then it is good to stand on the north side of the tree and to reach around the tree while facing south. The effects can be felt within a few minutes.

I could go on for some time about the symbolism of the plant kingdom, but perhaps these few examples give an idea of the great hidden wisdom of nature, which can even have unforeseen effects on our health.

---

94   The circle of course has other symbolic meaning levels as well. In itself it is a perfect geometric figure and thus also expresses perfection.
95   Hilarion, Other Kingdoms, p. 67-68.

Universal Laws and Spiritual Progress

The Many Symbolic Levels of Water

Symbolic levels can even be found in the world of micro-organisms. For example, certain vibrations that some organism has taken into use, unite symbolically with this host organism where the microbes operate and where they get their energy etc. We can well say that symbols cover the entire evolutionary scale on our planet

We have a good example of this in water, that supple liquid necessary to life on our planet. I have already considered matters concerning water in previous chapters, for example in connection with the Laws of Reflection, Permanence, and Love. It is easy to understand that the symbolism of water belongs as a matter of course in the Law of Symbols.[96]

Water is the circulatory system of our planet, and a magical mirror of our emotions, which carries within it many interesting matters. The significance of water for our survival is primary, but it has had an important role in for example Taoism and in the Bible. We can say that our relationship with water will be one of the crucially fateful questions in the near future both from the point of view of nutrition as well as from a deeper, more spiritual perspective.[97] However, for this, we need the help offered by symbolism.

Water is one of the four elements of antiquity, and one of the five elements of Chinese philosophy and medicine. In astrology, the water element relates to the emotions and the Moon, which for its part symbolizes, besides the emotions, also the streamings of our unconscious mind. Here we then find a connection to the oceans: after all, we do speak of the ocean of the unconscious, which has different levels.

---

96 The Law of Symbols is in some respects a corollary of the Law of Reflection in the same way that the Law of Speech is a corollary of the Law of Thought. Nevertheless it is reasonable to examine them as separate cosmic lawfulnesses because of their great explanatory power and their particular characteristics. And – as Hilarion mentions humorously – it is better to include twelve laws instead of ten, otherwise we would be treading on the toes of Moses.

97 Hilarion tells us that at this time it is especially desirable and blessed to send love to the water systems of our planet. You can easily do this in many different ways, for example through the powerful chakras at the bottom of the palms and through visualization.

The surface waters of the ocean are clear, and the animals that move in them are usually small and easy to recognize, so also are the matters in the surface waters of the unconscious. It is usually relatively simple to raise them into the light of consciousness. As we descend deeper, there is less light, and the fauna become ever stranger. Similarly, the individual and collective archetypes in the human unconscious mind can be compared to the peculiar inhabitants of these deeper parts of the ocean.[98] We have been able to acquaint ourselves with these for example through nature documentaries.

One of the exceptional characteristics of water, our life fluid, is its ability to appear in different forms: liquid, gaseous, and solid. We can extend our symbolic interpretation to these forms as well. First, the entire circulation of water can be seen, in the Chinese manner, as a symbol of the human incarnation process, where the water first rains out of "heaven", and then gathers experiences as it flows (among other things, information about the minerals that water meets on the way is stored in it), only to return to "heaven", enriched by experience.

The power of Sunlight, the symbol of God's radiance, transforms water from the liquid state into the gaseous, and raises it up into the air to form clouds – and eventually to rain back to earth. Similarly, the raising of human emotional nature also needs the gift of God's Light. The change of state from water to water vapor symbolizes the vibrational change that human emotionality has to undergo in order to rise to the purity of Christ-love.[99]

And what of the snow flake, where nature varies a certain basic theme, a six-pointed star, one of the holiest spiritual symbols of our planet? Every winter nature reminds us, inhabitants of the North, of the important spiritual truth symbolized by this sacred pattern. What is in question is of course the well-known structure that is often connected with Judaism under the name of the Star of David. But it is much older than Judaism.[100]

---

98 Hilarion, *More Answers*, pp. 42-43.
99 Hilarion, Tapestry, p. 52.
100 Hilarion, Body Signs, p. 11.

Universal Laws and Spiritual Progress

The human trinity (the physical, the emotional, and the mental, or, will, feelings, and thought, and the energy types that correspond to these) can be expressed with two triangles:

In this symbolism, the triangle with its point downward represents a person's lower self, the personality, which feels the pull of matter – and points toward the earth. The upward point on the other hand expresses the pull of spirit, or heaven, and thus represents the higher self, the soul. In this, an equilateral structure is the ideal case, where there exists a good balance between the physical, the emotional, and the mental nature of the being.

When these triangles are combined into a beautiful equilateral triangle, the star of David, we have at the same time illustrated one of the central goals of earthly life: to bring together our lower and higher being, that is, our personality and our soul, in such a way that the lower is governed by the higher. In this way the higher side can use the experience and practical know-how of the lower side, and correspondingly the wisdom and spirituality of the higher side are transmitted to the personality.[101] In this way the snowflake tells us through its symbolism about a very important goal in this university of heart and mind, in the interaction of earth and heaven.[102]

---

101 Hilarion, *Body Signs*, pp. 10-11.
102 In spite of their similarity of form, snowflakes are always individual. This symbolizes the fact that on the soul level a human being retains his individuality and is not merged into the masses.

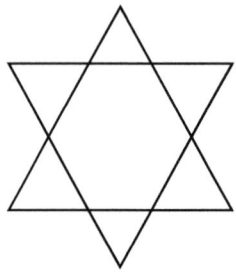

As you can see, even ordinary events such as a snowstorm may have behind them significant levels of symbolism, which reveal themselves only through reflection and insight. It is important to also consider the wisdom of the human body in this connection. Hilarion has treated this matter extensively in his book *Symbols* and *Body Signs* (see the bibliography).

The body of an adult human being is about 2/3 liquid by weight, and approximately the same amount of the surface of our planet (c. 71%) is covered by water. This numerical relationship has an important symbolic significance from the point of view of the evolution and the purification of the emotions. However, the amount of liquid in the body often diminishes with age, which symbolizes the drying up of emotional life.

The amount of water around us is a continuing reminder to humanity of its own decision to grow into its full measure on its chosen path - in love and about love. In Finland, the land of thousands of lakes, this symbolic reminder is close to the people every day.

Salt water, which covers the greater part of the surface of the blue planet, is nature's great symbol for worldly love. Thirst can never be quenched with salt water. This also represents the way in which the higher side of love becomes profane, earthy (salt is dug out of the ground), and how it appears in the relationship between a man and a woman.

Pure, crystal clear sweet water, which is much rarer on the planet, on the other hand symbolizes the highest dimension of love, unconditional Christ-love, which is the goal of humanity. That is, learning the kind of universal love that asks nothing in return, but only always wants to give of itself, and wishes the happiness of the beloved selflessly.

The rarity of pure water symbolizes the fact that very few people are able to express pure Christ-love. Most people are able to experience the romantic love between a man and a woman, which rather binds them to earth. Unconditional love is a peculiar thing in that it does not diminish as it is shared, but rather increases, grows, and flourishes. It can truly be called the water and source of life.[103]

In addition to water and the other things mentioned above, nature offers an immense, inexhaustible library of symbols for those who want to expand their vision of the profound mysteries of life.

The Large Spectrum of Symbol Doctrines

Master Hilarion has given us much information about various symbol systems in his books and channelings. Such systems have been central objects of my research since the mid 90's. Everyone is sure to find something for himself in these doctrines, and no symbol doctrine is superior to another – rather, each one forms a part of a great whole, where reality is examined from different points of view through symbols.

Symbols usually have many levels of interpretation, for example the number three refers astrologically to the planet Jupiter, to the basic trinity of divinity and of man, to the third alternative peeking out from behind a thesis and an antithesis, and to the important general lawfulness known as the rule of three. "The third time is the charm", and "Never two without a third" are sayings that hide behind them this lawfulness. I already wrote something about this in connection with the Law of Opposite Expression, but the matter deserves to be examined more precisely in connection with symbols.

This law of three operates in many ways in relation to symbols. One of the most central says that if a person does not understand a sym-

---

103 Hilarion, *Symbols*, pp. 9-10.

bol sent by his guides even by the third time, then the higher levels will spend no more energy on transmitting it. On the other hand, if you suspect that a symbol or message is coming from your guides, and it does not open to you immediately, have patience and express a request, for example telepathically, to be given another chance to understand the matter. At this, the guides will notice that you are awake in relation to the matter, and will usually arrange a second, and even a third, hint.

In a higher sense the law of three expresses symbolically the way in which the mental, the emotional, and the physical sides of your being cooperate within you. In general, the first two levels of interpretation have a meaning for you on the personal level, but the third level usually contains considerable influence from the guides. This extends beyond dualism and may for example reveal something of the person's own divine nature.

I will offer a personal experience of the law of three from many years ago. We were giving a training in the summertime in a spiritual center in Eastern Finland. In the evening, after teaching, we were driving slowly along a forest road to see how many orchids might be growing in the calcium-rich soil of the region (and there were quite a few). As we were driving at a walking speed in the evening light, a fox appeared on the side of the road, trotting along at the same pace. We followed with amazement as the fox kept on abreast of us, as if following us. Finally we stopped, and so did the fox. We were able to take a picture of it without a problem, after which it trotted off leisurely.

We might have forgotten the meeting with the fox, but when we started driving off after the workshop, a second fox appeared in a field. Now it slowly started to click in: really. What might there be behind this? At the time we already knew that animals are important messengers, and their appearing is never accidental.

Later that summer we were visiting our friends in France, and one day we were driving along a road in the middle of the huge Fontainebleau forest. Lo and behold, a fox (not the same one, for sure!) appeared and again begin to trot near the car. The third time is the charm! For us, the fox was a lucky charm: at that same time we received support from a completely unexpected quarter, support that made it possible to carry out an important project.

The law of three has been known for eons especially in the eastern tradition. When your inner work with symbols extends to the above-mentioned three levels, you may very well be able to bring up a very profound level of interpretation that relates to the symbol in question. This gives us an inkling of the effect of symbols on the microcosmic level.

It is good to remember, in connection with symbols, that people are in no way forced to understand them. Our free will is a question of honor to the guides, and we can choose to ignore the messages that come through symbols, or to work with them later, at a time that suits us better.

Especially when a symbol has a higher, spiritual meaning, and when it can offer something more than what is available in the three-dimensional world, it is given out in a way that does not give any concrete evidence of its existence or its meaning. Examples of such symbolic languages might be palmistry, astrology, some types of numerology, and predictive methods of the kind represented by the I Ching. The information given by them can often be dismissed as accidental. In this way the free will of the skeptics can also be protected.

If you nevertheless decide to work with a traditional system of symbols, or with one of your own devising, it will usually begin to work. In this connection it is good for you to start developing your own intuitive talents, since they have immense significance for your spiritual growth. When you open up your own knowledge and understanding in relation to some system of symbols, more knowledge and insight will begin to flow into your life. It is as if symbols opened new bridges and connections in your life. The passive receiver becomes the active doer.

You can create and activate your own symbols. But take care to avoid arbitrary images. Symbols transmit energy, and it is important for this energy to be as positive and constructive as possible. Then you can take these symbols along into your ritual work, meditations, or other spiritual practices. Working with symbols can change from passive receiving to active, creative doing. Besides, it is much more fun to work with them in this way.

Geometric symbols have always fascinated people, and an open-minded study of them can reveal much about the layers of the meaning of reality. I already alluded more than once to the many meanings of the triangle and the hexagram. The pentagram, the five-pointed star, has often been connected with occult doctrines, but it also has other levels of interpretation. Numerologically it of course refers to the number five, which is the number for balance in spiritual numerology, and is connected with the planet Mercury. This planet governs among other things communication, information search, mentality, and to a certain extent also travel, children, and trade. Mercury is the planet of France, and if we examine the geographic form of France, and use a cheese slicer on it a bit, we get a pretty exact pentagram.[104] Coincidence?

England, on the other hand, if treated with the same cheese slicer method, resembles a triangle with an upward point, while India has the form of a downward triangle.[105] These two nations have an important karmic bond, which I already referred to in connection with the cosmic Law of Karma, and even their geography seems to tell us something symbolically. England is sometimes connected with passionate and warlike Mars, while India has been perceived as a nation governed by Venus (and to a certain extent by Saturn). These are interesting matters, and someone who is willing to look can find even much more in them.

Symbols of The Body

In connection with the Law of Reflection in chapter 2, I examined the great wisdom of the human body in connection with various reflec-

---

104 Hilarion, *Symbols*, p. 20.
105 Hilarion, *Symbols*, p. 20.

tions, and in chapter 12 I will focus on the heart, our most important organ, and its immense symbolism. Our biography is truly written into our body, which is the experimental laboratory of all Universal Laws and therefore also a wise biographer.

Actually, everything in the body is symbolic. There is profound symbolism in facial features, in fingers, in teeth, in the vertebrae of the spine, in the internal organs, and in the structures of feet. This is only gradually becoming clear to people. Here I will only mention briefly some parts of the grammar of the human body.

Fingerprints – which do not change during a lifetime, unlike for example the lines of the palm – tell much about the highest levels of progress achieved in previous lives, where the five essential lessons are concerned. For example the lesson of the thumb is connected especially with the utilization of energy, with keeping or losing your temper, and with turning the other cheek, as this important lesson is expressed in the Bible. This is the classic lesson of controlling the energies of hotheaded red Mars, and the rounder the patterns on the tip of the thumb, the better this lesson has been learned in previous lives.

The index finger is connected with Jupiter, and with matters of faith in the most general sense of the word, the middle finger with Saturn and with building a positive self-image, the ring finger with Apollo, i.e. the Sun, and with our attitude toward money, and the little finger with Mercury and with our attitude toward sexuality. These are central points of growth in our times, and also crucial questions from the point of view of spiritual evolution.[106]

The message is usually aimed at our unconscious mind, which knows how to interpret such things, but even our conscious mind can learn to become skillful in this. You simply must dare to use your intuition, and also to ask the guides for the true deeper meaning of the matter. Often what is in question is confronting karma, and also some kind of spiritual chastisement whose time has come.

It is possible to find much symbolic information for example

---

106 Hilarion, *Body Signs*, pp. 51-65.

through the interpretation of dreams. Techniques that help you to bring some of your own ideas about symbols into a situation are useful. If your guides are with you in this, the method is even more powerful. Usually your guides have a greater influence on your consciousness when you are asleep, that is to say, when your consciousness is out of your physical body.[107] The symbols that your guides bring into the dreams that you remember the following day, generally tell you something very important and timely about your life. In the following meditation you can open and strengthen channels through which you can gain new information from your guides and helpers.

Symbol Meditation

Sit in a relaxed and comfortable position and breathe deeply a few times. Allow your breath to become a peaceful belly breath. Give your body a suggestion to relax and feel how a warm and healing relaxation spreads throughout your body from head to toe. Imagine that you are sitting in the middle of a beautiful emerald green column of light, which continues to grow brighter and stronger.

Then think of a symbol that has raised questions in your mind, and which you would like to receive some more information about. Or perhaps you want to take up a symbol you have worked with for some time, and which you now want to familiarize yourself with more deeply. In any case it is good if the symbol you choose is real, and something that you can use regularly. It might be a drawing that you find time and again on your pages as you are writing something, an image that comes to mind regularly as you are singing, a memory from times gone by which comes to mind now and then, but whose meaning is not quite clear, or a feeling that arises when you are socializing with people, and you are not quite sure why or what it really means.

---

107 One of the practical applications of the law of three usually appears after spiritual peak experiences and important learning events. The lessons are often tested and checked out three days after the experience or event.

Universal Laws and Spiritual Progress

Choose one of these symbols or matters and hold it in your consciousness for a while. Be with it, and then let the image go. A good way to let go is to recall the emerald green column of light. It rotates around you and sweeps the image down to the ground.

Now imagine a very special secret place. It may be in a forest where you are completely safe. Perhaps it is a place by the ocean where you feel deeply peaceful. Or the place might even be up in the air, for example on a particularly beautiful and radiant cloud. Choose a place like this for yourself and go there alone. Feel that you are completely safe there, that you are clear and surrounded by every kind of support and help.

Then I suggest that you invite your guide, your helper or your friend to be with you. As you sit quietly in this state of peace and calm, imagine that someone materializes in this place either knocking on a door, stepping onto the ocean shore, or coming on another cloud. This being is a beautiful, radiant and warm guide. This being does not say anything, perhaps he (she) only smiles. You remain together for a while. You sit close to each other, perhaps looking into each other's eyes, or simply remaining in each other's energy for a few minutes. Now become aware of your own breath again. Notice that breathing is now free and easy.

Then bring the symbol or matter that you chose into your consciousness again. Do this as you breathe in and notice how you feel the symbol forming. As you breathe out, the idea of the symbol expands and reaches your guide; at the same time he (she) feels, sees, experiences, or understands the meaning of that symbol in some way. Have a dialogue about this with your guide.

Then let the symbol go and simply continue breathing. You are sitting together with your guide, and you are again conscious of each other's energies. Notice your breath again. Feel your connection during the inbreath. When your outbreath is complete, pause for a bit before breathing in, in other words, breathe all the air out of your lungs and then hold your breath for a moment. Then allow the symbol to come in again, but in such a way that your guide has changed it. Breathe in again and notice how your guide has offered you a new point of view, or perhaps a new symbol, or perhaps some object that relates to the matter. You can repeat this if you like. You can simply remain in meditation with your guide and allow him (her) to bring you a present or to share it with you on some level.

Now I ask you to let go of all this. Your guide leaves you in the same way that he (she) came, and you yourself return from this secret place to the place where you are practicing. Do not worry if you did not yet receive a clear answer to your symbol, or a point of view that you could interpret. Just allow the symbol to be with you, and a higher meaning will gradually appear.

It may be that when you purposefully ask for help from your guide consciously, and in a safe place like this, you still feel a bit bewildered, and things do not become clear in the way that you perhaps expected. This is normal. Gradually things will begin to harmonize in such a way that you will be able to get much more out of them. This is why I suggest that you repeat this exercise every now and then, either alone or with your friends.

Summary

* Reality is full of symbolism that is only waiting to be discovered. Our guides produce plenty of symbolic things in our life every day.

* The individual's freedom of choice is respected also in relation to symbols: you can choose to ignore them, as many do.

* Symbols have more power and greater influence than has thus far been understood.

* A symbol is energy, and also transmits it.

* We can learn through the ordinary to understand the cosmic Law of Symbols.

* Symbolic dimensions can be perceived in world events, natural catastrophes, and economic crises.

* Nature is in itself a magnificent symbol, and the symbolism of the starry sky is immeasurable.

* The human unconscious contains regions where the individual and collective archetypes are located.

* The law of three is an important lawfulness in examining symbols.

* When working with symbols, it is good to develop your own intuitive talents, since they have an immense significance for your own individual spiritual growth.

* You can create and activate your own symbols. Symbols open up new bridges and connections in your life, and then you are no longer a passive receiver, but an active doer.

Literature:
Avanhov, Omraam Mikhaël 1988: *The Symbolic Language of Geometrical Figures*. Editions Prosveta, Fréjus Cedex.
Gurudas 1989: *Flower Essences and Vibrational Healing*. Cassandra Press, San Rafael, California.
Hilarion 1980: *Symbols*. Marcus Books, Agincourt, Ontario.
Hilarion 1981: *Other Kingdoms*. Marcus Books, Queensville, Ontario.
Hilarion 1982: *Vision*. Marcus Books, Queensville, Ontario.
Hilarion 1982: *Body Signs*. Marcus Books, Queensville, Ontario.
Hilarion 1985: *More Answers*. Marcus Books, Toronto.
Hilarion 1985: *Tapestry*. Marcus Books, Toronto.
Lehtiranta Erkki & Niemelä Leena 2007: *Suomen luonnon valkoista magiaa*. Smiling Stars, Helsinki.

11.

Progress

"Nothing remains stable or unchanging.
Things and beings must either progress
to a higher level or regress to a
more primitive level."

- Hilarion

THE COSMIC PRINCIPLE of progress is valid without exception for phenomena and processes of the physical, emotional and mental levels, as well as even higher levels. The Law of Progress is in addition an important background theme of this book, as the second half of the heading above tells us. In this I have particularly emphasized spiritual progress and furthering it.

In the course of natural evolution this cosmic lawfulness of course constantly finds various expressions in the framework of the evolutionary process, but the same is true for example in marriage or a comparable relationship: if it does not grow and evolve mutually, it will inevitably regress and weaken. It is actually not possible to freeze a relationship at some stable level.[108] In ancient Greece the philosopher of change, Heraclitus, expressed this cosmic principle with the words: "You cannot step twice into the same river". *Panta rhei kai*

---

108 Hilarion, *Vision*, p. 29.

　　　　　　　　Universal Laws and Spiritual Progress

ouden menei - everything flows, nothing stands still. According to this point of view, reality is like fire, it is constantly moving and changing its shape.

It is not by accident that this law and the Law of Love are the last ones to be considered, like sugar at the bottom, in the great law library of the universe, since progress and love form the direction and purpose of the universe. All the previously mentioned laws serve this purpose in their own way. However, free will means that a human being, humankind, and even greater entities make choices, and can also choose involution instead of evolution.

An inner resistance to change often acts as a great brake to progress. "You must never change" is the central message of a Finnish hit song of a few decades ago, echoing this resistance to change in its own way, with the means of entertainment. What is in question is by no means always laziness, but often rather a fear of change, and clinging to what is familiar and safe, and to what in itself belongs to the energies of the past.

No Use Resisting the Universe

If you nevertheless put the cart before the horse, your journey will slow down considerably. If on the other hand you begin to sail with the wind and steer your way wisely, you can go far, even if the wind occasionally intensifies into a storm. Change is in a direct relationship with your willingness to allow the flow of things and processes from the very first. Resistance never brings the best result.

Getting stuck in the energies and patterns of the past is of course understandable from a human point of view, but it does not serve our evolutionary needs and purposes. If we resist the universe and say that we will only do things in our own way, we are begging for difficulties for ourselves. The divine in us is constantly seeking new expressions, and is not satisfied with only the old, the familiar and safe. The explorers of spiritual space direct their gaze and their way toward new regions and vistas, where the richness and complexity of reality is visible in larger visions.

When you join this group of spiritual backpackers, you are not alone: there are ever more fellow travelers on this the higher path of pilgrimage. The alarm clock of the spirit rings more insistently than earlier, and many can hear its call in these important years for humanity and for the planet.

Progress is also seeing the possibilities and grasping them in this light of the spirit. Confucius alludes to this by saying that he who desires lasting happiness must change all the time. **Change is the central factor in progress**, and now we can see how the circle is closed in regard to the Universal Laws. We began with the majestic Law of Manifestation, which tells us that the worlds and the dimensions have been created simply so that spiritual beings could learn to know themselves.

The journey continues through reflections, opposites, karma, thought, and symbols toward ever-greater self-knowledge and the ability to express the love and light of our core being. This in turn eventually brings with it the maximum spiritual progress – which always includes helping other life forms with the means at our disposal. The Law of Progress takes us inevitably from serving ourselves and our ego to serving others. There is no other path into the light. But rising above ourselves requires courage and endurance.

Hilarion summarizes that our spiritual progress has three central goals: to learn the basic cosmic laws that govern all our experience, to find and to cherish the spirit of God in the heart of all beings, and to discover the secret of loving all of creation.[109]

When we look backward and examine the slow movement of human history, we can easily see how the flame of spirit and of progress has moved from one culture to another through the eons and according to its own evolutionary cycles. In this, the cosmic Laws of Cycles and of Progress come together. In relation to humanity, it seems that each evolutionary cycle has its own particular goals of progress.[110]

---

109 Hilarion, The Master Plan, p. 120.
110 I have examined some cultural cycles of evolution from the point of view of the different layers of the history of music in my Finnish book Musiikin korkeammat oktaavit, pp. 108-113.

Universal Laws and Spiritual Progress

Recent discoveries (I am writing this in the winter of 2011-2012) in particle physics and astrophysics also tell us of the Law of Progress, and of the fact that we cannot get stuck in place in science or in any other method of examining reality. The life domains, the countries and cultures that have tended to become stuck – here North Korea comes to mind – are forced to struggle more than others with friction and resistance.

Expansion on the Macro- and Micro Levels

The expanding nature of the universe gives us a fine symbolic representation of the universal Law of Progress and of its activity on the macrocosmic level. The new discoveries in particle physics on the other hand open the way to the microcosmic level. As in the small, so in the great, as below, so above, we could again say. These discoveries correlate with the collective expansion of human consciousness and with the unity of humankind and are at the same time connected with the Law of Reflection in an interesting way.

However, the expanding nature of the universe may be difficult to understand through the expanding, that is, separating, process alone. It is easier to understand it as an opening and expansion of consciousness, which is connected for example with obtaining a better idea of who we really are, and with our desire to open and to understand more about the world and about the nature of reality. In this it is pointless to allow physical distances to confuse us, since within consciousness we can connect with matters that are enormously far away in distance and also in time.

In other words, as the universe expands, greater unification and ability to receive and transmit information are occurring at the same time. This happens because along with growing expansion, a growing subtlety is also taking place, so that the ever-subtler nature of matter and energy becomes apparent. As you progress, a similar phenomenon takes place in your own bodies (in the physical body and the subtle bodies), in your consciousness, etc.

Consciousness is the key to these processes of expansion. I may be in sympathy with the idea of rising to the fifth dimension (or was it the sixth?), but if we imagine that this will happen without raising the level of human consciousness, without conscious spiritual progress, at the expense of learning the Universal Laws, then we are rather doing a disservice to the cause. **Progress is not a free drug**, which requires nothing more than the end of the Mayan calendar or of some other planetary or galactic cycle. Matters are truly in our own hands, as I already mentioned toward the beginning of my book. Besides, the future is in a constant state of change, which we influence with our daily actions.[111]

Progress Is the Most Important Product of The Processes

On the individual level the cosmic Law of Progress may have more profound and powerful consequences than any other lawfulness. What is in question is a coordinating law in relation to how the other cosmic principles come into your life and influence it. The lawfulness of progress is the most important "product" of the process. You can notice over and over again how you must confront the matters that you need to work on with patience and constancy, in accordance with the Law of Progress. Those matters may influence your entire life, and as you work on them, you may at the same time find some joy, gain some understanding and expand your consciousness. You may even laugh at those challenges as you understand the Law of Progress ever better. You will then find a smile and some humor at the core of progress, and you will no longer need to fight against reality with gritted teeth.[112]

Resisting progress is in direct ways connected with many health problems. This is also true of the other cosmic principles: if you re-

---

111 As for myself, I am leery of texts that give precise time limits, dates etc. to the progress of humankind. The Masters themselves do not do this, even though they have at their disposal a mighty cosmic-level technology.
112 I remind you again that humor is an integral part of spiritual progress.

sist them, you do it at the price of your own health. Most degenerative diseases are strongly connected precisely with resisting progress. A state of deterioration such as this, as well as the decomposition of biological materials and the decay of radioactive materials, illustrates well a descending spiral, which finally has great significance in the natural order.

The process of degeneration also shows that a state of balance has great significance for the biosphere. The old must at times "die" in order for the new to be born. An important feature in connection with the Law of Progress is that we are happy to take on the energies appropriate to progress and to work with them in such a way that we go forward when it is profitable, but we go backward when that happens to be convenient. In this connection it is again good to remember that stagnation and lack of movement do not exist, it is an illusion.

The Law of Progress helps us to understand how to confront and to work with difficulties. This has become obvious and familiar through the law of resistance, tension (voltage), and current, i.e. Ohm's law, where tension = resistance x current. However, this is not a universal law, but rather a lawfulness of the three-dimensional world, which I already wrote about in connection with the Laws of Opposite Expression and of Karma, in chapters 2 and 3. In those connections we also considered the superconductive state, where resistance diminishes and potential grows.

In practical terms, it is better to learn to work with whatever life throws at you, and eventually to make it a part of your own being, rather than start to resist it. Using the principle of resistance to end some process, or to start up something, does not usually work or bring about the desired result. It is wise to welcome all things, to use them in an appropriate way, and to see what all can be accomplished with them.

Here in the world of matter we could also attach to the Law of Progress the motto of the American General Electric Corporation: Progress is our most important product. We can find a deeper meaning even in advertising slogans like this. When we work with the law of resistance, we can see that it leads to progress. This formula, where the voltage equals the resistance multiplied by the current, can be understood without having to test it in all places and situations. In other words, we can make observations in the world. With the help of such observations and insights you can see that there is a constant movement toward tension, resistance, and current, or away from them. In its own way, this expresses how progress takes place: with the help of **movement.**

From Doing and Having to Being

In connection with the possibilities of the Law of Progress it is important to see the possibilities beneath the surface, since new psychological techniques, new ways of handling information, and new methods of understanding yourself and human life are arising, as the science and the psychological understanding of humanity are combined with spiritual wisdom and with the best ideas of the past. This is happening all the time in science, especially in its avant-garde circles, even though the "officials" of science often attempt to impede progress. But these wheels of progress can no longer be stopped.

The natural evolutionary journey of human life is from being to doing and from doing to having.[113] However, it has often been noted that as being gives way to doing and having, people usually have a tendency to place these in the wrong order, and in many ways to understand the nature of the process incorrectly.

Being always precedes *doing,* and *doing* precedes *having.* Subsequently the cycle returns to its beginning and starts over. When you examine some situation or phase of your own life where having played an important role, you can usually see that many things had already happened before that. Some of them may have been very subtle, perhaps even unconscious, but in any case they were very important to you.

---

113   To be - to do - to have –cycle.

If you nevertheless can refrain from doing and having, and remain in a state of being, you can note with interest how doing and having can be shared with others. It is precisely this state of being that the great saints and other masters have drawn on and from which they have shared with others. By remaining in a state of being, a state of conscious presence, they have delegated doing and having without any detailed instructions. It is as if energy itself had been transferred. What is in question is a very beautiful way of creating things in life, since it does not need any specific course.

You can try this out in your own life. Concentrate on your own being and allow the energy of your core nature to flow through yourself. This is not a static process, but rather the source of inspiration, from which the outbreath of being and the inbreath of doing begin. So if you want to use the outbreath to create for yourself progress in the direction of an expanding spiral, concentrate on being, which is always the core and the source of the process, the way in which it is initiated.

Begin Wisely – Things Proceed as They Began

Here we come to an important corollary of the Law of Progress, the idea that as things have begun, so they tend to continue. If, in the being-phase, you neglect something of the core of your being, of the higher integration of your own nature, you may have initiated a very problematic cycle. The resistances and rejections that you have created – ones that are directed at the core of your own being – will turn you back to the place where you began, and you will have to reconsider your motivations, your understanding, and your consciousness in relation to the matter.

In this way the trinity of being, doing and having will in any case be initiated, even if you were to turn the process backwards and concentrated only on doing or having, possessing. When you understand the course of this process better, it will bring you ever-greater peace at the same time that you are active. You can accomplish more, and you will feel good about it.

When you are more directed toward concrete doing and having, try at the same time to be deeply conscious of the meaning of being. **When you know who and what you are, your doing will at the same time become expansions of your being**. They will contain your loving side and your enthusiastic nature. You will see that the things that you accomplish as a result of the process are useful and practical.

What is then in question is something much greater than simply being conscious of the cycle of being, doing and having. It is admitting that constant progress and change exists, and that this change is in direct relationship with your willingness to allow things to flow in your life. This makes it possible for you to understand in your own life the nature of the Law of Progress, not only intellectually, but also experientially.

Here you can also examine phenomena of matter and the physical world. These physical phenomena are directly connected with the law of inertia, which could also be called the lawfulness of the resistance of matter. In this connection we can observe that what is at rest tends to remain at rest, and what is in movement tends to remain in movement. As you have begun some process, so it tends to continue.

A Vision of Evolution

Inertia also affects humanity strongly, as well as affecting how we can change the direction of evolution in matters that include negative and destructive factors. Here we can call on our own spiritual capacity to create positive visions even without going into the details or understanding them perfectly.

What will the world be like in 100 years? Create a vision of a world where there will be far fewer pollutants, where people will have more opportunities to connect with the animal kingdom, where dwellings will be more beautiful, where there is more food and other resources, and where everyone can pursue his own goals and evolution.

A vision like this can bring with it an opening of the heart, love, and also encouragement for all of humanity. With a vision like this we can see that an outcome like this is possible, that people can accept it as their goal and begin to work toward it. Then we can welcome evolution and expansion. This is what the collective consciousness of humanity wishes for; advances in the direction of evolution.

Therefore the delays of the physical level need to be taken into consideration as you work to further some project, work on a human relationship or work with other people. But on the subtler levels you have often gotten the idea or begun the process with inspiration received from your guides, even if you were not fully conscious of the fact. Therefore, if you meet with some problems or dead ends with your project it is good to remember that there are always more solutions than you had ever thought possible, as long as you are willing to apply the Law of Help and to ask your guides for assistance. It is their duty to help you. The next time life throws a challenge at you, you might ask: **What good will come of this** or what possibilities are hidden in this situation? These are the sensitive moments where important decisions are made.

The Law of Progress is actually more dependent on the other lawfulnesses than any other lawfulness. It coordinates the Law of Manifestation that governs beingness. But what happens after being? Always something more: doing, getting, studying, playing with things, and all the other things that come forth along with natural growth and evolution.

Your inner understanding of how the Law of Progress works is very important. The ancient Chinese principle of *Wu Wei*, the principle of "emptiness" or "action without doing", which is central to Taoism, is good to take into consideration: ride the horse in the direction that it is going. When you have learned to understand your horse and its direction, changes become much simpler.

Life demands the support of your consciousness in many ways in understanding the laws and yourself. This is in harmony with the Laws of Permanence and Manifestation, since as you strive to know yourself and to work with the energies you have manifested, you are at the same time expanding your consciousness, and in this conscious examination of the various laws you are guaranteed to get to know yourself.

Meditation on the "To Be – To Do – To Have" –Cycle

The Law of Progress can be approached from many different points of view, for example intellectually. In this meditation we will make a bold leap to the other side of the intellect. Relax your body again and calm your mind. Visualize around you a beautiful pure emerald green cylinder of light, which reaches down into the bowels of the earth as well as into the heights of heaven. For a moment breathe this protective, strengthening light energy into yourself.

Then just be. BE. For a moment imagine that some symbol connected with simply being is deep within you. For example visualizing bright sunshine may help you to feel your own being. What it feels like to just be. Just to be.

Draw into yourself sunshine that makes the whole room radiant, it warms your entire physical body with its radiance. It feels really good. Now just be in this light, breathe it in and feel its warmth.

Now you gradually begin to feel that there is something to do. It might be something very simple. Ask to be shown what you should do in the light. Let it be something simple, for example use this light to better hear or to understand this process or to bring energy into your body so it could be more alert and receptive.

As doing strengthens in you, maintain your being as well, and then unite it with your doing. Do not abandon being, but rather see it as the energy of sunlight, which activates you. See also how the light activates the things that you are now working with. As your thoughts become clear and you understand how to apply them in practice, see also how they are directly connected with your being and with the light.

A human being forgets too easily the principle of being and turns his back on it. As you understand these thoughts, return to the source deep within you and to the light. Let all other thoughts glide away, breathe this light and ask yourself, "What is this light?"

Now that you have had a small glimpse of doing and having, it is easier to understand the light within you, which is stronger than the Sun. It is a part of yourself, of the energy of your being, of your connection with the Earth – any one of these will do as an answer to your question. Some of the answers you get are not verbal when you are in this light. They are a consciousness that you are, that you exist. The "I Am"-principle is very beautiful and important to you.

Be in the light and smile.

You can find many of the things connected with the cosmic Law of Progress in previous chapters, and there is no need to repeat them here. In order for us to progress to the level of our possibilities, from our characteristics, we especially need patience.[114] It is not much appreciated in the modern world, where things must be accomplished as fast as possible. Our character, our greatest work of art within us, changes quite slowly. However, it is surely worthwhile to invest in refining it, since we have brought our character with us from previous lives, and we will also take it with us into future lives.

There is both permanence and progress in character, and it is the true indicator of our growth.[115] Indeed, the character measures each person. An old proverb says that our character is our destiny. There is much truth in this. Studying and applying the spiritual laws is a great help in the science and art of refining your character.

Summary

✳ Change is the only constant in life.

✳ We are on an evolutionary spiral, and we either progress upward or regress downward.

---

114 On the Spiritual Path, as well as in many mundane projects, the last ten percent or so of the task is often the most tedious. Patience helps to bring things to a conclusion.
115 The Finnish poet V. A. Koskenniemi has written in some context that character is the greatest multiplier of human talents. I could not agree with him more.

* Whatever life throws at you, make it a part of your being. Flow with it rather than resist it.

* Welcome the energies of change and use them in an appropriate way.

* Note the cycle of being, doing and having; it always conforms to this order.

* Change is directly related to your willingness to let things flow in your life.

* As something has begun, so it tends to continue.

* Understanding and applying the Law of Progress in your personal life causes more profound and more powerful changes than any other single cosmic lawfulness.

* If you apply the Law of Progress together with love, you will have positive, practical effects.

* You will have the maximum benefit if you apply the laws in coordination with each other.

* The Universal Laws do not order you to do things or to remain as you are, they are rather God's way of expressing his own nature to you. They are also the core of your own being.

Literature:
Hilarion 1982: *Vision*. Marcus Books, Queensville, Ontario.
Hilarion 1992: *The Master Plan*. Marcus Books, Queensville, Ontario.
Lehtiranta, Erkki 2004: *Musiikin korkeammat oktaavit*. Dialogic, Helsinki.

12.

Love

"The pain that you have suffered
is the love you have not offered."

- Wisdom of the Pleiades

THROUGH LOVE WE HEAR the heartbeats of the universe. It is said in the Bible that God is Love. Love elevates and transforms everything that it meets, and it is also the gate to the higher worlds. Also, the Law of Love has given a kind of background music to the long pilgrimage of humanity through the millennia, through the various cultural periods and through the tides of history. The Law of Love is the only "emotional" law in the most comprehensive, cosmic meaning of the word, and even just for that, deserves special attention. What is in question is the cosmic law that we have come to this planet to study and to express. That has not always been easy, as every one of us can understand. After all, love is the strongest emotion that we experience in our lives.

Few things have been so misunderstood among humanity in its evolutionary history, as love, even though we talk about it, write about it, and sing about it so much. Many people think that love is a madness, a blindness, an alternating current of feelings, and the tingle of erotic emotions that a new love relationship brings on. Or that love equals the desires of the physical or the emotional body, and their satisfaction. Or the name of love is given to something that in reality is duty or loyalty or commercial goods. One of the typical spiritual illusions of our time is the idea that sex equals love. To be sure, they have something to do with each other, but by no means always or in every case.

In its true form, love is none of these things. Real love is not made up of emotions as changeable as spring winds, it is as stable as the Sun or the Gulf Stream. It is the sustainer of life, which gives warmth, and like the Sun, it shines on everyone, "the good and the evil", as the Bible has it. Real love is also not blind as the pop songs tell us, but rather, only unconditional, true love makes us able to see.

Love – The Cosmic Glue

There are many definitions of love, and here is one of them: love IS. It is so good that "there are no words for it". When it exists in our lives in its true and complete form, time becomes eternity. Most people know from their own experience the difference in our consciousness when we are deeply in love, compared to when we are going to the dentist for a root canal.

The level of our consciousness changes at the same time. All experience is connected to consciousness. Father Anthony de Mello writes in his wonderful book *One Minute Nonsense:* "If God is love, then the distance between you and God is exactly the same as the distance between you and your consciousness of yourself."[116]

Seen from a higher point of view, love is literally **the glue that holds the universe together.** For love – which for example Christ felt and feels – is the real cause of the manifestation of the created worlds, of the different levels and areas of reality. It was precisely for this love that God created All That Is, and with this same love He beholds all his creatures. All comes from the same Source.[117]

---

116 de Mello, *One Minute Nonsense.*
117 Hilarion, *Vision*, p. 25.

When you learn to let this divine love fill your own being, you succeed in your ultimate task, that is, in expressing God's Love on the human level in this world of resistant matter. You are humanity in miniature. You matter. Your relationship with your fellow humans tells us something profound about your relationship to God. A loving relationship with yourself, or its lack, for its part tells us something about the sum total of rejecting or accepting love in your own life. You have actually countless good reasons to love and accept yourself, and it is also very important to accept love from others. You are a part of divinity, nothing less! You are valuable just as you are.[118] Are **you** able to accept love?

Love is energy that flows into us constantly as vibration. All beings and things in the universe share this vibration, which always flows through you in all directions and in all ways. This energy is made up of many parts, which have yet to be named, defined, or understood. Love is for us in many respects still an energy of unused possibilities. This is also the core nature of the vibrations of matter itself. When love flows through you, you change it in some way – and it changes you in some way. **In fact, love accelerates the movement of electrons around the atomic nucleus, and at the same time elevates the vibrational level of a human being.**[119]

Love is best weighed in practice and in ordinary life, through the small, or even the greater, deeds that we do every day in our own life environment. Once you start doing loving deeds, you find many paths that allow you to come closer to universal, all-encompassing love.[120]

Love can of course be discussed purely intellectually, as if from head to head. But love is rather the language of the heart, it is belonging, interrelating, forgiving – and being forgiven. "The heart knows better than a thousand books", I once wrote in one of my songs. No amount of intellect can compensate for a lack of love. The most efficient kill-

---

118 Maoshing Ni, M.D., gives excellent advice for loving yourself in his book *Secrets of Longevity*: every day, do at least one thing that helps you to love yourself more. Do something that makes you happy and remember to praise yourself regularly!

119 Starre, *The Diamond Light*, p. 39.

120 Ni, *Secrets of Longevity*.

ing machines created by man have been developed with intelligence that lacks love. You may stumble and feel lost in relation to love, but if your love is real and true, it will never attempt to harm its object.

Few people have understood love as profoundly as the Sufi mystic Rumi, who has written about the dynamics of love as follows in his book *Diwan e Shams*:

- Through love thorns become roses.
- Through love vinegar becomes sweet wine.
- Through love the stake becomes a throne.
- Through love the reverse of fortune seems good fortune.
- Through love a prison seems a rose bower.
- Through love a grate full of ashes seems a garden.
- Through love a burning fire is a pleasing light.
- Through love the Devil becomes a Houri.
- Through love the hard stone becomes soft as butter.
- Through love grief is joy.
- Through love ghouls turn into angels.
- Through love stings are as honey.
- Through love lions are harmless as mice.
- Through love sickness is health.
- Through love wrath is mercy.[121]

The Path of Love – The Choice of Humanity

Let us now perform a little time leap to the dawn of humanity. Humanity originated as a lifestream in the embrace of deep space eons ago. But the path and destiny chosen by humanity diverged from the choices and destinies of almost all other galactic races and civilizations. Where the other lifestreams decided to grow through developing mentally, the lifestream known as humanity took on a much more challenging task: to grow through love and in love.

---

121 See Dehlvi: *Sufism: The Heart of Islam*, p. 62.

The other galactic races had in fact rejected this route because it was considered so dangerous, and because the possibilities to go wrong were so great. There had been previous failures. But the Creator of Love welcomed humanity's collective decision (at that point we were something like individual cells in the body of a great being) with cosmic joy: a lifestream that is able to express the love aspect of God in all its glory, is at the same time able to bring out the side or characteristic of divinity without which the created world would be imperfect.[122]

The place that humanity obtained for its home was like Paradise: a blue planet whose surface was mostly water. Water is also the symbol of emotions, and of the most beautiful one – love. The amount of water was, and still is, a continuing reminder to humanity of its own decision to grow into its full galactic measure in love and from love. Thus, water is an important sign on humanity's path of pilgrimage toward divine love, and the wisdom that comes with it. Let us, then, allow the refreshing, healing waters of love flow in everything that we are, do, or seek.

However, we never reach this only and exclusively for ourselves. Through humanity's efforts, and through our evolution into full adulthood, our planet is becoming a kind of great **love generator**, whose purpose is to produce this infinitely important spiritual element for the needs of the entire galaxy. Humanity will show to the Milky Way Galaxy the beauty, the power, and the majesty of God's love. There is only one way to learn this: by teaching it to ourselves![123] Again, if you read these words with your heart, you can feel how they resonate with the deep streams of your being.

Only love, the love of people for each other, love for nature, for our planet, for all beings, love for the Creator, can save humanity. Neither our intellect, nor our money, nor our modern technology can do this. We must find a new path to love. Our conception and our

---

122 Hilarion, *Seasons of the Spirit*, pp. 12-14.
123 Hilarion, *More Answers*, p. 64.

understanding of love must change in some fresh, radical, and profound way. At the same time, we must purge the concept of love of all that is inessential, false, and unnecessary, that has been attached to it over the centuries and millennia. We must return to the gold standard of love.

It is high time for us – the real prodigal sons of humanity, our planet, and our galaxy – to find again the love and respect for the other natural kingdoms, such as the mineral, plant, and animal kingdoms. Many "undeveloped" peoples have known how to do this. Have you, for example, sent love to the trees in the forest? As incredible as it may seem, trees answer our love in a very beautiful way, as I myself have had an opportunity to experience many times. In Finland we have a saying: the forest answers in the same way as you shout into it. But in this case, we would rather speak to it with tenderness and love.

Exercise: Sending Love Energy

We can use our will and our creative imagination to send and to strengthen love energy between ourselves and a "difficult" person. This exercise is from Master Hilarion's inexhaustible exercise collection.

Sit comfortably in a peaceful place and calm your mind with some method that you have learned. When you have reached as calm and clear a state of mind as possible, visualize on the screen of your consciousness a clear and bright image of the face of some person that inspires great, deep and lasting love in you.

Then allow love to flow between the two of you from heart to heart. So that your heart might open even more to this wonderful loving interrelationship, think of some characteristic in your friend that particularly warms your heart. See your friend at his best, radiant, beautiful, full of vitality, youthful, etc.

The purpose is to get the stream of love to flow as freely as possible between your friend and yourself. Explore what this wonderful flow feels like, and where you feel it. Then remove the image of your friend from your consciousness, and at the same time imagine yourself turning off the current.

After a moment, start again, and notice how love begins to flow again, perhaps even more easily and faster than the first time. Repeat this on/off switch at least ten times, and you will notice that it is possible for you to learn how to turn on the love flow **with the will.**

Next, raise on the screen of your consciousness the image of a person that you only like somewhat. Now, when you try the same process that you visualized with your dear friend, you may notice that the love energies flow less easily at first.

Perhaps your heart center is a little more closed in this case. But you can, with your will power, strengthen the flow of love again, and feel the same warmth and love for this person that you felt a moment ago for your dear friend.

If you like – and if it is difficult to reach the same kind of love vibration – you can from time to time bring back into your mind your dear friend's face and strengthen the flow in this way. You will come to see that through your will and your determination, you are able to feel exactly the same kind of love for both people.

Then, when you have learned to control and to direct your love energies well enough, you can next choose from your life's portrait gallery someone for whom you feel little in the way of either positive or negative emotions. This might for example be some chance acquaintance from your work place, or from some other mundane situation.

Make the image of this person equally bright and clear in front of your inner gaze, and again try to reach the same kind of strong, intense, and pure love that you felt for your dear friend. If this is difficult, you can again bring your dear friend's image onto the screen and feel how easily love flows between you. Then again exchange the "neutral" person for him. After practicing for some time, you will notice that you can feel the same intense love for this person also, if you so wish.

Then comes the real challenge, as you no doubt have already realized. Change the image of your chance acquaintance for the image of a person that in some way has the role of an "enemy", a rival, or an adversary in your life. Perhaps you feel that he wishes you harm or tries to trip you up in this phenomenon called life.

What is in question here is a great test, which accurately measures your ability to bend your love nature to your will. For, if you are able to channel an unobstructed flow of love even to this person, you will have learned the most important ability that it is possible for you to gain: the ability to send love to any person or any thing, **if** only you so will! If you **will**. With this ability you will have a direct connection and will be able to send love to your enemy.

It is worth your while to practice this ability to send love energy consciously by visualizing, and with the help of your will power, when situations arise where you feel a desire to speak or think negatively about some person. In this, also, practice makes perfect.

The Purifying Streams of Forgiveness

Christ exhorted us to love our enemies. Immense wisdom, and also great opportunity, is contained in this. When we learn to open our hearts to a person that we previously considered our enemy and adversary, we at the same time find the ultimate key that lets us escape the wheel of *samsara*, of reincarnation, of the necessary return to the chain of physical lives on our planet Earth. It is actually impossible for hatred, jealousy, fear, resentment, or other negative emotions to reign together with authentic love. **Love smooths out conflicts and is also the most beautiful and the most important thing in us.** It is being and living in the pure vibrations of the heart.

It is worthwhile to remember the unbreakable law that if you die in this incarnation while feeling the slightest amount of resentment or dislike toward even a single other soul, you will have to return to the physical plane to meet that person. At that time the same old conflicts and resentments will again arise – so that they could now finally be confronted and conquered. Love – and only love – can conquer these old enmities.

Universal Laws and Spiritual Progress

We can make a choice here: either we learn this quickly and go forward consciously, with the help of our will and our love, to neutralize our human relationships that are still in a negative state, or else we can put off this lesson of neutralizing negativity till later. But that would be as silly as moving masses of snow forward with a plough, rather than pushing them to one side, where they belong.

An essential part of the process is forgiving yourself as well as others. When a person allows forgiveness to penetrate deeper into his own consciousness, the principle of manifestation begins to arise. It helps him to accept with natural ease the parts of life that support and love him. At the same time there may be an opening of the immense energy reserves of our own breath, which may have been blocked, perhaps for numerous lifetimes.

The 2010 decade has potentially been a decade of forgiveness, as I have written in my Finnish book on astrological cycles.[124] Indeed, forgiveness opens the gates to the higher evolution of humanity and to the Age of Aquarius. It is good to remember, in this connection, that in the final analysis, forgiveness operates on an on/off principle: either you have forgiven 100%, or you have not really forgiven at all. Therefore, there is no point in bargaining with forgiveness – like love, it is not a commercial good, but rather a realization born with the help of love and will.

Actually, these matters of loving and forgiving are the most central lessons for travelers on the spiritual Path. It is not wise to put them off and slow ourselves down on our future path, not even for comfort's sake. The lessons brought by experience in relation to the Law of Love, as well as to the other Universal Laws, are extremely valuable, because they illuminate the laws in a way that is useful in real life.

When it comes to the Law of Love, there is often a difficulty here, which could be resolved by uniting the mind and the heart. Finding the **heartmind** in every area of life usually means letting go of the past and the future, and focusing **just now** on the present moment, and on

---

124 Lehtiranta & Stenberg, *Astrologiset syklit ja elämänhallinta*, p. 234.

your own breath, exactly as if you were allowing your heart and your mind to melt together pleasantly and naturally. You then allow answers and new possibilities to come into your life, and you see energies, and everything else, in a new way. That brings light to the heart.

The Symbols of Love in the Human Body

There are interesting connections with love in esoteric human anatomy and in human physiology.[125] In various cultures, the heart and the circulatory system have classically been connected with the emotions, and specifically with love. It is not difficult for a student of the secret wisdom to understand that the problems that arise in the sphere of the heart and the circulatory system always hint, in one way or another, of the individual's inability to express and to feel love in daily life.

Let us take a couple of illuminating examples here. High blood pressure usually indicates that the individual's love nature is undeveloped, and that he has attempted to limit or to reserve his love for only a few objects. When the love energies are blocked in this way, it is clear that the pressure to express them grows, and eventually something must happen to let the pressure release. It is good to take note of the wisdom of the body: as in the inner, so in the outer. Where health problems are concerned, it is always worthwhile to keep in mind the relationship of the outer to the inner. This usually brings up at least the Law of Reflection and the Law of Karma, and in connection with the heart, the Law of Love.

Arrhythmia suggests a capricious love nature; anemia, that is, an inadequate number of red blood cells in the blood, suggests the individual's inability or unwillingness to use his God-given talents and gifts in a wholehearted way in deeds of love, in helping and serving his fellow man. Arteriosclerosis symbolizes a hardening of the emotional part of the person, which often takes place with advancing age. The young are usually able to keep some emotional channel open, which

---

125 Hilarion, *Body Signs*, pp. 31-34.

protects them from this problem. Of course such things as diet and life style have a part to play in these health problems, but we should not forget that there are even more important causes behind them.[126]

The heart is reflected in for example the lips, the left eye, and the nails of the index fingers, so you can gain additional understanding of this subtle equation between the Law of Love and the Law of Reflection. The heart is also reflected in the arms, as is well known in connection with many heart problems. But the arms and hands can be used to do much good by helping one's fellow man, or for example the natural environment.

The connection of the heart with the heart chakra is direct. An opening of the heart center accelerates deep consciousness, and an understanding, of all the Universal Laws in a grounded way. In general, the chakras are a kind of **windows of the soul**, through which our Higher Self energizes us.[127] An open heart chakra can easily receive the love energies which come from a higher level, and which also strengthen the physical heart and the circulation at the same time.

The heart has its own inner intelligence, which always strives for coherence, unification and consistency. Understanding coherence is one of the central keys to understanding the true nature of the Law of Love, which extends beyond the verbal and intellectual level. The heart also has its own electromagnetic field and power, which is considerably greater than the field of the brain, and which extends far beyond the physical body. For example, the research results of The Institute of HeartMath in California are both perplexing and encouraging.

The spine is one of the central anatomical structures of our body, and each of its vertebrae has its own spiritual symbolism. The Law of Symbols, the Law of Reflection, and the Law of Love meet at the four lower thoracic (T-7 – T-10) vertebrae. These vertebrae are purely and

---

126 Hilarion, *Body Signs*, pp. 31-34.
127 Of the central energy centers only the root chakra at the base of the spine receives its energy from Mother Earth. In the case of all the other chakras, we are in an energetic interrelationship with our higher Self. Open and bright centers tell us that this interchange of energy is going well. The openness and brightness of the chakras is also in direct relationship with our health and our well-being. Hilarion, *Seasons of the Spirit*, pp. 66-67.

simply connected with love. Everyone who has a problem with these vertebrae – whether minor or major – must ask himself whether he allows pure love to flow from his heart center without any thought of sexuality, physical pleasure, or conditionality.

It is important to understand this. Nowadays too many people think they love, while in fact their experience is at bottom based on the desire body and the tendencies of the physical body. This is why many people give the name of love to what is merely physical infatuation. I already wrote about this in the beginning of the chapter.

Love does not desire, it simply loves. Love does not always seek the company of the beloved, but rather seeks the happiness of the beloved. Love is not conditional, nor does it expect anything in return. Love does not expect to be reciprocated with an emotion of loyalty or affection, it only sends out loving rays, knowing that all love eventually returns to the Source of All, God.[128]

Anyone who is unable to create this feeling of unconditional love, may notice that one of the vertebrae in question is somehow imperfect, or has health problems, it is out of alignment, or simply causes back aches.[129] Body therapists report that many back problems are found precisely in the area of these vertebrae.

Cleansing the Emotional Body with Love

Cleansing the blood is important for people who start on the spiritual Path. It is very difficult to reach emotional purity if the blood is polluted by poisons and other refuse. A positive life – especially a wholesome and unblocked emotional life – cleanses the blood effectively of its negative prana vibrations.

A slightly more esoteric connection between the symbolism of the body and love is found in the human emotional body (the astral body, as it has sometimes been called, a bit misleadingly.) The emotional

---

128 Hilarion, *Body Signs*, p. 41.
129 Hilarion, *Body Signs*, p. 41.

Universal Laws and Spiritual Progress

body is in every cell identical with the physical body, but it is made up of a subtler material, the substance of the emotional level.

The emotional body corresponds to the emotional nature of humans. This subtle body is actually the seat of all emotions, which feeds itself with emotions. All a person's emotions are born in this body and it is the first one to be affected by them. The effect on the physical body follows later.

Understanding this mechanism is crucially important because the emotions that are allowed in Earth life have an immense effect on the structure, the integrity, and the "health" of a person's emotional body.

When an individual dies on the physical level, he only leaves his physical vehicle, while his conscious ego-personality moves into the emotional body. If the person has allowed himself to experience and express many negative emotions during his Earth life, his emotional body is deformed – it may even lack some parts.

There is only one emotion that clearly brings health to the emotional body – love. It does not necessarily have to be cosmic or Christ-love. The manifestation of any emotion based on love, such as affection, kindness, tenderness, or similar emotions, produces very positive effects on our emotional body.[130]

Negative emotions of course have their own physiological effects on the physical body, as we already observed in connection with some typical disorders of the heart and the circulatory system. However, there are even deeper and more esoteric dimensions to the matter. For example, if a person feeds himself mainly with hatred, resentment, jealousy, and similar emotions (according to Hilarion, this situation pertains to approximately 95% of humanity at this time), the negative effects are initially focused on the systems and the internal organs of the emotional body.

The principal damage is to the stomach of the emotional body.[131] When the emotional body, which is nourished by emotions, is con-

---

130 Hilarion, *Other Kingdoms*, pp. 6-7.
131 Hilarion, *Body Signs*, p. 26.

stantly given only negative, destructive nutrients, the stomach of that emotional body may eventually completely refuse to function – it can no longer process the food it is given. The analogy to the physical stomach and physical nutrients should be obvious.

After a time the negative effects then migrate to the physical body. According to Hilarion, it usually takes a change in the emotional state about nine months before the effects are visible in the corresponding organs of the physical body. The emotional body is comparable to a person's ability to produce, store, and express a large amount of heat energy. The emotional body is precisely the stored energy supply that is symbolized by for example the high specific heat of water. But **the only emotion that warms the emotional body is love.** Most people have noticed that profound love experiences give you a warm feeling and bring a pleasant sense of opening and love to the heart area.

All negative emotions (hatred, fear, self-pity, guilt, etc.) only chill and weaken the emotional body. Therefore people who feed themselves with negative emotions usually have less energy and drive than those who are able to express positive emotional states like love, friendship, affection, and so on. In this way the emotional body can directly nourish the physical body with its own love energy, particularly where endurance, drive etc. are concerned. And in fact it must do so, if the person is to express fully all of his possibilities and positive abilities.[132]

The Powerful Symbolism of Gold

Gold is a wonderful symbol of love, and there are many interesting examples of the connection of love to gold. One of these is **the incarnation of children of the golden ray**, which is currently taking place around the world. It behooves all of us to know what kind of beings of light have just been born or are about to be born, especially into the families of seekers on the spiritual Path. More liberal ideas, a heightened consciousness, and the activation of new rays, have re-

132 Hilarion, *Symbols*, p. 13.

sulted in the gradual adjustment and transformation of former rules and doctrines. The truths of today are the half-truths of tomorrow. The rays as such represent new forms of energy, new potential, and people of the golden ray are bringing an entirely new understanding of love to our planet.

The golden ray is thus bringing new, different characteristics to humanity. They are especially connected with new ways of loving that have previously not been understood. This is particularly connected with group consciousness and the ability of a group to know itself – and to love. The time has ripened for an energy that allows an individual a stronger connection with the collective consciousness than has ever previously been known on this planet. People are simply able to know the correct way to proceed in various matters.

The energies of the golden ray are in some ways reminiscent of the energy of the pink ray, and also of the energies of other warm rays that people are working with. But the golden ray enlivens the group, more so than the individual. This is particularly true in the Scandinavian countries, where much hard work has been done during the past millennium, for the cause of understanding groups and group work.

Astrologically the golden ray is strongly connected with the energies of the Sun, which is easy to understand. It is good to tell these children, already at a very young age, about gold and the golden light. It has a similar effect on these children as does for example ringing a bell. It catches their attention suddenly, and they listen.

The golden ray has powerful symbolic messages for our time. Gold is the most noble of the metals, but the so-called **golden rule** ("do unto others as you would have them do unto you") is also a most powerful energy, and the children of the golden ray are conscious of this. They are not yet able to put this into words, but they will do so as they grow into adults. When you talk with them about these things, you will be surprised to see how it touches some sensitive place in their being. It can even bring about a transformation.

The children of the golden ray have come here to teach us, among other things, how the powerful energy of that golden rule can at last be anchored on our planet. Opening up this understanding has been the goal of various religions for centuries, but in spite of that, people still do to each other what they would by no means want to have done to themselves. It is as if the golden rule applied to others, but not to themselves. This is going to change!

The price of gold has climbed to peak values in the past few years. This is no accident, but rather what is in question is a message from the collective consciousness that gold has more value than has been appreciated. What is in question is not commercial value but symbolic value. *Love over money* might be a fitting saying to describe this value.

We are going to notice that among the children born in the coming months and the next few years, some represent the so-called rainbow ray, others the golden ray. A majority of these children of the golden ray will be girls, because they are more willing than boys to ask for directions when they come to a crossroads of life; this is not as easy for boys or men. When these girls ask for directions, the collective consciousness is ready to give them advice. At that point the universal Law of Help – at this time perhaps the most misunderstood of all the Universal Laws – will be activated.

Children of the golden ray are especially sensitive to noise, to ultrasound, to movement, to all kinds of things that were previously not thought to have any particular effect. For example a fetus may even react to the food the mother eats during pregnancy. Sometimes the reaction may prompt the mother to leave a certain food out of her diet.

It is good for a mother to send the child positive, useful vibrations, especially during pregnancy. This has a good effect on both. It is good for the mother to think about everything that is highest and best in humanity, love, care, etc. It is beneficial for the child, as well as for the mother, for example, when going for ultrasound examinations, and after them. Golden energy can be visualized through the imagination as a healing ball of light which is directed through the hands into the fetus. The energy of golden light has recently become stronger and clearer than ever before, and it is good to send it to animals and plants as well.

Because more and more golden children are being born, we suggest that some strong, protective energies should be used before and after ultrasound examinations. These could be for example the healing golden light mentioned above, or a combination of the inert gases argon and krypton. Immediately after the ultrasound imaging, it would be good to listen to, for example, ocean waves or any moving waves that could be visualized as traveling through the mother's body. Even just producing waves in a bath would be adequate for this. This clears the body of any toxins that have accumulated in it through the ultrasounds. Ultrasound produces a sequence that can damage a golden ray child's connection to the collective consciousness.

Many of the children born these days are so-called old souls, who have had intensive training between physical incarnations. For many souls, this time is spent only in digesting the experiences of the previous life. On the other hand, an evolved individual seeks out the teachings that are available on the spiritual level, which enhances his capacities in the next Earth life. Raising these so-called old souls from childhood to the threshold of adulthood is a challenging and valuable thing, and it is important for expectant mothers to gain a better connection with their unborn child, for example through symbols – gold is a wonderful example here. These children have been careful in choosing their own parents, with whom they often have a karmic tie. **Gold balances this karma**, and gold used as a vibrational remedy helps in this process.

Summary

✳ Humanity has come onto this planet expressly in order to study and to express the universal Law of Love. We chose love as our lesson.

✳ Love is God's loving energy, care, and understanding.

✳ Love is the energy of potentiality.

✳ Love heals.

✳ Love energy has many parts that are yet to be named, defined, or understood.

✳ Love is vibrational glue, which concretely holds the universe together.

✳ In the end, only love is able to save humanity from its self-inflicted problems.

✳ Knowing universal love is in direct relationship to free will.

✳ The symbolism of love is strongly present in the human body.

✳ Opening the heart center greatly speeds up a profound consciousness and understanding of all the Universal Laws on a practical level.

✳ Cleansing your emotional life and your blood is one of the central lessons on the Path of a spiritual seeker.

✳ Gold has a strong symbolic connection with love.

✳ Children of the golden ray anchor a new kind of understanding of love on our planet.

✳ Love is the best and the highest in us.

✳ Love increases the speed of electrons around the atom, and thus raises our vibrational level.

✳ Love is the high call and destiny of humanity.

Literature:

Charlton, Hilda 1989: *Master Hilarion*. Golden Quest, Woodstock, New York.
Dehlvi, Sadia 2009: *Sufism: The Heart of Islam*. HarperCollins Publishers India, Noida.
Gurudas 1985: *Gem Elixirs and Vibrational Healing, Vol. I*. Cassandra Press, San Rafael, California.
Gurudas 1986: *Gem Elixirs and Vibrational Healing, Vol. II*. Cassandra Press, San Rafael, California.
Hilarion 1979: *Seasons of the Spirit*. Marcus Books, Queensville, Ontario.
Hilarion 1980: *Symbols*. Marcus Books, Queensville, Ontario.
Hilarion 1982: *Vision*. Marcus Books, Queensville, Ontario.
Hilarion 1982: *Body Signs*. Marcus Books, Queensville, Ontario.
Hilarion 1985: *More Answers*. Marcus Books, Queensville, Ontario.
De Mello, Anthony 1986: *One Minute Nonsense*. Doubleday, New York.
Lehtiranta, Erkki & Stenberg, Sven 2010: *Astrologiset syklit ja elämänhallinta*. Smiling Stars, Helsinki.
Ni, Maoshing 2006: *Secrets of Longevity*. Chronicle Books, San Francisco.
Starre, Violet 2000: *The Diamond Light* (Djwahl Khul channeled through Violet Starre). Light Technology Publishing, Flagstaff, Arizona.

Epilogue

Steps on the Diamond Path of Reality

This book tells about universal principles, but equally about You, my dear reader, and about me. The basic questions are: How do we meet these Laws in our daily lives and in more solemn moments, how can we ease our journey by following them, how do we learn to live in such a way that we do not break the eternal rules of life? In the previous pages I have attempted, with the help of Hilarion, to answer these questions in many ways. We people are often very different, so I have consciously tried to present different points of view and consideration.

What do you take with you from here, is one of the fundamental questions that we should remember to ask, preferably every week. If you take with you a good spiritual tool kit, which contains tested means for understanding the basic structures and requirements of reality, I believe you have made an excellent journey. The years and decades spent in the stresses of the physical level have not been thrown away in vain.

The English language has a couple of excellent sayings about taking your teachings into practice, living them as reality: *Practice what you preach* and *Walk your talk*. This is a fundamental matter in the spiritual sphere as well.

On our journey of pilgrimage we filter wisdom out of knowledge, we test the teachings we receive on the practical level, and we take with us only what has passed the acid test of practical use. From then on it is our permanent possession, and it will also help us in the challenges of our future lives.

In the preface I compared human life with the journey of fragile coal into strong clear diamond. On the diamond path of reality the most important thing is the journey, not the goal (though that may be very pleasant, too). The process is more important than the result, and what stays with you as experience is more important than the product. In the West we live in a culture of accomplishment, but have we forgotten a more fundamental thing, BEING? Being, especially being like a real human being, is a true art form, which demands being literate in the reading of reality, having an open mind and a warm heart.

I hope my book will help you in acquiring and working with these matters. May working with these universal lawfulnesses help you to strengthen the best and the highest in yourself, and may these Laws give you direction and guidance in your life. May the Powers of Good give you blessings, protection, guidance and inspiration on your journey!

OM – SHANTI – SHANTI – OM

Appendix A

Some Nations and Their Governing Universal Laws

The Law of Manifestation	Estonia
The Law of Reflection	USA
The Law of Karma	India, North Korea
The Law of Permanence	Australia, China, Portugal
The Law of Opposite Expression	Russia, Spain
The Law of Cycles	Many aboriginal nations/tribes, for example the Hopi
The Law of Thought	Canada, Denmark, Finland, Italy
The Law of Help	Tibet
The Law of Speech	France
The Law of Symbols	England, Japan
The Law of Progress	Germany, Greece, Holland
The Law of Love	Sweden

These governing laws of the nations are subject to change in the long run. For example, the governing law of the United States changed from the Law of Opposite Expression into the Law of Reflection about 35 years after the Civil War, whereas in Finland the Law of Karma was replaced by the Law of Thought as the governing law at the end of the World War II. At the moment Germany is in a period of transition from the Law of Progress into the Law of Love and in Portugal the governing law is changing from the Law of Permanence to the Law of Reflection.

The governing law always gives some distinct quality to a nation and can be combined with the governing rays and astrological information for a fuller picture.

Appendix B

Master Hilarion

From the most ancient times esoteric science has included writings and discourses on the great souls who have journeyed to the end of the human path of pilgrimage and graduated from this planetary school with the aid of their own endeavor, love, patience, and wisdom. Sometimes these great beings are called Masters of Wisdom and Daughters of Light. These high initiates belong to the Great White Brotherhood/Sisterhood, whose sacred duty it is to further the progress of humanity, as well as of other natural kingdoms, in the great divine plan that exists for our planet.

It is easier for us to understand the concept of spiritual Masters if we accept as underlying assumptions a couple of basic ideas that are commonly accepted in spiritual circles, that is, the doctrine of reincarnation and the law of cause and effect connected with it, and the idea of the path of spiritual progress and the refinement of character associated with it. Human life leads actually inevitably to this mastery when a person has worked through his negative karma, escaped the sphere of resistant matter and gravity, learned to govern his own powers and energies, and become a strong servant of humanity and finally its teacher. This is possible for all of us. The masters have said: "Where you are, we have been, and where we are, you someday will be."[133]

One of these great teachers of humanity is Master Hilarion, also known as Master H. His name is familiar to many students of esoteric knowledge. For example, Light on the Path, a book published in 1885 in England, which is small in size but great in significance, comes from Hilarion, who transmitted it telepathically to Mabel Collins.

It is said of Hilarion that he is the great Master, or Chohan, of the fifth ray, who channels the energies of this divine ray to our planet.

---

133 Charlton, *Master Hilarion*, p. 4.

The rays are the basic energies, or qualities, of the universe, which can also be seen as tools of creation and as expressions of the divine. The fifth ray – which is connected with the emerald green color – is the ray of concrete knowledge, of science, and of spiritual inquiry, whose influence is very strong at present on our planet. The breathtaking progress of science and technology is partly connected with the energies of this ray, and with the inspiration and teachings given by Master Hilarion.

Hilarion often uses the pronoun "we" when he speaks. This may of course be confusing to many, but it is good to understand that the Masters also work with and through their soul group, their students – or as is sometimes said – their ashram. Hilarion has told us that he has over 900 students in Finland, most of whom work in the field of technical knowledge. Among them are many engineers. Most of them are not aware of this connection in their conscious minds. There are also a few astrologers among these students.

The work usually takes place through inspiration and telepathy, and also during astral projection, outside of the physical body, at which time the student can receive teachings at higher frequencies when in one of his subtle bodies. This method of working has been familiar to many esoteric groups throughout the ages, and safe ways of leaving the body and working consciously on other levels of reality, is taught these days for example in Finland.

Some of the phases of Hilarion's life are obscure, but some are known. It is said that he was a scientist of the same name in the late period of Atlantis, and he has given knowledge of the two sides of the science of Atlantis, the day side and the night side, in many reliable channeled books. Hilarion also has many incarnations on Venus in lifestreams that are completely different from humanity. "Lifestream" is Hilarion's word for the galactic races.

Closer to our own age the best known incarnations of Hilarion are probably Plato and Paul the Apostle. Plato, or "the Athenian", as he is sometimes called, is of course one of the foundation pillars of western culture. At one time there flowed through him an immense energy of philosophical clarity and spiritual inspiration to the awakening Hellenistic culture – and through that to the entire western civilization.

Plato is also the person who, in two of his later writings, Kritias and Timaios, brought forth the vision of Atlantis, the high culture that was located in the area of the present Atlantic Ocean, and that belongs to the basic myths of the west.

The influence of the Apostle Paul can scarcely be overestimated. His significance to Christianity has been notable. It is interesting that Hilarion himself has commented on Paul's writings in his book The Letters of Paul (Triad Publishers, 1989), which gives a much deeper and more esoteric interpretation of the apostle's thought. The Apostle John is also often mentioned in connection with Hilarion.[134] Gurudas alludes in his books to John's group, through which much knowledge has flowed to humanity, concerning for example healing.

A very significant incarnation was the Neo-Platonist Iamblikhos (ca. 245-325), who lived in the area of Chaldea, and was a notable white magician. His "theurgy" has been studied in our time by among others Gregory Shaw in his book Iamblichus. Theurgy and the Soul (The Pennsylvania State University Press, 1995). There is a picture of the Master in the form of Iamblikhos on the cover of Hilda Charlton's book Master Hilarion (Golden Quest, 1989). Iamblikhos himself wrote a biography of Pythagoras, among other things. Other books available in English include On the Mysteries of the Egyptians, Chaldeans, and Assyrians (The Prometheus Trust, 1999) and The Exhortation to Philosophy (Phanes Press, 1988).

Master Hilarion's ashram is said to be located in the higher levels above the island of Crete. Many of his lives are connected to the sphere of the eastern Mediterranean, to Egypt as well as to the cultures of Greece and Chaldea. For example Saint Hilarion (291-371) is included in Hilarion's chain of incarnation. This hermit monk who lived in the area of the eastern Mediterranean was one of the greatest

---

134 What may be in question is a great individual's simultaneous incarnation in two or more bodies. Bertolucci's movie "The Little Buddha" tells of this possibility. We do not as yet have sufficient knowledge of the factors and principles connected with incarnation.

healers of his time, whose help was sought by many that came from far away. Hilarion's castle still exists in Cyprus.

In recent decades Hilarion has given much knowledge and wisdom through various channels. We already mentioned the classic, Light on the Path. In the beginning of the 20th century Hilarion worked a great deal through The Temple of the People, which was located in Halcyon, California. Teachings from that time have been collected in books published by that organization: Teachings of the Temple 1-3, Temple Messages, and Theogenesis. These books are still available.

Closer to our own time we can find several Hilarion channels. One of the most productive has been the Canadian businessman and raja-yogi Maurice B. Cooke, to whom Hilarion transmitted more than 15 books between the years 1979-1992. These books, published by Marcus Books, consider for example the nature of reality (The Nature of Reality), the secret history of humanity (Seasons of the Spirit), the possibilities of the new technology (Einstein Doesn't Work Here Anymore), the karmic characteristics of nations (Nations), spiritual astrology (Astrology Plus), esoteric anatomy and physiology (Body Signs), New Age communities and universal lawfulnesses (Vision), and the secret characteristics of edible flowers (Wildflowers).

The knowledge in these books is compact, often easy to understand, but never superficial. The true greatness and measure of the brilliant thoughts may only become clear after many years.

An important channel for Hilarion in the latter part of the 20th century has also been Helen Merrick Bond, pen-named Pensatia, through whom Hilarion has given about a dozen books. These works, published by The Euclid Publishing Company, are poetic, inspiring writings on the spiritual Path, its challenges and possibilities. A most moving book is Master H (1976), in which Hilarion tells of his own experiences and challenges on his journey toward spiritual mastery.

The Stone and Elixir (1970) describes the alchemy of the soul and the opening of soul consciousness on the spiritual Path, while The Inner Signature (1977) is a work on the inner signature of all extant things, which is written into the Akashic records. Pensatia's books are notes on out-of-body visits to higher levels of consciousness with the guidance of Master Hilarion. As such they are rare works in esoteric literature.

Since the 1980's one of the most prominent Hilarion-channels has been the Californian engineer and inventor Jon C. Fox, through whom there has flowed much channeled material. Because of his technical background and through his extremely clear channeling, Fox is perhaps the ideal channel for information that contains a great deal of technical material, some of it very detailed.

Among other things, Jon C. Fox has channeled a part of Gurudas' books Flower Essences and Vibrational Healing (Cassandra Press, 1989) and Gem Elixirs and Vibrational Healing, Vol. I & II. (Cassandra Press, 1985, 1986). The book The Spiritual Properties of Herbs has mainly come through him. However, perhaps the most massive book channeled through Fox is Rubenfeld and Smulkis' classic Starlight Elixir and Vibrational Healing (The C. W. Daniel Company Limited, 1992), where a gateway is opened into the history of the races, or lifestreams, that have lived and now live in various galaxies, and into the influence of these lifestreams on the destinies of humanity. The visions offered by this book are dazzling, cosmic in many senses of the word. I consider this one of the most significant works of our time in the sphere of literature that is connected with spirituality.

In this book Hilarion also guides us into the use of starlight elixirs. What is in question is perhaps the area of vibrational healing with the highest vibration, since these elixirs are connected with the consciousness of the stars themselves, and with the consciousness of the evolved galactic races, or lifestreams, that live in the planetary systems of the stars. Many of these races are dizzyingly far ahead of the current phase of humanity in their evolution.

According to Hilarion it is partly explained by the fact that these civilizations have chosen a different path of progress, the path of intellectual and mental evolution, while humanity long ago chose the path of progress through emotion and love, which, in the galactic and cosmic point of view, has been considered a particularly difficult and risky route of evolution. I have written about this choice in connection with the universal Law of Love in chapter 12. In some sense humanity is a kind of experiment, which, if it succeeds, can produce a great deal of light and love energy for the needs of the galaxy. It is also a much-desired experiment, as Hilarion has told us in Rubenfeld and Smulkis' book.

At the end of this short introduction I wish to borrow some of Hilarion's own words from this book, where he clarifies his work among humanity:

We have had a number of lifetimes on this planet, as well as several incarnations in completely different lifestreams on the planet Venus in your solar system. In our lives, we have experienced many important beings of great light and teaching. We have also experienced many of the dramatic and amazing changes that the human race has gone through. Having deep compassion and connection with human beings, we have become as human a soul as is possible for such evolution and have tied our karma and understanding to human evolution.

From such we are able to have a unique dualistic viewpoint. One of these is the point of view from understanding universal consciousness, Universal Laws, and the essential principles of the cosmos, what are essentially just mathematical principles. At the same time, we have a viewpoint from the heart, from what human beings know, from the essence of what it is to be alive and part of the human lifestream, encompassing those elements of human development including incarnations as mountains, as dinosaurs, as beings of the sea, and as beings of the land.

By understanding this from both points of view, we are able to make some interesting and unique choices and note that most of the information is valuable only from the point of view of where it opens you to your own heart, to your own awareness, to your own human qualities. It is the human condition that is admirable here, and not ours. […]

We are acting as guides for many, as well as acting as guides for certain guide beings who can transmit or translate that energy. But nevertheless it is up to you to choose how you would wish us to work with you. It is indeed up to each person and what they would wish to create. Then it is up to us to understand the best way we can fulfill such requests. Our true purpose is to provide information and help in a way that assists not just one individual but all people everywhere, and even beyond that perhaps to the beings that co-inhabit the planet with you: the nature kingdom, the animals, the plants, the guide beings of a nonphysical nature, and of course all aspects of the Earth herself. Therefore an answer to a question may not come at just one level. By allowing the unfolding and opening of your consciousness, this inspiration can touch the consciousness of others. (Rubenfeld & Smulkis, *Starlight Elixirs* p. 306-308)

About the Author

Erkki Lehtiranta, M.A., is a Finnish professional astrologer, an explorer of reality, a valued instructor, lecturer, musicologist, journalist, raja yogi and writer. For over 40 years, he has studied the spiritual dimensions of life and traveled on five continents. These studies have generated 12 books and hundreds of articles, lectures and courses.

Having studied astrology for over 40 years, Erkki has been a professional astrologer for the last twenty. His speciality is spiritual astrology. He is a member of the Finnish Professional Astrologers' Association.

The foundation of all Erkki's courses is spirituality. His courses and personal interpretations give guidance for self-knowledge, spiritual development and much needed support. They also open up an understanding of consciousness, life cycles and our karmic boundaries. Though dealing with deep issues, Erkki's training always has a warm and humorous atmosphere. He has trained groups in Crete, Estonia, the Canary Islands, India and England, as well as organizing spiritual and cultural trips to Nepal, Tibet, Bhutan and France.

In recent years, his key training topics have included:
- Astrology and well-being
- Astrology and the spiritual path
- Spiritual Laws - the Traffic Rules of the Universe
- The karmic grammar of the body
- Palmistry and spiritual development
- Karma, reincarnation and spiritual development
- Reading reality
- On the doorstep to a new world view
- Star contacts – the galactic roots of mankind
- Flower essences, vibrational remedies and well-being
- The spiritual effects of music
- The Spiritual Grammar of symbols

Erkki's 12 books deal with the following topics:

- Astrology and Wellbeing - Find Your Own Success Codes (2017)
- How to Read Reality - Tips for Enlightenment (2017)
- Music, Spirituality and Wellbeing (2015)
- Fire – The Element of Change and Creativity (2014)
- Water – Messenger of Life (2012)
- Universal Laws and Spiritual Progress – A Manual for a Meaningful Life (in Finnish 2012)
- On the Road and Under the Sky - Writings on a Seeker's Path (2011)
- Astrological Cycles and Life Management (2010)
- Plant Wisdom, Rock Memory – The Effects of Flower and Gemstone Remedies (2009)
- Astrology and Spiritual Path - Pilgrimage under the Stars (2008)
- The White Magic of Finland - The Effects of Finnish Flower Essences (2007)
- Higher Octaves of Music - Sound and Music in Us and in the Universe (2004)

For more information, visit Erkki's website at www.smilingstars.fi or contact info@smilingstars.fi.